MW01629593

More Praise for *Tainted Money*

Reflecting his long experience in uncovering and analyzing the financial networks and business practices of terrorist organizations, Jorisch has distilled the essentials of both into a well organized and lucid presentation. His book can help in developing strategies and designing tools to disrupt the financial activities of terrorist and other criminal groups. It should therefore be on the required reading list for any law enforcement, intelligence, or military personnel who investigate the financial networks of criminals and terrorists, as well as banking compliance groups and business intelligence companies.

—**Dr. Jeffrey Starr**, *former deputy assistant secretary of defense and senior advisor for special operations and threat finance at the Pentagon; former vice president of business intelligence, Goldman Sachs*

Jorisch asks the question that policymakers are afraid to confront. Eight years after 9/11, there is increasing evidence that we have spent an inordinate amount of resources attempting to identify illicit finance in many of the wrong places, and that we persist in the use of countermeasures developed in an era very different from the challenges of today. Jorisch brings impeccable credentials and personal passion to this well-researched and reasoned book. *Tainted Money* should serve as a wake-up call for policymakers, national security bureaucracies, and concerned citizens.

—**John Cassara**, *former U.S. Treasury special agent and author of* Hide & Seek: Intelligence, Law Enforcement, and the Stalled War on Terrorist Finance

Tainted Money provides the nuts-and-bolts knowledge that prosecutors worldwide need in order to build cases against terrorists—and secure convictions. These groups cannot sustain their activities without steady funding, and Jorisch has laid out the blueprint for cutting off that flow in the United States and abroad.

—**Dr. Alberto Nisman**, *chief Argentinean state prosecutor, 1994 AMIA bombing case*

Tainted Money

Are We Losing the War on Money Laundering and Terrorism Financing?

Avi Jorisch

Red Cell Intelligence Group
Washington, DC

Visit our website: **www.redcellig.com**

Published in 2009 in the United States of America by Red Cell Publishing, 2200 Wilson Boulevard, Suite 102-310, Arlington, VA 22201

ISBN 978-0-9841747-1-3

First edition 10 9 8 7 6 5 4 3 2 1

Design by Daniel Kohan, Sensical Design & Communication

Jacket photos: Stefan Klein/iStockphoto. Photo on part openers: Image by Kevin Dooley under Creative Commons license (www.flickr.com/photos/pagedooley/3301817899).

PRINTED IN THE UNITED STATES OF AMERICA

Table of Contents

Acknowledgments

This book is the culmination of more than two years of service at the U.S. Department of the Treasury and two years of independent research. I am grateful to Becker Family Trust for providing me with the resources and time to complete this study. In particular, I am indebted to Newt Becker, who believed in this project from the beginning and painted a vision of what it could eventually become. I would also like to thank Cliff May, president of the Foundation for Defense of Democracies, and Mark Dubowitz, the foundation's executive director, both of whom supported this study and have played an important role in my career. My appreciation also goes to Toby Dershowitz for her time, energy, and encouragement.

I am grateful to Jonathan Schanzer, Paul Dergarabedian, Ahmed Qureshi, John Cassara, and my father, Henry Jorisch, for reading the manuscript and editing it at various stages. These five individuals have played an invaluable role in shaping my understanding of both illicit finance and human nature, and in guiding me during my time at Treasury and following the founding of Red Cell IG.

I am also thankful to Jeff Starr, who has continued to act as my coach; to David Thompson for our insightful conversations during my assignment at Immigration and Customs Enforcement and for teaching me about the ins and outs of trade-based money laundering; to John Davidson for his keen eye; to Khairi Abaza for the gift of friendship; and to Lisa Mendelow and Los Warith.

This study required an immense amount of work on the part of my editor George Lopez, whose professional skill and patience are without rival; and on the part of Dan Kohan for design and layout. My sincere thanks also go out to the many other friends, family members, and colleagues who contributed to this work. Finally, to my wife, Eleana, who was at my side from the beginning of this journey, for her tireless support, steady encouragement, and wise counsel.

Avi Jorisch
Washington, D.C.
August 2009

Executive Summary

During the 1980s, Colombian drug lords produced massive amounts of narcotics, shipped them into the United States, and laundered the resultant billions of dollars in profits through U.S. banks—often bringing cash by the bagful to local bank tellers. In order to make it more difficult for the cartels to conduct their business, Washington policymakers and the law enforcement community focused on devising strategies to interdict the drugs and reduce their use. Meanwhile, the various schemes by which the cartels cleaned their tainted money and remitted it back to Colombia continued unabated, largely because few policymakers understood the inner workings of the financial and law enforcement sectors. Had more of Washington's decisionmakers examined the cartels' methods in the 1980s and 1990s, we might have been better prepared for the latest entrants in the financial battle: terrorists and rogue regimes that use the same time-tested ways of moving money and disguising its origin.

Combating money laundering and terrorism financing—two species of crime that were conceptually and administratively bound together by the September 11 attacks—is a complex challenge due in large part to the diversity of methods used. All of these methods center on exploiting vulnerabilities in the financial system to disguise the movement of funds. Money launderers make their money illegally and try to clean it in order to conceal its criminal origins. Terror financiers can make their money legally or illegally—their aim is to conceal both its origin and its ultimate intended use. In essence, then, money launderers convert dirty money into

Show Me the Money!

The International Monetary Fund has estimated that money laundering comprises 3–5 percent of the world's gross domestic product (GDP). According to the World Bank, global GDP was approximately $72.3 trillion in 2007, which would place international money laundering somewhere between $2.17 and $3.61 trillion per year—in other words, potentially larger than the U.S. budget!

Similarly, the amount of money available to terrorists, while impossible to calculate precisely, is clearly in the billions, if not trillions.

clean money, while terror financiers take money and make it dirty by funding acts of violence.

Only in recent years has the international community begun to realize the enormity of the problem and call for the establishment of comprehensive "anti–money laundering/combating the financing of terrorism" (AML/CFT) regimes. At the center of these efforts lie three goals: (1) protecting the integrity of the international financial system; (2) identifying, disrupting, and dismantling the financial networks that underpin international criminal and terrorist organizations; and (3) making it more difficult for criminals and terrorists to profit from their crimes.

HOW IT ALL HAPPENS

In general, criminal organizations and terror financiers move and disguise their money through four primary means:

- The formal financial sector (e.g., banks)
- The informal financial sector (e.g., "hawala" and other money services businesses)
- Physical movement (e.g., cash smuggling)
- The movement of goods through the trade system

Over the course of twelve chapters, this book covers these sectors in detail, providing a step-by-step guide on how each is exploited to further illicit activity.

THE INTERNATIONAL FRAMEWORK

Although some countries have taken the offensive in cracking down on illicit actors who hide the movement of their money, others are doing much less to meet this threat. The more serious governments have taken the lead by creating international organizations whose sole mandate is to combat money laundering and terrorism financing. The most important of these organizations is the Financial Action Task Force (FATF), established by members of the Group of Seven (G7) in 1989. Over the years, FATF has issued a set of standards on effective AML/CFT efforts and created a framework to assess individual countries' compliance with these benchmarks. Although the organization has limited membership and no enforcement capabilities, it has been surprisingly effective on certain fronts.

FATF's principal contribution to the field has been its oft-updated "Forty Recommendations on Money Laundering and Nine Special Recommendations on Terrorist Financing," or the "40 + 9." Typically referred to as "the international standard" for AML/CFT efforts, the 40 + 9 were issued with the intention of universal application, to serve as a comprehensive framework against the movement of illicit money. The standard rests on three principles. First, countries must improve their national infrastructure to combat money laundering and terrorism financing. Next, each country is obligated to strengthen its financial systems. Both banking and nonbanking institutions must set up procedures to identify clients and detect suspicious transactions, as well as develop secure and modern transaction protocols. Finally, countries must strive to improve international cooperation by collecting, analyzing, and sharing AML/CFT-related information at the administrative and judicial levels. This includes sharing information on international currency flows and developing mutual judicial-assistance programs in order to investigate, freeze, and confiscate illicit funds.

> If a country wishes to be taken seriously on the AML/CFT front, it must implement FATF's recommendations in full. More often than not, countries pick and choose which standards to implement based on their national interests and the resources at their disposal. This piecemeal approach to compliance is not a recipe for effective international action against money launderers and terrorists.

FATF's official policy is to blacklist countries that either fail to comply with the international standard or refuse to have their financial system evaluated. Despite the fact that it has no enforcement mechanism, the blacklist has been remarkably effective in changing the behavior of designated countries in the past. For example, many financial institutions and other good corporate citizens have been reluctant to do business with or in countries shunned by FATF. Moreover, blacklisted countries that have refused to take remedial action have at times lost significant international investment as a result. In fact, the International Monetary Fund and World Bank have sometimes chosen to downgrade a blacklisted country's credit rating—a significant punishment in today's interconnected financial world. As discussed in chapter 3, however, FATF has attempted to reform its designation system in recent years, and the delays in fully implementing these reforms have diminished the blacklist's effectiveness and minimized the agency's use of the technique.

ENFORCEMENT

Criminalizing money laundering and terrorism financing is the basis of any effective AML/CFT regime, as it gives governments the legal authority to pursue illicit actors, prosecute them in court, and freeze their money. Unfortunately, many countries have yet to take even this most basic of steps.

The United Nations has tried to give countries the impetus to do so. In addition to a number of conventions that encourage member states to set up their own AML/CFT mechanisms, the UN maintains the primary international terrorist-designation

A Word about "International Standards"

The UN and other international organizations have issued standards on countless important issues—from piracy to child pornography to human smuggling, just to name a few. Undoubtedly, the world would be a much better place if every country implemented all international standards to the letter. This has not been the case, of course.

Although it is unrealistic to expect countries to treat the international standard on money laundering and terrorism financing much differently, this book aims to show how even imperfect AML/CFT efforts can have a measurable effect against one of the most significant threats of our time—provided the United States and other key members of the international financial community are willing to lead the way. This entails setting the appropriate example by fully implementing FATF's recommendations, pressuring other countries to do the same, and facilitating the sort of international cooperation and information sharing that law enforcement needs in order pursue criminal and terrorist schemes that have become global in scope.

The obstacles to such initiatives are obvious: bureaucratic constraints, finite resources, and, most recently, an unexpected economic downturn. But even incremental improvements can go a long way—policymakers need only understand where to begin.

list. Yet, these measures have several serious shortcomings that have kept them from achieving anything more than limited success. For example, the UN terrorist list is based on Security Council Resolution 1267, which targets only those individuals and groups associated with the Taliban, al-Qaeda, and Usama bin Laden. No other terrorist groups have been designated or otherwise targeted by the UN—in fact, the organization has not even managed to adopt a clear international definition of terrorism. Moreover, some countries completely ignore the "1267 list," while others have simply not allocated resources toward providing their financial institutions and law enforcement agencies with updated information on those designated.

In light of these issues, the Security Council adopted Resolution 1373, which "obligates" countries to institute domestic sanctions programs targeting *all* global terrorist organizations. Among the resolution's most promising provisions was a call for member states to empower authorities to freeze these organizations' assets without delay. As with many other Security Council resolutions, however, most countries have decided to completely ignore this obligation. And the UN has taken little action to rectify this state of affairs or punish noncompliant member states.

For its part, the United States has done a relatively good job on the AML/CFT front—it was one of the first countries to criminalize money laundering and terrorism financing, and it has lodged a high number of prosecutions and successful convictions. In addition, it has taken steps to inform the private sector about designated terrorist organizations and rogue regimes. Persons found to be doing business with such entities face heavy fines and jail time.

IMPLICATIONS AND POLICY RECOMMENDATIONS

U.S. officials have made clear on numerous occasions that the AML/CFT fight is a high priority. When President Bush issued Executive Order 13224, empowering Treasury to block the transactions of entities associated with terrorism, he stated, "We will starve the terrorists of funding, turn them against each other, root them out of their safe hiding places, and bring them to justice."[1]

Although tremendous progress has been made in recent years to implement AML/CFT controls, there are still a number of crucial steps the U.S. government—and willing global allies—must take in order to make life as difficult and costly as possible for launderers and terror financiers:

1. The United States should strongly encourage other countries to criminalize money laundering and terrorism financing and effectively pursue those who engage in these activities. Countries that refuse to do so should be penalized—in particular, they should be barred from receiving American foreign aid or technical assistance. They should also be publicly taken to task through appropriate public diplomacy outlets. In addition, Congress should mandate the annual publication of a list of countries that have made progress on criminalization in accordance with FATF's international standard and associated list of "predicate offenses." Doing so would serve as a catalyst for national authorities that have not already begun to take action.

2. The United States should insist that European Union member states comply with their UN obligation to maintain domestic targeted sanctions programs and freeze without delay the funds of all terrorist organizations. FATF

> The Treasury Department's Office of Foreign Assets Control (OFAC) publishes the "Specially Designated Nationals" list, which compiles the names of individuals and organizations targeted by sanctions programs focusing on terrorism, weapons of mass destruction, narcotics, and other issues. In addition to publicly naming these designees, the government freezes their assets and prohibits Americans from conducting business of any sort with them.

has found most EU countries to be out of compliance with this portion of the international standard—instead of instituting their own sanctions regimes, these states tend to rely on the super-national authority of the EU.

3. The U.S. government should provide additional resources to those agencies tasked with investigating and monitoring criminal abuses of the informal financial sector (e.g., "black" hawala, bulk cash smuggling, trade-based money laundering). Such abuses will continue to pose a major threat to our financial system unless the current oversight system is enhanced.

4. Washington should strongly encourage FATF to issue international standards on trade-based money laundering—a practice in which the basic mechanisms of international trade (e.g., container shipping, company-to-company invoicing, currency exchange) are exploited in order to conceal, transfer, convert, or otherwise legitimize large quantities of tainted money. Most jurisdictions around the globe have done very little to counter this phenomenon, creating a major vulnerability in the international financial system.

5. Washington should also encourage FATF to add gold and diamond smuggling to the list of "predicate offenses" to money laundering. Both commodities are among the most compressed forms of wealth in the world and are frequently used in laundering, terror financing, and drug trafficking.

These are only a handful of the policy recommendations offered in the concluding chapter of this book, all of which are geared toward concrete legislative, departmental, and diplomatic action.

In sum, there are infinite ways to disguise illegally obtained money and integrate it into the financial sector. Given the threat that such activity poses, countries must do everything they can to counter it. Implementing measures to prevent and detect illicit financial activity, coupled with a robust ability to enforce financial controls, will be vital. Only then will the international community be able to make serious headway against money laundering and terrorism financing.

Introduction

In New York City's Chinatown, restaurateur Chen Chui Ping establishes a successful informal banking business, then uses it to launder the millions of dollars she earns from one of her other enterprises—smuggling and exploiting illegal immigrants. In Colombia, the Chiquita banana company pays protection money to the AUC—a U.S.-designated terrorist group and drug cartel responsible for the deaths of untold Colombian citizens—in order to continue operating unmolested. In Iran, government authorities use state-owned banks and an array of front companies and other deceptive techniques to evade the controls of responsible financial institutions and further their nuclear and terrorist efforts. On the island of Macau, the obscure, family-owned Banco Delta Asia circulates millions of dollars in counterfeit U.S. currency on behalf of North Korean diplomats, some of whom are engaged in drug trafficking, arms deals, and other illegal activities. In Indonesia, al-Qaeda affiliate group Jemaah Islamiah uses cash couriers to deliver thousands of dollars to operatives in Bali, who use the funds to conduct a suicide bombing attack that kills more than 200 people.

These are just a handful of the abuses perpetrated by drug cartels, human smugglers, terrorists, rogue states, and other illicit actors who exploit the international financial system to further their goals. Although some of these specific activities have been successfully prosecuted or otherwise halted, such abuses continue to threaten both U.S. national security and the global economy. Accordingly, fighting them has become one of the most important struggles of our time.

Today, that fight centers on money laundering and terrorism financing—two terms that were inextricably linked by the attacks of September 11, 2001. Following those attacks, policymakers in the United States and elsewhere came to realize that one of the best ways to prevent future catastrophic incidents was to deny terrorists the financial means of sustaining themselves. The domestic and foreign mechanisms already in place to counter wider financial crime offered the best means of doing so. At the same time, by highlighting the ways in which al-Qaeda and other terrorist groups funded their activities, authorities brought greater attention to the fact that other criminals were exploiting serious gaps in existing enforcement systems—to the tune of billions and perhaps even trillions of dollars a year.

As Washington reaches out to financial and foreign ministries around the globe, policymakers and laymen alike should be keenly aware of the financial dangers that will need

Who is the book written for?

This study is aimed at a number of different audiences involved in setting and implementing policies to combat terrorism and crime in general, especially the financial aspects of these issues. It was principally written with the U.S. policymaker in mind—whether as a refresher course for experts or a primer for legislators and other nonspecialists. At the same time, international legislators and officials working in finance ministries, foreign ministries, customs agencies, police departments, and militaries should also derive tremendous benefit from various chapters, as should financial professionals and laymen hoping to understand the scope of the problem and potential solutions.

to be countered—whether they stem from rogue regimes like Iran and North Korea, the Usama bin Ladens of the world, or criminals engaged in a myriad of illicit activities. Unquestionably, one of the most serious public policy challenges that the United States will face in the foreseeable future will be how to use every tool in its arsenal to make progress against those who exploit tainted money. Given the global nature of the financial system, the only way to make it harder, costlier, and riskier for illicit actors to conceal and move their funds is for countries to adopt and implement a coordinated set of "anti–money laundering/combating the financing of terrorism" (AML/CFT) controls.

This book is intended to serve as both a guide and a policy monograph: first, describing the methods used by money launderers and terrorism financiers to move money; second, detailing the international standards already established by organizations such as the Financial Action Task Force to counter the flow of illicit money; and third, reviewing the implementation of those systems by the United States. In addition, the study will highlight those parts of the international and domestic systems that are not fully functional, as well as the organizations that are effectively addressing these gaps.

Many countries around the globe have struggled—or deliberately refused—to understand their international obligations and implement the necessary legal and financial controls. Hopefully, this book will help relevant policymakers and curious laymen alike better envision the sorts of concrete steps needed to combat this problem in each jurisdiction.

HOW THIS BOOK IS ORGANIZED

Although the book was meant to be read cover to cover, the author is well aware that much of its intended audience—namely, the policymaking community—rarely has the opportunity to read large studies in full or all at once. Thus, while there is a great deal of interesting material in each chapter, not everything is essential to your overall understanding of money laundering and terrorism financing. Readers should feel free to consult individual chapters or subsections at a moment of need, using the glossary to help clear up any previously defined terms.

In terms of content, the book aims to answer fundamental questions such as:

- What are money laundering and terrorism financing?
- Who is engaged in this type of activity?
- What have the U.S. government and international community done about it, and have their efforts been effective?
- Can money laundering and terrorism financing be stopped?
- Which are the most important international organizations currently dealing with the issue?
- How do illicit actors raise and move money through the various financial sectors?
- What are the basic building blocks of these schemes?
- Why are charities such a popular vehicle for raising and moving illicit money?
- If countries are serious about money laundering and terrorism financing, what can they do to counter it?
- What are the countries and regions of greatest concern?

In order to effectively answer these questions, the book is divided into four parts.

PART I: THE BIG PICTURE

The opening chapters are meant to set the stage for the reader's understanding of the subject. Since the September 11 attacks, a plethora of experts have appeared in the media to describe money laundering and terrorism financing, but there is still an immense amount of ignorance and misinformation in the public domain regarding both phenomena. Therefore, if you are a newcomer to the subject, it is recommended that you spend some time with Part I (and the glossary, described below) to get comfortable with the basics. Seasoned government officials looking for a refresher course should begin here as well.

In chapter 1, the principal actors are defined, and their methods of raising and moving money are explored at a macro level. In chapter 2, the reader is taken through a practical primer on basic money laundering and terrorism financing schemes as carried out by fictional characters. This will help the reader get oriented on how criminals try to stay one step ahead of law enforcement. In chapter 3, the major international organizations dedicated to AML/CFT monitoring and enforcement are described. This will help the reader understand who does what in the international community, and what resources are available.

PART II: MOVING MONEY

Part II is for those who need to get up to speed quickly in understanding a technical expert, or who wish to start down the path toward becoming experts themselves. The reader is taken through the various means by which illicit actors move their money, with each chapter organized the same way, offering (1) an overview of a given tactic and the advantage criminals gain by using it, (2) a highlighted country/region of concern in a story box, and (3) the international standards and U.S. domestic mechanisms currently in place to counter the tactic. The reader will also find case studies sprinkled throughout the chapters.

Chapter 4 introduces the reader to abuses within the banking sector—the most logical starting point for Western readers accustomed to using that part of the financial system themselves. In chapter 5, the informal financial sector is described. Understanding this sector and the international rules governing it is imperative to grasping the other informal ways of moving money described in the subsequent three chapters. Chapter 6 is dedicated to bulk cash smuggling, while chapter 7 describes trade-based money laundering. Chapter 8 delves into charities and their role in money laundering and terrorism financing. This chapter appears last because charities are uniquely potent targets for abuse, allowing terrorists and other criminals to use all of the major tactics described in the previous chapters.

PART III: ENFORCEMENT

Enforcement is the cornerstone of any AML/CFT regime. Criminalizing money laundering and terrorism financing while sanctioning those who engage in such activity is essential to fighting the problem. As with part II, aspiring technical experts should read part III carefully. Chapter 9 describes in detail how countries that are truly serious about AML/CFT should implement criminalization standards. Chapter 10 reviews targeted economic sanctions, how they have been used to date, and how the United States carries out its targeting process. Case studies are provided to illustrate each issue. Chapter 11 describes the international effort to assess how countries are doing with regard to implementing the latest standards.

PART IV: CONCLUSIONS

This final section outlines a number of policy recommendations specifying how the United States could carry out the financial war against illicit actors more effectively.

GLOSSARY

In order to simplify things for the reader, we have included an in-depth glossary at the end of the book, before the endnotes. International and domestic institutions love using acronyms and technical jargon, and readers wishing to participate in or influence the AML/CFT discussion will definitely need to understand these terms and use them in context. Moreover, some of the terms defined in early chapters appear unglossed in later chapters, so readers may need to consult the glossary if perusing chapters individually, or if they simply need a refresher.

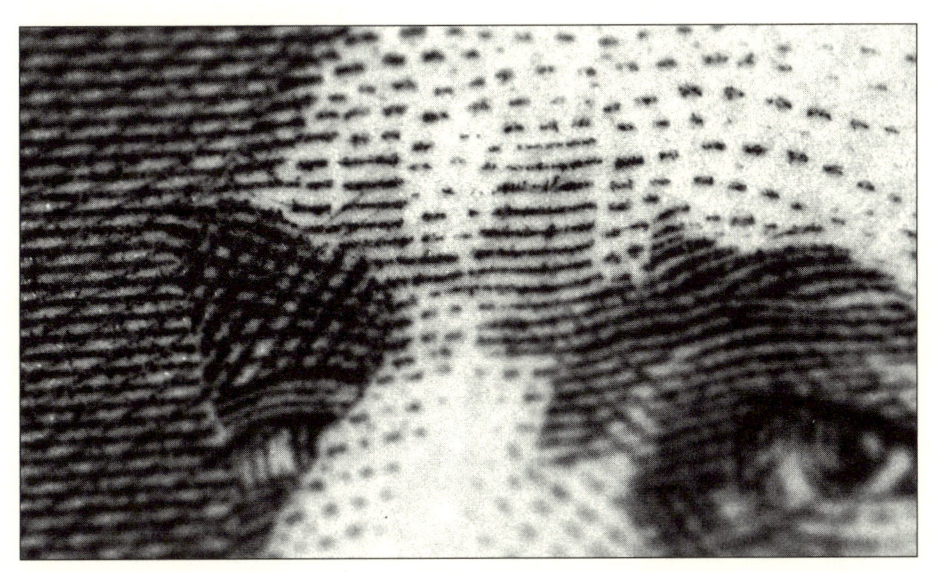

PART I

The Big Picture

Chapter 1
Why Should We Care?

In this chapter:

- Defining the problem
- Are money laundering and terrorism financing really such a big deal?
- Raising and moving money: an overview
- Following the financial trail

Money laundering and terrorism financing are global problems that transcend borders. Those who engage in such activities are constantly adapting their techniques, while law enforcement agencies try to catch up.

Efforts to precisely quantify the magnitude of global money laundering have proven elusive—by their very nature, illicit actors tend to carry out their activities in secret. Nevertheless, the amount of such activity carried out worldwide is by all accounts huge. The International Monetary Fund has estimated that money laundering comprises 3–5 percent of the world's gross domestic product (GDP). According to the World Bank, global GDP was approximately \$72.3 trillion in 2007, which would place international money laundering somewhere between \$2.17 and \$3.61 trillion per year—in other words, potentially larger than the U.S. budget![1] Similarly, the amount of money available to terrorists, while impossible to calculate precisely, is clearly in the billions, if not trillions.

In Simple Terms

Money Laundering: Giving "dirty" money the appearance of having been earned legitimately.

Terrorism Financing: Financially supporting individuals or groups that plan, encourage, or engage in terrorist acts, using money earned either legitimately or criminally.

Both concepts are fundamentally simple. Money laundering is the process of converting money derived from criminal activity in order to give it the appearance of having been legitimately obtained—in short, changing dirty money into clean money. By distancing ill-gotten gains from criminal activity, launderers make it difficult for law enforcement to confiscate and for lawyers to prosecute.

Terrorism financing is the monetary support, in any form, of those who plan,

Case Study

The "Mother of All Snakeheads"

Human smuggling is a lucrative business in China. The global industry in human smuggling is worth an estimated $7 billion per year,[1] with Chinese traffickers alone reportedly making between $2.4 and $3.5 billion.[2] Smuggled Chinese arrive in the United States by land, sea, and air. Some travel directly, while others transit through Mexico or Canada and then cross overland illegally. Although exact figures are unavailable regarding how many Chinese are smuggled into the United States, credible estimates put the number at 50,000 arrivals annually. Those who pay for this service report that they come to the United States to earn an elevated status and a better salary in order to provide for their families back home.[3]

The number of Chinese smuggling groups worldwide is not known, with estimates ranging from seven to 50.[4] The Chinese use the terms "snakehead" and "human snake" to describe smugglers and those being smuggled, respectively. These terms stem from the image of slithering from point to point along clandestine routes.

Smugglers reportedly prefer to be paid in full before they embark. For those unable to pay up front, the snakehead's organization contacts their relatives upon arrival at the destination. If the family refuses to pay, male human snakes are often sold to labor camps, while young women are often sold to prostitution rings until the smuggling costs are paid in full.

In 2006, the "mother of all snakeheads" was convicted of conspiracy to smuggle aliens into the United States, hostage taking, money laundering, and trafficking in ransom proceeds, among other charges.[5] Federal judge Michael Mukasey sentenced Chen Chui Ping, also known as Dajie Ping (in English, "Big Sister Ping"), to the maximum 35-year jail term. Over the course of her smuggling career, she is reported to have netted more than $40 million.[6]

The sentencing of the Chinatown grandmother and shopkeeper marked encourage, or engage in terrorist acts. The source of the funding can be clean or dirty—the criminal nature of the act is based on the ultimate intended use of said funds. In other words, terrorists take money and make it dirty by carrying out acts of violence.

the end of a sad New York–China saga. Ping had become "one of the most powerful and one of the most successful alien smugglers of our day."[7] According to court documents, she established her international ring as early as 1984 and smuggled hundreds, perhaps thousands, of aliens into the United States, principally from China's Fujien province. In one notorious incident, she arranged and paid for a ship named the *Golden Venture* to transport 282 Chinese immigrants to America. The boat's 100-day journey has been described in harrowing detail—the immigrants, who paid up to $40,000 each, endured squalid conditions and were reportedly abused physically and sexually by their guardians.[8] On June 6, 1993, the ship arrived off the coast of New York and ran aground on a sandbar 600 feet from the Rockaway shore. Six drowned in the 53-degree surf, while two others died a few days later of their wounds.

Ping used a money remitter business and a restaurant to launder the proceeds of her smuggling activities and to facilitate her operations. Located at 47 East Broadway in New York City's Chinatown, her money laundering operation sat directly across the street from a branch of the Bank of China, Beijing's central bank.[9] She reportedly built up such an effective underground banking system that it eventually became one of the principal competitors to the Bank of China. One female immigrant who used Ping's services told reporters, "The Bank of China took three weeks, charged a bad foreign-exchange rate and delivered the cash in Yuan. Sister Ping delivered the money in hours, charged less and paid in American dollars. It was a better service."[10]

According to New York City police, Ping's money remitter service allowed snakeheads in China to lend money to those who could not afford to pay up front for the trip to America, or who did not have U.S.-based relatives to sponsor their trip. Ping reportedly charged 30 percent annual interest on such loans.[11]

One of the keys to Ping's success was corruption. New York City police report that she put the pieces of a global smuggling network together by buying off corrupt immigration, tourism, and other officials and using fake or purchased papers to transship clients to America.[12]

WHAT CONSTITUTES MONEY LAUNDERING?

The term "money laundering" is thought to have originated in the United States sometime in the 1920s. Criminal gangs headed by Al Capone, Meyer Lansky, and other infamous figures began disguising their dirty money by abusing cash businesses such as launderettes. They took money acquired from alcohol sales, gambling revenue, and other organized crime and mixed it with clean money, making their ill-gotten gains appear legitimate. In terms of basic tactics, very little has changed since then. Today, money launderers tend to choose businesses that are both cash-intensive and service-oriented in order to appear as legitimate as possible. Examples include hotels (e.g., who is to say how many guests actually stayed?), small grocery stores (e.g., did the owner actually sell that many cigarettes?), restaurants (e.g., did the cook really make 40 grilled cheese sandwiches that day?), and nightclubs (e.g., were there really more than 200 patrons last Friday night?).

Money laundering is a key component of criminal and terrorist activity. Readers must keep in mind that the majority of criminal acts involve obtaining money illegally, which then needs to be laundered in some fashion. Some of the more prominent examples of criminals who launder money include narco-traffickers, human smugglers, weapons proliferators, kleptocrats, organized crime figures, and prostitution rings. Terrorists can also become money launderers if they raise money through criminal activity and need to hide its origin or ultimate purpose.

WHAT CONSTITUTES TERRORISM FINANCING?

Although there is no internationally agreed-upon definition, terrorism is generally understood as a violent act intended to create fear for an ideological or political purpose, and deliberately targeting (or disregarding the safety of) noncombatants. In the U.S. Code of Federal Regulations, terrorism is defined as "the unlawful use of force and violence against persons or property to intimidate or coerce a government, the civilian population, or any segment thereof, in furtherance of political or social objectives" (28 CFR section 0.85).

There are only two internationally recognized ways to label a group or individual as a terrorist entity: designation by the United Nations or through a national government authority. To date, only two organizations have been designated using the first means: al-Qaeda and the Taliban. Domestically, the United States has designated a number of organizations (see chapters 3 and 10 for a detailed account of these designations).

RAISING MONEY

Criminal and terrorist organizations vary widely—some are small, decentralized, and self directed, while others are large and state-like, with enormous operational capabilities and access to funds. All types, however, need to raise money for their activities.

They have several options for doing so:

- Illicit means
- Legal means
- State sponsorship

Raising money from illicit sources and hiding its origins automatically categorizes one as a launderer. In many other cases, however, terrorists and other criminals earn some of their funds legitimately, whether through legal businesses or donations. Terrorists may also turn to state sponsors for their money. No international organization has ever designated a country as a state sponsor—to date, only the United States and a handful of other countries have done so individually. This is not surprising given the international community's inability to reach even a universal definition of terrorism.

In the United States, the State Department is responsible for designating countries that "have repeatedly provided support for acts of international terrorism."[2] As of November 2008, four countries hold that designation: Iran, Syria, Sudan, and Cuba.[3] Several other countries have appeared on the list but were eventually removed: North Korea (removed in 2008), Libya (2006), Iraq (2004), and South Yemen (1990).

MOVING MONEY

The time-tested ways of moving money and disguising its origin are still effective, though each method has vulnerabilities. Criminals and terrorists conduct billions of dollars in transactions each year through four principal means: the formal financial sector (e.g., banks), the informal financial sector (e.g., "hawala"), the trade system (e.g., commodities), and physical cash smuggling. In recent years, terrorists and their supporters have also perfected the abuse of charities, which use all of the aforementioned methods.

Over the past two decades, the international community has developed a blueprint standard to limit the amount of money being laundered. Although not yet legally enforceable by any international

Dollars vs. Euros

Traditionally, the U.S. dollar has been the most popular currency for money launderers due to its acceptance worldwide. Since its introduction in 1999, however, the euro has gained a strong foothold in the laundering business. Experts predict that the euro will eventually supplant the dollar because it has tremendous volume, crosses borders with little difficulty, and is the common currency for 16 of the 27 European countries.

body, this standard mandates that governments criminalize money laundering and terrorism financing, target those engaged in such activities, and put measures in place to ensure that illicit actors are trapped in a "financial box." New legal and financial tools based on this standard, if used, could prove very powerful.

No country is immune to the problem. Money launderers and terrorism financiers have moved funds into all jurisdictions, including those with robust laws in place to counter such activity. Paradoxically, some criminals believe that successfully integrating laundered money within countries that have strong countermeasures can actually improve their prospects. That is, if they are able to move their money into countries like the United States, they are less likely to arouse the suspicion of law enforcement agencies elsewhere in the world. At the same time, nations that fail to put strong legal safeguards in place invite a host of other negative consequences; in particular, crime tends to become more entrenched, and foreign investors shy away. Experts have also

Case Study

Chiquita Pays Colombian Terrorist Group

In March 2007, Chiquita Brands International, based in Cincinnati, Ohio, pled guilty to one count of engaging in transactions with a Specially Designated Global Terrorist (SDGT).[1] For more than six years, the company made payments to the violent, right-wing terrorist organization United Self-Defense Forces of Colombia—an English translation of the Spanish name "Autodefensas Unidas de Colombia" (AUC). The AUC has executed some of the worst massacres in Colombia's history. It also exports a sizable percentage of the country's cocaine.[2]

From 1997 to 2004, Chiquita made payments to the AUC through its wholly owned Colombian subsidiary Banadex, focusing on the two regions of the country where it had banana-producing operations: Urabá and Santa Marta. Chiquita paid the AUC in monthly installments at least 100 times, for a total amount of more than $1.7 million.[3]

This unethical practice became officially illegal in late 2001, when the U.S. government designated the AUC as a Foreign Terrorist Organization (FTO) and an SDGT. Both designations made it a federal crime for any U.S. citizen or corporation to provide money to the group.[4] The AUC's designation was widely reported in both the American and Colombian press. In addition, Chiquita "reportedly knew about the AUC's designation as an FTO through found a direct correlation between the proceeds of crime and the increasing strength of transnational crime organizations.[4]

LIMITATIONS OF CONTROLS

As long as countries fail to implement the international community's blueprint for effective financial controls—as detailed in the Financial Action Task Force's "40 + 9 Recommendations" (see chapter 3)—illicit actors will retain access to financial systems worldwide. Many policymakers, experts, and international organizations have pointed out that effective implementation of these controls could significantly reduce the amount of money laundered, increase the chances of detection, and make illicit transactions more difficult and costly to carry out. The international community, however, has a long way to go before it reaches a state of "effective implementation."

a paid Internet-based, password-protected subscription service" that helped the company keep abreast of such developments.[5]

Prior to the designation, Chiquita paid the AUC through various intermediaries and recorded the payments in its corporate accounting books using terms such as "security services."[6] From 2002 to 2004, however, Chiquita paid the AUC directly in cash in order to conceal the practice entirely.

In April 2003, after internal legal deliberations, the company voluntarily disclosed to the U.S. government that it had been paying the AUC since 1997. The Justice Department advised Chiquita that such payments were illegal and should cease immediately. The company continued the practice until February 2004, however, making 20 payments totaling more than $300,000 even after its disclosure.[7]

Following Chiquita's eventual plea agreement, the federal sentence included a $25 million criminal fine, a promise to implement and maintain an effective compliance and ethics program, and probation for five years. The company also agreed to cooperate in ongoing investigations.[8]

Chiquita sold Banadex, its most profitable operation, to a Colombian buyer in June 2004.[9] The company continues to buy Colombian bananas, reportedly from independent suppliers.[10] In addition, Chiquita faces a $7.86 billion lawsuit filed in November 2007 on behalf of nearly 400 Colombian families who hold the company responsible for the "torture and murder" of their loved ones.[11]

To be sure, even if every country fully implemented every recommendation, a number of factors would still work in favor of those who wish to abuse the system. The international standard is not a panacea for money laundering and terrorism financing—it is simply the most promising tool available at present.

One of the biggest loopholes in the international standard—and in the U.S. anti-money laundering/combating the financing of terrorism (AML/CFT) framework in particular—remains customer identification and recordkeeping procedures for certain types of transactions. These vulnerabilities cannot be completely rectified. Regarding wire transfers, for example, institutions are required to carry out such procedures only when the transaction exceeds $3,000. This means that multiple small deposits of illicit money—a practice known as "smurfing" or "structuring" (see chapters 2 and 4)—can be easily placed into the financial system.

Moreover, American financial institutions are not required to report suspicious activity unless the transaction is above a certain amount: $5,000 in the case of the formal financial sector (see chapter 4), and $2,000 in the case of the informal financial sector (see chapter 5). These somewhat arbitrary thresholds effectively allow suspicious activity below these amounts to take place unhindered. There are several reasons why the United States has been unable to close this loophole:

- **Cost.** The financial burden associated with recording transactions below a certain amount and repeatedly carrying out customer identification procedures would be very high. Accordingly, the United States uses a risk-based approach to regulate the financial system—in the government's view, the risk associated with small, unmonitored transactions is acceptable compared to the cost of monitoring them. Launderers and financiers can therefore carry out their activities in small amounts, even if they eventually add up to very large sums. The law enforcement community strongly believes, however, that forcing criminals to resort to complicated small-transaction schemes eventually increases the chances that they will be detected.

  Interestingly, the formal financial sector has determined that it is in its own best interests to maintain records below the government's reporting threshold. It also reports suspicious activity below the threshold requirement to the Financial Crimes Enforcement Network (FinCEN), America's primary "financial intelligence unit" (see chapter 3 for a full discussion of this term). Moreover, individuals who do not have an account at a given bank are generally not permitted to transact business there as a result of the associated risks. The most problematic loophole therefore lies not in the formal financial sector, but rather in the informal sector. For example, even if every money services business (MSB)—i.e., a non-bank institution that conducts monetary transactions (see chapter 5)—in the country registered with FinCEN and followed every regulation (most MSBs do neither), anyone could still walk in off the street and send money in amounts smaller than $3,000. Unlike the formal financial sector, most MSB operators do not feel internally obligated to go beyond the legal thresholds or institute their own risk-management measures.

- **Limited human resources.** The law enforcement community, the Justice Department, and FinCEN each have limited resources, and they would not relish the prospect of being flooded with additional financial reports related to normal or suspicious transactions—they are already inundated with millions of such reports annually. Moreover, prosecutors typically seek to pursue the "big" cases, reasoning that going after small-time criminals is not always the best use of time, energy, or resources.
- **Immigration issues.** Many policymakers fear that placing too many strict controls on the formal financial sector will drive much of America's large immigrant population to the informal sector. The more people who use this sector, they argue, the easier it will be for terrorists and money launderers to blend in and abuse it. The reasoning behind this line of thinking is faulty, however. Despite the government's best efforts to get as many people as possible to use the formal financial system, millions of people still use only informal MSBs, for a variety of reasons (see chapter 5). Therefore, the informal sector's more troubling loopholes will remain a problem regardless of changes made to the formal sector.

LOOKING AHEAD

In light of these limitations—some of which would be insurmountable even under a robust monitoring and enforcement regime—one might ask why the United States and other countries should expend the resources necessary to fortify the international system against money laundering and terrorism financing. After all, illicit activity has been a socioeconomic problem for hundreds of years, so why should policymakers pay special attention to this particular facet?

Clearly, the sheer volume of tainted money corrupting the system today is ample motivation in of itself, as described at the beginning of the chapter. More important, however, the techniques used to launder and move money enable a motley crew of criminals—terrorists, weapons proliferators, human traffickers, armed robbers, organized crime figures, kleptocrats, prostitution rings, and forgery artists, just to name a few—to avoid getting caught, to enlarge their bank accounts, and to reinvest these funds in further crimes. The continued growth of such activity is cause for concern on several fronts:

- **Effect on business.** The marketplace depends on the perception that it is operating according to the highest legal, professional, and ethical standards. For financial institutions, reputation is invaluable. Moreover, if these institutions are abused for criminal activity, they become part of the problem rather than part of the solution.

- **Effect on economic development.** Developing economies tend to attract illicit actors because, as a general rule, such areas do not possess adequate financial controls. These conditions ease the money laundering process. Some observers have argued that developing economies cannot afford to be selective about their sources of funding. But in the long term, the opposite is true: the easier it is to launder money in a jurisdiction, the more entrenched organized crime becomes there. And countries where organized crime is rampant can expect a dampening effect on foreign investment, since their financial institutions will be viewed as being subject to the control of illicit organizations.
- **Effect on society.** Clearly, crime weakens the underpinnings of a well-functioning society. And allowing money laundering—the lifeblood of criminals—to continue relatively unhindered is one of the surest ways to enable crime itself.

In light of these concerns, policymakers and citizens alike have a vested interest in detecting and drying up illicit funds to whatever extent possible.

There are no easy solutions to these problems—governments will have to strike the right balance of prevention, detection, and enforcement in order to tackle them effectively, and AML/CFT controls are only one of several tools needed to do so. Nevertheless, following the financial trails left behind by illicit actors is one of the most powerful means that governments and law enforcement agencies have at their disposal in the fight against crime and terrorism.

Chapter 2

How Criminals Raise and Move Money

In this chapter:

- The different stages of laundering
- Meet Sanjay and Sanya, money launderers and terror financiers extraordinaire
- Breaking the bank
- Using "Papa Smurf" to hide money
- Hawala is happening
- Physically moving money
- Faking the invoices
- Advanced schemes: Black Market Peso Exchange and charities

There are a multitude of ways to launder money and just as many to disburse it to terrorists. Launderers and terror financiers often use the same clever methods to make their funds appear as clean as possible and attract the least amount of attention from law enforcement. Although it is impossible to describe every such method, we can review some of the most common ones.

In general, simple operations serve as the building blocks for more complex schemes. As noted Internal Revenue Service expert John Madinger put it, "The most convoluted, detailed scam in history can still be broken down into its component parts."[1] Isolating and explaining these components is one of the best ways to understand the overall process.

Typically, the laundering and terrorism financing cycle is divided into three distinct phases:

- Placement
- Layering
- Integration

The placement stage is the first and most vulnerable. At this point, launderers/terror financiers move money or change it from one form to another in order to cover their tracks. Methods include but are not limited to: (1) physically moving the money—e.g., Mr. Illicit stuffs a suitcase full of cash into the trunk of his car, drives down to Mexico, and deposits the money at an exchange house, no questions asked; (2) depositing the money into the financial sector—e.g., Mr. Illicit takes the money to a bank and deposits it in small amounts so that the bank teller doesn't ask intrusive questions, or even in bulk via a complicit teller whom he can trust (whether via bribery or prior friendship) to conceal both his identity and the suspicious aspects of the transaction; (3) mixing legitimate and illegal money—e.g. Mr. Illicit takes drug money and mixes it with the legitimate earnings of his grocery store. Illicit actors can carry out these schemes on their own or in concert with others.

In Simple Terms

In the placement stage, the only difference between money launderers and terrorism financiers is that the latter may get their money from legitimate sources.

The second phase, layering, typically involves moving the "placed" money to other institutions, further obscuring its origins. For example, Mr. Illicit creates a shell company and then uses it for a series of simple and complex transactions, or he converts his cash into a different monetary instrument like a travelers check.

The last and most important step is integration. If the first two phases were successful, the tainted money now appears legitimate and can be used for any purpose. Once money has reached this stage, it is very difficult for law enforcement to investigate or detect. In many cases, the illicit money is now returned to the legitimate economy (e.g., Mr. Illicit buys a piece of real estate or invests the money in the stock market). Some of these legitimate investments can in turn be abused for further criminal enterprises (e.g., Mr. Illicit concocts an invoice scam using one or more front companies). Whatever the case, the illicit proceeds of crime are now well hidden and can be used or reinvested by the criminal organization. As for terrorism financiers, by this stage they have gotten the money to their intended party, often with deadly consequences.

MOVING MONEY 101: SANJAY AND SANYA'S STORY

The following story of Sanjay and Sanya is fictitious but is meant to illustrate some of the more common ways money launderers and terrorism financiers raise and move money. Their story begins with a simple banking transaction, a sector that most readers will intuitively understand. The reader will then be guided to less familiar, informal sectors such as hawala, bulk cash, and commodities—all used heavily in immigrant communities and throughout the developing world. Their story ends with complex schemes such as the Black Market Peso Exchange and charities, which combine several means of moving money to further obscure illicit activity.

Sanjay and Sanya's various schemes will correspond directly to the in-depth explanatory chapters that appear in Part II of this book.

THE BANKING/BUSINESS TRANSACTION

One of the most basic and effective means of laundering money is to establish a business, whether large or small. Criminals can then use (what appear to be) legitimate business transactions to obscure their illicit money. In other words, money laundering can be as simple as performing ordinary bank deposits.

Let's take the example of Sanjay and Sanya. Originally from India, they now own a grocery store in Washington, D.C. On the side, they also run a successful drug trafficking operation. Each year, Sanjay and Sanya launder approximately $1 million.

Their grocery is popular and sells a variety of goods, including CDs, cell phones, and movies, among other things. As in many grocery stores, customers often pay in cash. One of the ways Sanjay and Sanya launder their drug proceeds is by mixing the clean and dirty money. And as in many other cases, exploiting banks is their first step toward broader laundering operations.

> The United States has very strict reporting requirements for banks. A Currency Transaction Report (CTR) must be created and sent to the U.S. Treasury's Financial Crimes Enforcement Network (FinCEN) every time a bank carries out a currency transaction that exceeds $10,000 (see chapter 4).

Sanjay and Sanya hold five bank accounts in five separate banks: one in Sanjay's name, one in Sanya's, and the other three in the grocery store's name. Given the amount of money they have to launder every day, they need multiple accounts to make their deposits appear normal. They deposit as much of their money as possible below the federally mandated reporting requirements for banks (see box). They also frequent multiple branches of each bank so they do not appear suspicious. If and when they do trigger the reporting threshold, their business provides adequate justification for depositing large amounts of money. Once the deposits are made to their various accounts, they can further launder the money.

Because their business is cash intensive, Sanjay and Sanya have a relatively easy means of creating the illusion that all of their financial affairs are legitimate. If they need to launder more money, they can simply add more accounts and/or more banks. As mentioned in chapter 1, however, law enforcement has discovered that Murphy's Law often holds in this case—the more transactions Sanjay and Sanya carry out, the greater the likelihood they will eventually get caught.

SMURFING AND STRUCTURING

After a few years, Sanjay and Sanya's drug operation has grown exponentially. They know the chances of getting caught will increase greatly if they continue personally depositing large sums of money in local banks, no matter how small the individual transactions are. Accordingly, they decide to employ ten Indian friends as "smurfs" for the operation—trustworthy but expendable individuals who are in need of a good salary.[2]

Sanjay and Sanya devise a plan that calls for their smurfs to travel to a different U.S. city each week. There, these smurfs are instructed to structure $100,000. Their job is to deposit the money into bank accounts in amounts well below $10,000. They are also instructed to purchase financial instruments such as travelers checks or cashier's checks in amounts under $3,000. As described in chapter 1, for such purchases under this amount, banks and money services businesses (MSBs) are not required to verify a customer's information (including identification), to record the transaction information (i.e., amount, date of sale, or serial numbers for each instrument), or to keep long-term records of the transaction (see chapter 5).[3] Once purchased, these instruments can then be deposited anywhere in the world, anytime.

Smurfing is often the first step in placing illicit money into the financial system. Although illegal in the United States, it remains a popular tactic in part because of vulnerabilities in the U.S. system (described here and in chapter 4).

MORE COMPLICATED BANKING SCHEMES

Once their money is placed in the financial system, Sanjay and Sanya decide to start layering it, the second step in the money laundering cycle. Specifically, they begin transferring funds back and forth between various accounts in a practice known as "churning." This is done in the hope of concealing the money trail from law enforcement.

Once the couple has effectively layered the money, they move to the third step of the cycle, integration. First, Sanjay and Sanya decide to begin investing in real estate. They buy four small commercial buildings in Baltimore and pay contractors cash to renovate them. In addition to helping them process illegal funds, the buildings (and any other real estate they purchase) will eventually give the couple another legitimate cash source.

Sanjay and Sanya understand that the likelihood of successfully laundering their money increases if they move funds to a jurisdiction that does not have strict banking controls and that provides customers with banking secrecy. Taking money offshore in this manner makes it very difficult for investigators to follow the financial trail.

Using a simple internet search, Sanjay and Sanya discover that incorporating a business and opening bank accounts in the Comoros Islands, off the coast of East

In Simple Terms

The term "smurfing" is derived from the image of the cartoon characters the Smurfs, a large group of many small creatures. Smurfing describes the act of dividing a large amount of money into smaller sums to make money laundering easier. These sums are deposited into one or more bank accounts either by multiple people (smurfs) or by a single person over an extended period of time. One of the main purposes of a smurfing operation—technically called "structuring" by the U.S. government—is to avoid the Currency Transaction Report threshold of $10,000.

Miami-based lawyer Gregory Baldwin is said to have coined the term in the 1980s.

Africa, can be done very easily. They contact an agent who, for a very reasonable price, can accommodate them. The agent even offers them help in acquiring Comorian passports.

There are many offshore jurisdictions where this practice is not illegal or even frowned upon. For the host country, there are many advantages to allowing such activity. In particular, it is a source of tremendous revenue for very little work, requiring a government to simply file some paperwork and collect licensing and registration fees.

Sanjay and Sanya establish a new Comorian corporation called the IGAS Resort Company. Although IGAS conducts legitimate business as part of the Comorian tourism industry, it primarily serves as a laundering front for the couple's American drug profits. Having accumulated a sizeable amount of money, Sanjay and Sanya wire $1 million to their account in the Comoros Islands. If anyone were to investigate the couple there, it would appear they had made their money legitimately in the United States through their real estate investments and grocery business. And if U.S. law enforcement were to conduct a cursory domestic investigation, it would likely conclude that the couple's money stemmed from legitimate ventures in Baltimore/Washington and the Comoros Islands.

HAWALA: A PRIMER

Another popular way to launder money is via the informal financial networks known by many names throughout China, East Asia, and the Arab world. Examples include hawala (Southeast Asia and the Arab world), fei chien (China), padala (Philippines), hundi (India), hui kuan (Hong Kong), and phoe kuan (Thailand). For the purposes of this study, all such networks will be referred to as hawala, an Arabic word that means "to transfer." In addition to ease of reference, using this term exclusively is appropriate for this book because hawala networks in the United States, Europe, and the Middle East are of greatest concern in the fight against terrorism financing.

There are two main components of hawala. The first is the sending/receiving process, which takes place between two hawaladars, or brokers. The second is the settlement process. Hawala expert Patrick Jost explains, "What actually happens is, as in improvised music, 'variations' on a theme. The hawala system is very flexible, so many variations occur."[4] The easiest way to understand the hawala system is to examine a single transaction.

In Simple Terms

Informal financial systems were created by merchants and traders to avoid the dangers of traveling with gold and other forms of payment on routes beset by bandits. These systems remain popular today because they are:

- Cheap
- Fast
- Easy
- Efficient
- Frictionless
- Convenient
- Reliable

Amit emigrated from India and now lives in Washington, D.C. He wants to send USD 5,000 to his family living in Mumbai. First he goes to a major bank, where he is told the following:

1. He has to open an account
2. There is a USD 100 fee to send money to India
3. The official rate is 50 Indian Rupees (INR) to the dollar
4. Delivery to his family's house requires an extra USD 40 courier fee

Once the fees are removed, going through the conventional banking system would allow Amit to send INR 243,000 to his family.

Amit believes he can get a better deal by going to a hawaladar. He knows that his local Indian grocers—our friends Sanjay and Sanya—also remit money to India. Sanjay and Sanya tell Amit they can give him the following terms:

1. There will be a 1 percent commission for the transaction (USD 50)
2. They can give him a rate of 60 Indian Rupees to the dollar
3. Door-to-door delivery is free.

In other words, Amit can send his family INR 297,000 instead of the INR 243,000 offered by the bank—clearly a much better deal!

Amit gives Sanjay and Sanya USD 5,000. They then communicate with their Indian counterpart—generally in the form of a fax, email, or telephone call that details the amount of the transaction and gives some information indicating the recipient's identity (e.g., a banknote serial number). In this case, Sanjay calls his sister Rupa in Mumbai and provides her with the details of the transaction. Rupa delivers INR 297,000 to Amit's mother's home within 24 hours.

RECONCILING HAWALA TRANSACTIONS

The way hawaladars settle their accounts poses major challenges to the law enforcement community. International hawaladars use both simple and complex settlement methods to reconcile their debts. Hawaladars are not restricted by specific rules on who they can do business with. They are informal and therefore have the flexibility to bend or even break laws in order to conduct their business.

As hawaladars send payment instructions to one another, they create an informal debt or loan, and settlement must eventually take place to reconcile the accounts. Because this system requires trust—hawaladars need to know that they will eventually get their money back from the other broker—they generally use networks of family kinship, ethnic ties, and business associates. Below are some illustrations of how hawaladars typically settle their affairs, using Sanjay and Sanya's transaction with Rupa as an example.

> **White/Black Hawala**
>
> International law enforcement authorities have developed useful terminology for distinguishing between different types of hawala transactions:
>
> **White Hawala:** Transactions involving legitimately earned money
>
> **Black Hawala:** Transactions involving illicitly earned money
>
> These terms help authorities focus on how a given sender earned the money being sent.[1]

- **Scenario 1:** Rupa owes money to Sanjay and Sanya. By remitting INR 297,000 of her own money to Amit's family, she is paying off her debt—Sanjay and Sanya will simply retain the USD 5,000 given to them by Amit.
- **Scenario 2:** Sanjay and Sanya have a certain amount of money in India, and they would like to transfer it to the United States. Rupa can help them do so indirectly through the transaction with Amit's family. That is, Rupa

uses Sanjay and Sanya's Indian money to make the payment to Amit's mother, while Sanjay and Sanya collect dollars from Amit in Washington.

- **Scenario 3:** Sanjay, Sanya, and Rupa do business together on a regular basis, and transferring money is a normal part of that relationship. Accordingly, they often commingle the cash from their regular businesses and their hawala businesses. For example, Rupa may send Sanjay and Sanya CDs and specialty foods from India, while they may send her phone cards and cellular phones from the United States. As money laundering expert Nikos Passas explains, "The settlement process can be intentionally broken up in ways that each jurisdiction only gets to see or detect a small part of the total picture. In this way, substantial amounts and serious misconduct can be masked."[5]

- **Scenario 4:** In addition to indirect methods, one of the simplest ways to reconcile accounts between established hawaladars is via direct bank-to-bank wire transfers. Using the example above—and to keep things simple—at a certain point Sanjay and Sanya will want to balance their books with Rupa. If no other transaction took place that month, Sanjay and Sanya could wire Rupa USD 4,975, keeping USD 25 (i.e., their half of the USD 50 commission).

The reconciliation process is often far more complicated than the above scenarios. Frequently, the bigger hawaladars have bank accounts in other parts of the world, including places like New York, London, Hong Kong, and the United Arab Emirates. Hawaladars will often aggregate the money they collect in one central location that acts as a clearinghouse—this reduces costs and is more efficient. Another advantage to aggregating money in important financial centers is access to hard currency, which does not fluctuate radically in short periods of time (at least under normal conditions) and therefore provides stability.[6]

LAUNDERING MONEY THROUGH HAWALA

Using the case of Sanjay and Sanya, one can see that it is relatively easy for illicit actors to launder their money through hawala. For example, instead of going to the bank themselves or employing Smurfs, Sanjay and Sanya might find it simpler—and perhaps even less dangerous—to employ the services of a hawala network. A hawaladar could send their money to their offshore company in the Comoros Islands, or to a trusted family member who could place the money more easily in the banking system. Indeed, illicit actors have a variety of possibilities to choose from when using a transfer system that lacks long-term recordkeeping—effectively giving them a better chance of evading detection by law enforcement.

HAWALA AND TERRORISM

Hawala is easily abused by terrorism financiers as well. For example, in addition to their distinguished career as drug traffickers and money launderers, Sanjay and Sanya happen to be staunch supporters of Lashkar-e-Tayyiba, also known as the Army of the Righteous. This group is the armed wing of the Pakistan-based religious organization Markaz-ud-Dawa-wal-Irshad—a Sunni anti-American missionary movement formed in 1989. Lashkar is one of the three largest and best-trained groups fighting in Kashmir against India, conducting numerous operations against Indian troops and civilian targets there since 1993. To demonstrate their support, Sanjay and Sanya instruct Rupa to give regular donations to the group in the natural course of their hawala deals.

CASH SMUGGLING

Physically moving money is an oft-used tool in the hawala settlement process, and it too can be abused by both money launderers and terror financiers (see chapter 6). For example, if Sanjay needs to send money to Rupa, he may decide to use one of two possible cash smuggling methods to settle his debt.

One method involves cash couriers. Sanjay has a friend, Ayman, who works for a professional courier service. He is planning a trip to India and agrees to carry the money in his briefcase and give it to Rupa when he arrives. Traditionally, couriers who move illicit money use a variety of methods to hide the funds. Examples of ingeniously concealed money include swallowed condoms filled with currency, false compartments in shoes or luggage, hidden sections of a vehicle, and special money belts or other garments specifically designed to hold money.

Couriers and Bulk Cash Smuggling

Cash Couriers: Couriers move large quantities of cash but are limited by what they can carry on—and in some cases inside—their person. Cash couriers moving illicit proceeds are always considered to be in breach of the law. Other cash couriers are not linked to criminal activity, however, and are considered legitimate as long as they abide by the host country's reporting obligations. At the same time, hawaladars and other informal operators may use smuggling techniques even when dealing with strictly legitimate money, if only to avoid the red tape or fees associated with reporting large amounts of cash brought into a given country.

Bulk Cash Smuggling: This type of smuggling, which often involves containerized cargo shipments, is traditionally associated with criminal activity.

Alternatively, Sanjay arranges to use a container on a ship traveling to India, which he fills with cellular phones and CDs. Since this is part of his normal business exchange with Rupa, there is nothing strange about sending such goods. He then takes apart one of the phones and hides money in it in order to settle his debt to Rupa—he need only tell her exactly which phone to take apart.

Cash smuggling has been used to disburse money to terrorists as well, of course. For example, Sanjay could easily instruct Rupa to give some of the hidden cash to Lashkar-e-Tayyiba.

SHELL COMPANIES

Sanjay and Sanya's drug business is doing so well that they decide to further diversify their risk by contacting another agent and setting up another offshore company, this time in Panama. Unlike the Comorian IGAS Resort Company, the sole purpose of this new company, called GIPPER Investments, is to hold and/or move their money—it does not conduct legitimate business. In places like Panama, the law permits secrecy in banking relationships and conceals companies' true ownership, making it easy to establish shell companies like GIPPER. As the name implies, shell companies simply have a name, address, and bank accounts. Clever money launderers will also fabricate and maintain financial records to reinforce the illusion of a real company, without the need to conduct any actual business.

Sanjay and Sanya send money to their agent in Panama via couriers who make several trips to the country carrying amounts under $10,000. By structuring the money in this manner, they avoid the U.S. "Report of International Transportation of Currency or Monetary Instruments" (CMIR) threshold (see chapter 6). The agent then places the money in GIPPER's Panama account in exchange for a small fee.

TRADE-BASED MONEY LAUNDERING

As their businesses diversify, Sanjay and Sanya decide to cook up an invoice scam with a few trustworthy customers. Their goal is to send $1 million abroad without raising any red flags. The couple has done a lot of business with Pablo Diaz, who owns a Colombian import-export company. Together, they concoct a simple plan to move the money using their legitimate businesses as a front.

Sanjay and Sanya ship one million pencils worth $2 each to Pablo, but on their invoice, they list a price of only $1 each. Pablo pays them for the pencils by sending a wire transfer for $1 million. Pablo then sells the pencils on the open market for $2 million and deposits the extra $1 million (the difference between the invoiced price and the "fair market" value—minus his fee) into a bank account to be disbursed according to Sanjay and Sanya's instructions. This is a classic example of an under-invoicing scheme.

Over-invoicing works in reverse: Sanjay and Sanya ship one million pencils worth $2 each, but this time they invoice Pablo for $3 million. Pablo pays them for the pencils by sending a wire transfer of $3 million. They then deposit the money in an account of his choosing in the United States.

Research suggests that under-invoicing exports is far more common than over-invoicing. Accordingly, most customs agencies are currently set up to "stop the importation of contraband and ensure that appropriate import duties are collected."[7] Exports are less rigorously monitored than imports.

FALSE INVOICING

After carrying out a number of these types of deals, Sanjay and Sanya decide that they no longer need to involve Pablo or anyone else—they can control both sides of the transaction via their own Panamanian shell company, GIPPER Investments. The couple wants to move yet another $1 million out of the country. The first step in their new scheme is to "order" 500,000 bathing suits worth $2 each from GIPPER Investments. They have GIPPER send them an invoice, which they pay by sending money to the company's bank account in Panama. No bathing suits are ever sent, of course, but Sanjay and Sanya record the transaction in both their and GIPPER's books as if the goods had changed hands. The money has effectively been laundered. If investigators dig, they will find that nothing was shipped, but both parties' books would appear legitimate under cursory investigation.

Another type of false invoicing is used to misrepresent what is actually being sent. For example, Sanjay and Sanya again wish to send $1 million to Pablo. They ship him a container and declare that it contains scrap metal worth close to nothing. In fact, they include several gold bars worth $1 million in the container, hidden among the scrap metal. This type of transaction is often called "falsely described invoicing."

In Simple Terms

Typical invoices list item quantities, prices, billable hours, service descriptions, and other information relevant to transactions between two companies. Of course, the goods and services listed on an invoice possess whatever value the buyer and seller wish to assign. This leaves plenty of room for abuse and manipulation, especially if both parties are in on the scam or if one party controls both sides of the transaction. In essence, manipulating invoices gives illicit actors a paper rationale for sending money abroad, which facilitates money laundering. The most basic invoice manipulation scheme involves over- or under-invoicing goods—i.e., stating that an item is worth more or less than its actual price.

BLACK MARKET PESO EXCHANGE

Simple schemes become complex when illicit actors abuse the formal and informal financial sectors in conjunction with, for example, bulk cash smuggling, narco-trafficking, or tax evasion. One of the largest and most pernicious money laundering schemes in the Western Hemisphere is the Black Market Peso Exchange (BMPE).

Typical BMPE transactions involve a number of important actors who must depend on one another for a given scheme to succeed:

1. Colombian drug cartels, which smuggle narcotics into the United States and have various operations in both countries
2. Colombian peso brokers, who have representatives in both countries
3. Legitimate Colombian businesses
4. Legitimate American businesses

The process begins when a Colombian cartel smuggles drugs into the United States. After selling the drugs, the cartel's U.S.-based traffickers have a tremendous amount of cash and need to dispose of it. At this point, the cartel's Colombian operators approach a peso broker. According to money laundering experts John Madinger and Sydney Zalopany, peso brokers typically agree to buy cash from cartels at a 15–25 percent discount.[8] Once an arrangement is reached, the broker gives "clean" pesos to the Colombian operators—the cartel is now completely out of the transaction and does not have to devise a means of smuggling the drug proceeds from the United States to Colombia. Instead, the broker has a network of American operators who collect the cash directly from the traffickers.

The broker can then take one of several steps. For example, he can "smurf" the collected money into the financial system by instructing his agents to purchase monetary instruments or cashiers checks—all well under the reporting requirements. Once the money is integrated into the system, the broker can use various means to aggregate it into a central account.

The peso broker then looks for a buyer willing to purchase the "clean" U.S. dollars—an option that exists largely due to restrictions in Colombian foreign exchange laws. These laws require all domestic importers and exporters to conduct their business via the official currency exchange market, and such transactions are also registered with the Colombian customs and tax authority. The resultant red tape, along with less favorable exchange rates, import/export duties, and taxes, has led many companies to prefer peso brokers for their financial needs.[9]

Specifically, when a legitimate Colombian company buys the right to use the peso broker's newly acquired dollars, it gives the broker pesos in exchange—this is how the broker accumulates the pesos needed by drug cartels. And the broker has made money from "the spread" between his transactions with the drug cartel and the legitimate company.

> **In Simple Terms**
>
> The Black Market Peso Exchange is an advanced money laundering scheme that is used to launder an estimated $5 billion worth of drug proceeds per year from Colombia alone. The most remarkable part of this system is that dollars never leave the United States and pesos never leave Colombia. This type of scheme is used all over the world.

For its part, the company can now buy American goods or conduct other transactions at less than the official exchange rate. In order to avoid detection, however, it must do so indirectly. For example, the company could instruct the peso broker to purchase a certain quantity of American goods such as refrigerators, stoves, consumer electronics, alcohol, tobacco, or used auto parts. There are several ways to get these goods into Colombia. In one popular method, major U.S. companies ship their goods to another U.S.-based company owned by the peso broker. The broker's company then ships the goods to Colombia and over- or under-invoices them as needed to conceal the transaction. Other options include smuggling the goods into Colombia covertly or bribing customs officials to look the other way. To make matters even more complicated, some Colombian firms further muddy the financial trail by using companies in a third country to move goods.

It is important to underscore that these types of schemes take place all over the world, not just in Colombia. It is also worth remembering that those who engage in tax evasion and capital flight often use the same mechanisms to move their money. The key difference between such activity and a BMPE-style scheme is that the former moves legitimately earned money across borders, while the latter involves the proceeds of crime.

CHARITIES

Any sector that is not properly regulated can be abused using all of the techniques described in this chapter. The charitable sector is particularly vulnerable (see chapter 8 for a full discussion of the challenges it poses).

In Sanjay and Sanya's case, they could conceivably send money to their favorite terrorist group, Lashkar-e-Tayyiba, via a charity sympathetic to the organization or its ideology. Given the dearth of regulations governing international charitable activity, most charities can do whatever they please with donations. In some cases, illicit or complicit charities provide support to terrorists or other illicit actors using all of the aforementioned techniques—hawala, bulk cash smuggling, over- and under-invoicing, or any combination thereof. Terrorism financiers like Sanjay and Sanya are quick to take advantage of such opportunities.

CONCLUSION

Today, money can be moved anywhere in the world with speed and ease using a variety of methods—some high tech, others ancient. Money launderers and terrorism financiers generate and transfer substantial sums of money to further their activities. Like our fictional criminals Sanjay and Sanya, these actors understand that by moving funds through numerous financial sectors and across international borders, they decrease their chances of being detected and prosecuted by law enforcement.

Chapter 3

International Monitoring and Enforcement

In this chapter:

- The Financial Action Task Force
- FATF-style regional bodies
- The United Nations
- Egmont

In recent years, the international community has come to realize the enormity of the problem posed by money laundering and terrorism financing. Accordingly, some countries have begun to wage a global fight against the phenomenon. At the same time, a number of international organizations have been tasked with providing policy guidance to this fight.

THE FINANCIAL ACTION TASK FORCE

In 1989, seven of the world's leading industrial nations—Canada, France, Germany, Italy, Japan, the United Kingdom, and the United States—jointly created the Financial Action Task Force (FATF) to address their increasing concerns about money laundering's threat to the international financial system. Also known by its French name Groupe d'Action Financière (GAFI), this intergovernmental, policymaking task force was given the mandate to examine money laundering techniques and trends, review domestic and international action, and set the international standard for anti–money laundering/combating the financing of terrorism (AML/CFT) efforts.[1]

Although FATF has reportedly had more success than any other organization in coordinating international AML/CFT initiatives, it has also faced challenges in convincing individual countries to implement its blueprint for countering illicit activity. As such, FATF has arguably not met its mandate in full.

Currently, FATF is composed of thirty-two member states and two international bodies.[2] Although these members are relatively limited in number, they represent a high percentage of the world's financial activity. Moreover, FATF's reach extends

In Simple Terms: Recommendations or Obligations?

According to U.S. deputy assistant Treasury secretary Daniel Glaser, the international community has a "collective obligation" to (1) protect the integrity of the international financial system, (2) identify, disrupt, and dismantle the financial networks that underpin international criminal and terrorist organizations, and (3) make it harder for criminals and terrorists to profit from their crimes.[1] The sad fact remains that these responsibilities are unenforceable by any single organization—it is for this reason that the international standards are officially called the "40 + 9 *Recommendations*" (see below), not "Obligations." Individual countries may, however, take unilateral steps to protect their own financial systems from abuse, and the international standards provide an excellent blueprint for doing so.

beyond its members and observers to the international law enforcement community, financial institutions, and regional "FATF-style" organizations.

BEGINNINGS

FATF has developed and improved its international standards gradually. The year following its founding, the organization submitted a comprehensive report at the 1990 Arch Summit on money laundering, held in Paris. It was at this point that FATF issued the first version of its "Forty Recommendations on Money Laundering," meant to serve as the basic framework for preventing, detecting, and suppressing illicit financing. And in October 2001, as a direct response to the September 11 attacks, FATF adopted the "Nine Special Recommendations on Terrorist Financing."[3] These recommendations—known as the "40 + 9"—are collectively referred to as "the international standard" for AML/CFT.[4] Although not binding as law or treaty, the 40 + 9 Recommendations have been widely endorsed by countries around the globe and by several prominent relevant organizations, including FATF-style regional bodies, the United Nations, and other international bodies such as the Egmont Group and the International Monetary Fund (IMF)/World Bank.[5]

FATF's initial recommendations were purposefully imprecise in order to accommodate different legal systems and institutional environments. As the organization evolved, its nonbinding recommendations became increasingly precise, enhancing the legitimacy of both the standards and FATF itself. In addition to the special recommendations of 2001, the standards have been significantly revised twice: in 1996 and 2003. FATF also issues periodic "Special Interpretative Notes" and "Best Practices" in order to clarify provisions and facilitate greater compliance. This increased precision has been implemented with the intention of "narrow[ing] the scope for reasonable interpretation, detailing conditions of application and elaborating required or proscribed behavior."[6]

FATF-STYLE REGIONAL BODIES

In addition to FATF, there are currently nine FATF-Style Regional Bodies (FSRBs) that serve as regional centers for matters relating to AML/CFT:

1. Asia/Pacific Group on Money Laundering (APG)[7]
2. Caribbean Financial Action Task Force (CFATF)[8]
3. Council of Europe–MONEYVAL[9]
4. Eastern and Southern Africa Anti–Money Laundering Group (ESAAMLG)[10]

FATF's 40 + 9 Recommendations have three primary goals:

- **Improving national efforts to combat money laundering:** Countries are encouraged to criminalize all aspects and forms of money laundering. For many years, only a limited range of laundering activities—e.g., those related to drug trafficking—were targeted by law enforcement. As FATF's international standards have developed over time, the organization has also expanded its list of "predicate offenses" that can serve as grounds for a laundering prosecution—in other words, the underlying criminal activity that generates the proceeds to be laundered, whether it be corruption, bribery, human smuggling, or a host of other offenses. In addition to criminalizing all laundering schemes tied to such activity, FAFT also urges countries to set up effective confiscation procedures.
- **Strengthening financial systems:** Banks and non-banking financial institutions alike are encouraged to set up procedures for identifying clients, to detect suspicious transactions, and to develop secure and modern transaction systems. This includes prohibiting anonymous accounts
- **Improving international cooperation:** Countries are encouraged to analyze, collect, and share all laundering-related information at the administrative, law enforcement, and judicial levels. Countries are also encouraged to share information on international currency flows and develop mutual judicial-assistance programs in order to investigate and seize illicit funds.

5. Intergovernmental Action Group against Money Laundering in Africa (GIABA)[11]
6. Financial Action Task Force on Money Laundering in South America (GAFISUD)[12]
7. Middle East and North Africa Financial Action Task Force (MENAFATF)[13]
8. Eurasian Group (EAG)[14]
9. Offshore Group of Banking Supervisors (OGBS)[15]

The primary purpose of these bodies is to promote AML/CFT regimes through the implementation of the 40 + 9 Recommendations. Although they are not directly affiliated with FATF, they attend FATF meetings and are linked to the organization through a shared mandate.[16] Membership in an FSRB is voluntary, and any country within a geographic region may join; many FATF countries also participate in FSRBs, for example. Since FATF has comparatively small membership, FSRBs are uniquely positioned to work on and solve the issues FATF has been addressing since its inception. In the past few years, these bodies have provided creative ideas regarding charities, bulk cash smuggling, hawala, and training seminars.

INTERNATIONAL COOPERATION BLACKLIST

As mentioned previously, countries are not obligated to implement FATF's standards as they are simply recommendations. But even without an enforcement mechanism, FATF has given itself the "right" to ask its members to sever financial ties with any jurisdiction found to be largely out of compliance with its standards. This is done to protect the international financial system. FATF's official policy is to blacklist countries that either fail to comply sufficiently with the standards or refuse to have their financial system evaluated.

In the past, the blacklist has been remarkably effective—many financial institutions and other good corporate citizens have been reluctant to do business with entities placed on it. Blacklisted countries that have refused to take appropriate remedial action have reportedly lost significant international investment. In addition, the IMF and World Bank have at times chosen to downgrade a blacklisted country's credit rating. In today's interconnected financial world, this can constitute a significant punishment.

FATF has put forth two iterations of lists targeting any country that "continues not to apply or insufficiently applies the FATF Recommendations."[17] The first was known as the list of "non-cooperative countries and territories" (NCCTs). The second is the list of the International Cooperation Review Group (ICRG).[18] The goal of both has been to secure the adoption of FATF's international standard and prod designated jurisdictions into cooperating more fully in efforts to prevent, detect, and punish money laundering.[19]

FATF began adding countries to the NCCT list in 1998.[20] From 2000 to 2002, the list identified 23 countries "with shortcomings in their anti–money laundering provisions or an obvious unwillingness to cooperate in this area."[21] Most of the designees had either deficient AML/CFT regimes or none at all. The list included the Bahamas, Cayman Islands, Cook Islands, Dominica, Egypt, Grenada, Guatemala, Hungary, Indonesia, Israel, Lebanon, Liechtenstein, Marshall Islands, Myanmar, Nauru, Nigeria, Niue, Panama, Philippines, Russia, Saint Christopher and Nevis, Saint Vincent and the Grenadines, and Ukraine.[22]

The NCCT process was incredibly successful. Each and every one of the blacklisted countries passed significant legislative measures and remedied many of their deficiencies. All have since been removed from the list and have functioning AML/CFT regimes.[23] Nevertheless, the NCCT process was halted in 2002 due to one glaring criticism—FATF had modified the international standard significantly throughout the 1990s but was still assessing countries based on old criteria. When the IMF and World Bank joined the international effort to create a uniform assessment methodology in 2002, FATF agreed to stop adding countries to the NCCT list until the new methodology was in place and countries had been evaluated against it for a few years.

FATF Blacklist

As of the beginning of 2009, there were six countries on the FATF blacklist:

- Iran
- Pakistan
- Sao Tome and Principe
- Turkish Cyprus
- Turkmenistan
- Uzbekistan

In 2007, the blacklisting process began anew following the adoption of an agreed methodology that evaluated countries uniformly. FATF and its partners established the ICRG to carry out the process, and this body has since named six countries and jurisdictions publicly: Iran, Pakistan, Sao Tome and Principe, Turkish Cyprus, Turkmenistan, and Uzbekistan.[24] The ICRG list has major problems of its own, however:

1. There are no clear procedures or criteria for nominating countries for review. In the past, countries have been nominated for lacking an AML/CFT regime, for refusing to be assessed, or for representing a terrorism financing risk, but there are no written guidelines to encourage, mandate, or define such decisions.

2. Following a review, there is no clear procedure for adding countries to the list.

3. For countries that are listed, there is no clear procedure on how to get themselves off the list.

These problems represent a major deficiency. One of the reasons why the NCCT was so successful was because it had clear and consistent procedures for listing and delisting countries. For reasons that are not entirely clear, most of these procedures were not carried over to the ICRG list. FATF will need to remedy this situation if it wishes countries and financial institutions to view its blacklists as credible and fair.

FATF EFFICACY?

As the world's premier AML/CFT organization, has FATF been effective in fulfilling its mission? To date, it has received mixed reviews.

First and foremost, the 40 + 9 standards have not been implemented in full. They were issued with the intention of universal application, to serve as a comprehensive framework against the movement of illicit money. Although the international community as a whole has made significant strides on the AML/CFT front since 1989, the vast majority of countries continue to pick and choose which parts of the 40 + 9 they implement.

Second, the collective international standard itself is deficient. In particular, FATF has been unable to make headway against one of the key ways criminals move money—through commodities. Trade-based money laundering remains a vital component of many informal financial schemes, including "black" hawala (see chapter 2), the Black Market Peso Exchange, and the smuggling of precious metals and gems. Indeed, trade schemes are often the method of choice for criminals looking to balance their books or, in more technical terms, provide "counter-valuation" (see chapters 2 and 7). FATF has not issued a standard regarding this problem nor encouraged its members to address it. This omission is akin to sticking one's head in the sand—it constitutes a major liability in the international financial system, and FATF will be unable to fulfill its mission until it rectifies the problem. Doing so will require an international mechanism capable of detecting trade anomalies.

The international standard also lacks a clear means of addressing or rating a country's effectiveness in combating money laundering and terrorism financing. Currently, a country could implement all of FATF's recommendations yet not carry out a single arrest, prosecution, or freezing procedure—and still receive high ratings. Instituting a more practical rating tool could have a major effect on how such a country was viewed by law enforcement agencies, financial institutions, and other countries.

In contrast to these deficiencies, blacklists have been the most effective tool in FATF's arsenal. As described above, although nonbinding on countries, agencies, or financial institutions, these lists have been able to bring many governments into better compliance with the international standard.

THE UNITED NATIONS

In addition to FATF's efforts, the United Nations has been given a particularly important role to play in the fight against terrorism financing. In 1998, the international community placed the UN in charge of the global blacklisting system for financiers of al-Qaeda and a number of other terrorist organizations. According to counterterrorism officials in Europe and the United States, however, this sanctions system is currently at risk of collapse as a result of legal challenges and waning political support in many countries. In September 2008, the Luxembourg-based European Court of Justice declared that the UN blacklists violated "fundamental rights" of those targeted and made it "almost impossible for people to challenge their inclusion."[25] In addition, French and British courts have questioned whether they can enforce the UN obligation to target entities on the international list without "violating local laws, including a defendant's right to see evidence." Other countries do not possess the political will to fight terror financing and have simply ignored their UN obligations.

To its credit, the UN has been attentive to issues surrounding tainted money since well before 1998. It was the first international organization to mount an effort against money laundering. In 1988, the UN Drug Control Program (UNDCP) drafted the Convention against Illicit Traffic in Narcotic Drugs and Psychotropic Substances, also known as the Vienna Convention.[26] With 170 signatories to date, this convention facilitates "confiscation of the proceeds of drug trafficking" and aims to "restrict the freedom of movement of drug traffickers."[27]

This was only the beginning of what eventually became the 40 + 9. The Vienna Convention's primary provision focuses on the tracing, freezing, and confiscation of income and property derived from drug trafficking. Although the agreement never actually uses the term "money laundering," it does define the concept and calls on signatories to criminalize the proceeds of narcotics.[28] In subsequent years, the UN expanded the definition of underlying criminal offenses to which money laundering could be

In Simple Terms

Once a person or organization is placed on the UN terrorist list, member states are prohibited from allowing certain transactions involving that entity. This obligation includes: (1) ensuring that frozen funds or any other financial assets or economic resources are not made available, directly or indirectly, for the entity's benefit (this mandate extends to governments, nationals, and anyone else within the country's territory); (2) preventing the entity from entering or transiting through the country; (3) preventing the direct or indirect supply, sale, or transfer of arms or related materiel to the entity.

tied and prescribed steps for meeting this emerging threat (see chapter 9). Although UN members are obligated to criminalize laundering according to this expanded definition, many have not done so.

It took the UN ten years to turn its attention to the business of targeting terrorists. In 1998, it published its first terrorist blacklist in an effort to prevent al-Qaeda and Taliban supporters from raising or transferring money. With this list, the "1267 Committee"—named after Security Council Resolution 1267 and including representatives from each of the council's member states—has the power to add or delete targets based on public evidence or secret intelligence reports.[29] According to U.S. and UN officials, many of the names that have been added have been at the urging of the United States. Procedurally, nominations are approved as long as no Security Council member objects.[30]

To date, the 1267 Committee requires member states to impose a travel ban and freeze the assets of 503 individuals, businesses, and groups. Enforcement, however, is spotty. Some countries have quietly permitted alleged al-Qaeda supporters to travel within their jurisdictions and retain access to their bank accounts. At the same time, the designation program has resulted in member states freezing approximately $85 million in al-Qaeda and Taliban assets.[31]

Criteria for Designation

The criteria for determining "association with" the Taliban, al-Qaeda, or Usama bin Laden and adding an individual or group to the 1267 List include the following:

- Participating in the financing, planning, facilitating, preparing, or perpetrating of acts or activities by, in conjunction with, under the name of, on behalf of, or in support of designated entities
- Supplying, selling, or transferring arms and related materiel to designated entities
- Recruiting for designated entities
- Otherwise supporting the activities of designated entities

Once entities are on the list, the UN requires member states to take specific action—mainly, freezing their assets, including "funds derived from property owned or controlled, directly or indirectly, by them or by persons acting on their behalf or at their direction."

The UN also obligates its members to take action beyond those two groups. Security Council Resolution 1373 requires them to create domestic sanctions programs that target individuals and entities associated with *any* global terrorist organization.[32]

MIXED REVIEWS

Many counterterrorism officials claim that blacklists are a vital, if imperfect, tool for fighting al-Qaeda and other terrorist organizations. In particular, the UN sanctions program is important because it is the only one that governments and banks are "compelled" to enforce worldwide. Critics, however, claim that sanctions are actually not that effective because many terrorist organizations avoid using the international banking system and require only small amounts of money to carry out actual attacks. Others cite the fact that the UN targeting program is one of several blacklists—including those maintained by the United States, United Kingdom, and European Union. Sometimes these lists overlap, and sometimes they clash, creating confusion about who is actually designated by whom. For example, Hizbollah is considered a terrorist organization by the United States and Britain, but not by the European Union or the UN. And even Britain has recently considered engaging certain Hizbollah elements, further complicating the issue.[33]

Perhaps most sadly, few countries have taken their UN counterterror obligations—whether under Resolution 1267 or 1373—seriously and implemented a robust targeted sanctions program. Some have claimed problems with how the various blacklists are compiled, while others have blamed judicial obstacles or a lack of resources. Even some U.S. officials have cited problems with current designation procedures. According to Victor Comras, a former State Department official who served at the UN, the international system of designating terrorists is "weak, under attack, and needs to be reformed."[34] In addition, a number of European countries and human rights organizations have claimed that the blacklists maintained by the UN, EU, and others are "totally arbitrary and have no credibility whatsoever."[35] Their opposition is partly based on the blacklists' reported lack of judicial due process—specifically, they argue, designated entities cannot examine the evidence against them because it is classified, and they can be kept on a blacklist indefinitely without an automatic right of appeal.

Problems have arisen on the law enforcement side as well. For example, a number of European criminal investigations of accused, UN-designated al-Qaeda supporters have been dropped for being based on evidence that would not stand up in court, or for lacking evidence altogether. For example, Italian prosecutors have dropped cases against three people on the UN blacklist because they did not find grounds to press criminal charges.[36]

The UN has tried to respond to these criticisms. In June 2008, the Security Council adopted a resolution that will eventually require blacklisting authorities to publish a narrative summary of their reasons for designating a given target on the internet.[37] And in 2006, the UN began to allow designees to approach the council directly to appeal for a review of their cases—previously, they had to ask their country of nationality to take up their case. Even so, the UN's procedures still fall short. The Security Council

Case Study

Collapse of the UN Sanctions System? The Case of Yasin al-Qadi

Yasin al-Qadi is a Saudi businessman who was has been designated on various blacklists, including the UN's 1267 list (added in 2001), the U.S. Treasury Department's Specially Designated Global Terrorist list (2001), and the European Union's "Consolidated list of persons, groups, and entities" (2004). The United States claimed that al-Qadi used charities to fund terrorist organizations such as al-Qaeda and Hamas. The UN designated him at Washington's request, and with Saudi Arabia's support. Accordingly, the relevant Security Council resolutions legally require every member state to freeze all of al-Qadi's assets and impose a travel ban. To date, he has not been delisted despite his best efforts to prove his innocence.

Not everyone in the international community agrees with this particular designation. In 2006, for example, Turkish prime minister Recep Tayyip Erdogan stated, "I know Mr. Qadi...I believe in him as I believe in myself. For Mr. Qadi to associate with a terrorist organization, or support one, is impossible."[1] Perhaps the most crucial aspect of the al-Qadi case, however, is its potential implications for the designation process in general.

In September 2008, the European Court of Justice ruled that UN sanctions against al-Qadi infringed on his basic rights and were illegal under EU law. The ruling was largely based on the fact that blacklist designees are not given the actual evidence of their wrongdoing (often because it is classified material) or allowed to put their case before an independent body that can review said evidence. According to Richard Barrett, this ruling has "far reaching consequences, for not only the EU but also the entire UN system of targeted sanctions." If the EU does not find a way to implement the sanctions and at the same time enforce the court ruling, the "UN sanctions regime may collapse."[2]

has no obligation to take the views of the designee into consideration or to respond to any petition. And according to Richard Barrett, former coordinator of the UN's Taliban and Al-Qaida Monitoring Team, it is unlikely that the council would ever allow an independent panel to review its designations—a measure called for by many critics.[38] As he and others have concluded, the debate on how to address these concerns will continue for some time.

A POLITICAL TOOL?

Perhaps the most serious criticism of the international blacklisting system centers on accusations that the designation process is subject to political influence. Some critics believe that this influence can drive individual designations. According to Armando Spataro, deputy chief prosecutor in Milan, a person "can be added to the list for political reasons, without any serious evidence of wrongdoing."[39] Others point out broader effects, as when diplomatic developments influence counterterror cooperation at the national level. According to Michael Chandler, a British government official who headed the UN's 1267 Monitoring Team from 2001 to 2004, political issues—not a lack of due process—are perhaps the primary reason why European countries do not want to play ball when it comes to U.S.-backed designation requests. Chandler views the 2003 invasion of Iraq as a turning point in this regard: "Once we got into the middle of 2003, we found that people were not so supportive [of U.S. requests] anymore."[40] Another European critic—Alexander Alvaro, a German member of the European Parliament—has argued that politics sometimes overshadows security concerns in the designation process: "Is the purpose to actually prevent terrorist attacks and cut off funding for terrorist organizations, or is it to please who it might serve to put them on the list?"[41]

More often than not, unfortunately, political factors serve to keep deserving illicit actors off of blacklists. One recent case demonstrated that the UN does not always add a name to its lists even when there is overwhelming evidence in support of doing so.

For a number of years, U.S. terrorism financing trackers noted suspicious financial transactions coming out of South Africa that seemed to benefit al-Qaeda. Junaid Ismail Dockrat, a Johannesburg dentist, and his cousin Farhad Ahmed Dockrat, a Muslim cleric, were reportedly donating money to a charity that supported the Taliban and al-Qaeda. The United States reached out to South African law enforcement, but beyond monitoring the Dockrats' activities, the local authorities were reluctant to take action.

By January 2007, Washington had run out of patience and approached the UN to add the Dockrats to the international targeting list. Among other pieces of information, the United States presented evidence that Junaid paid for other South Africans to travel to Pakistan in order to train in al-Qaeda camps. According to the Treasury Department, the two had also personally raised more than $180,000 for "Al Akhtar Trust, a globally recognized al Qaida fundraiser."[42] Nevertheless, South Africa used its rotating membership on the Security Council to place an indefinite hold on the U.S. request, arguing that the evidence was insufficient. On January 26, 2007, the Treasury decided to take unilateral action and designated the pair itself. According to former Treasury official Jonathan Schanzer, however, this move may mean little without South African cooperation: "while American sanctions might freeze any of the Dockrats' assets that reach U.S. banks (the likelihood of that is now extremely low), the terrorist-funding cousins continue to do business in South Africa with impunity." In his view, although "America may be a tougher place for terrorists to move money, terrorists see growth opportunities around the world."[43]

EGMONT GROUP

In recent years, there has been a proliferation in the number of financial intelligence units (FIUs) around the world, in large part because the FATF international standard mandates their creation in order to more effectively combat money laundering and terrorism financing. FIUs began forming in the early 1990s but were isolated from one another at first. Countries quickly realized the utility of forming a new international body to alleviate this problem.

The Egmont Group was created in 1995 with the express purpose of serving as a center for overcoming the "obstacles preventing cross-border information sharing" between FIUs."[44] The organization was named after the palace in Brussels where the initial meeting occurred. To date, Egmont's membership includes 108 FIUs.[45] Countries are encouraged to join but must have the necessary national measures in place before they are admitted. Egmont provides technical assistance and know-how in order to help countries establish functioning FIUs.

Unfortunately, this body has not met its full potential. To date, Egmont has emphasized increasing its membership, not sharing intelligence—in other words, it has equated a large number of members with effective international cooperation. In reality, however, there is no direct correlation between membership numbers and information sharing. Egmont simply gives countries and their FIUs a forum in which to hold face-to-face meetings and get to know their international counterparts. Some members do not share information or cooperate with other members. Conversely, there are FIUs that are not Egmont members but that excel at sharing financial information with FIUs around the world through bilateral agreements and memorandums of understanding.

Egmont was ostensibly set up for operational units, not policymakers, and it should begin functioning as such. In recent years, the organization's meetings have attracted primarily financial regulators and policymakers—very few members of the law enforcement community have participated. This is unfortunate because FIUs were created to bridge the gap between banks and law enforcement. Egmont cannot

In Simple Terms

What Is a Financial Intelligence Unit?

According to the FATF international standard, countries must establish a financial intelligence unit that collects, analyzes, and disseminates financial information regarding potential money laundering or terrorism financing activities. This body should act as a control tower of sorts, mediating between financial institutions and law enforcement in order to provide whatever information is needed to conduct financial investigations.

Specifically, FIUs were created to empower authorities seeking to re-create the financial trail left by illicit actors. Countries are therefore required to collect a tremendous amount of financial intelligence records. As described in chapters 2 and 4, financial institutions of all kinds, and certain other designated professions, are required to keep customer identification records and Currency Transaction Reports above selected thresholds, and to report suspicious activity. The central collection point for all of this intelligence is the FIU.

become a force to be reckoned with unless law enforcement figures are involved in a serious manner. For example, the organization could conduct more operational activities in which members carry out joint targeting exercises. It could also hold more exercises that allow members to jointly analyze transnational Suspicious Activity Reports and Currency Transaction Reports (see chapters 2 and 4).

In addition to these problems, Egmont has begun to drift outside its mandate in recent years. For example, when considering a new member, Egmont assesses whether the candidate nation has criminalized money laundering and terrorism financing. Yet, this evaluation does not include an assessment of the country's record against terrorism itself. More to the point, Egmont does not necessarily have the expertise to judge either issue. This problem is only exacerbated by the organization's vested interest in green-lighting candidates in order to increase its membership.

Predictably, then, Egmont has made some poor choices in regard to new members. For example, Syria's FIU was admitted in 2007, despite the fact that MENAFATF, the FATF-style regional body for the Middle East, gave the country failing marks for its AML/CFT efforts.[46] According to Matthew Levitt, former deputy assistant secretary of the U.S. Treasury's Office of Intelligence and Analysis, extending membership to Syria—a country Washington regards as a sponsor of terrorism—"raises serious questions about Egmont's standards and continued efficacy" in the fight against illicit money.[47]

CONCLUSIONS

There are a number of international bodies whose primary mission is to help countries fight money laundering and terrorism financing. Some are more effective than others, and they all have their strengths and weaknesses.

FATF has done an outstanding job in creating an international standard and moving countries toward implementing its recommendations—but only when it takes a clear stand regarding blacklists. For its part, the UN has tried—albeit with only limited success—to give countries the impetus to freeze terrorist funds. In addition to a number of resolutions that require countries to set up their own AML/CFT mechanisms, the UN maintains the primary international terrorism list. But the resolutions have thus far been unenforceable, and the list faces serious opposition from some members of the international community who are more worried about infringing on the rights of individuals than protecting society as a whole from terrorist attacks. Unfortunately, the Egmont Group has also failed to meet its full potential of facilitating international cooperation, given its overemphasis on membership numbers rather than intelligence sharing.

In short, although there is a framework in place for those countries that wish take the offensive and crack down on illicit actors who hide the movement of their money, countries that do not wish to join the fight can easily shirk their responsibilities.

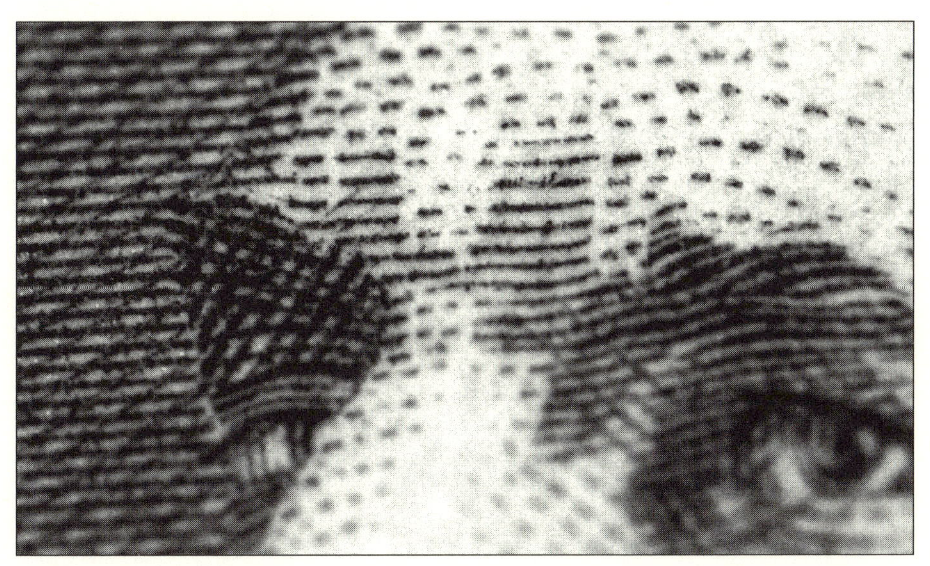

PART II

Moving Money

Chapter 4

Breaking the Bank

In this chapter:

- Country of concern: North Korea and Banco Delta Asia
- Know your customer
- Keeping good records
- Reporting requirements
- U.S. regulatory structure: successes and failures

As described in chapter 2, money launderers and terrorism financiers worldwide exploit some of the most common methods of moving funds, including:

- the formal financial sector (e.g., banks)
- the informal financial sector (e.g., hawala)
- the physical movement of money (e.g., cash couriers)
- the physical movement of goods through the trade system

This chapter takes a more in-depth look at abuses targeting the first sector, and how governments and formal financial institutions have attempted to safeguard their banking systems from such activity. The last half of the chapter focuses on the U.S. regulatory system, detailing both its strong points and shortcomings.

A KEY SECTOR

The formal financial sector is crucial to the success of launderers, terror financiers, and even rogue states because it gives them a means of legitimately transferring funds and exchanging currencies. Their ultimate goal in using this sector is to convert the proceeds of criminal activity into various types of financial instruments and assets in order to hide their illicit origin.

The Financial Action Task Force (FATF) has established a number of preventive measures applicable to all formal financial institutions (see chapter 2 for an introductory overview of FATF).[1] To make money laundering and terrorism financing as difficult as possible, FATF encourages countries and individual banks alike to implement compliance and auditing programs, in addition to recurring

Country of Concern

Tightening the Noose around Banco Delta Asia and North Korea

For decades, the United States has applied pressure on North Korea in order to reduce the regime's ability to invade the south and spread communism. The most prominent of these measures have included country sanctions, an arms embargo, and restrictions on trade and travel. Less well known is Washington's successful financial battle against North Korean activities in Macau, a small island off the coast of China.

In September 2005, following two law enforcement investigations colorfully named "Royal Charm" and "Smoking Dragon," the U.S. Treasury Department blacklisted Banco Delta Asia (BDA), an obscure Macanese family-owned bank, for its role in laundering money for the North Korean regime. Through BDA, North Korea reportedly circulated tens of millions of counterfeit USD 100 bills, known as supernotes. U.S. law enforcement agencies contend that North Korean employees of the Zokwang Trading Company, all carrying diplomatic passports, brought the bills into Macau and deposited them at BDA.[1] In addition, some of the bank's North Korean clients engaged in drug trafficking, unconventional weapons sales, and counterfeit cigarette smuggling.[2]

Treasury designated BDA under section 311 of the "Uniting and Strengthening America by Providing Appropriate Tools Required to Intercept and Obstruct Terrorism Act of 2001," better known as the USA PATRIOT Act. This section permits the department's secretary, in consultation with other agencies, to single out foreign banks, jurisdictions, transactions, or accounts that are of "primary money laundering concern." Once the government institutes a 311 designation, American financial institutions are required to take protective measures, including cutting ties with designees (see below and chapter 10 for more on the PATRIOT Act and section 311).[3]

According to the Treasury website, within six days of the designation, thousands of BDA's customers withdrew approximately $133 million, or 34 anti–money laundering/combating the financing of terrorism (AML/CFT) training for employees to keep them up to date on processes, laws, developments, and internal procedures.[2]

percent of the bank's total deposits.[4] BDA lawyers also noted that about 50 entities had closed their accounts, "including 20 North Korean banks, 11 North Korean trading companies, nine North Korean citizens, eight Macau-based companies that conducted business with North Korea and two Macau residents." In addition, all of BDA's correspondent banks in the United States, which handle the institution's international business, closed their accounts. European and Asian banks quickly followed suit.[5]

Subsequently, the Macanese government took control of BDA and began investigating its dealings with North Korea. The authorities immediately froze approximately $25 million in accounts related to North Korea and cut the bank's ties with the country.

Meanwhile, the U.S. investigation led to criminal activity in Northern Ireland. In October 2005, Sean Garland, a longtime senior figure in the Irish Republican Army, was arrested on charges of distributing North Korean–made supernotes. Garland, who has been linked to several KGB operatives and North Korean intelligence agents, reportedly distributed the counterfeit bills throughout Europe. Both he and North Korea vehemently denied the charges, while the Justice Department requested his extradition to the United States.[6]

The U.S. designation of BDA had a huge diplomatic impact. In contrast to Washington's failed efforts to secure broad international sanctions against North Korea in the past, financial institutions worldwide were willing to comply with the action against BDA, particularly when faced with losing access to one of the world's most important markets.

For its part, Pyongyang refused to return to the six-party talks regarding its nuclear program until its BDA funds were unfrozen and the United States ceased pressuring the bank. Negotiations failed for more than a year, and were renewed only after Washington agreed to hold separate talks on the BDA issue. In the end, intense American pressure led some two dozen financial institutions around the world to voluntarily cut back or terminate their ties to North Korea.[7] The Zokwang Trading Company shut its doors in Macau and disappeared—it is rumored to have relocated in mainland China.[8]

FATF believes that leaving a financial trail for investigators to follow is one of the keys to safeguarding the financial system from abuse. All AML/CFT programs must therefore include the following measures:

- customer identification and "due diligence"
- recordkeeping
- suspicious transaction reporting
- currency transaction reporting

CUSTOMER DUE DILIGENCE

The first step a financial institution must take to detect and deter money laundering and terrorism financing is to identify its customers and understand their financial activities.[3] FATF puts such a premium on due diligence—i.e., identifying and verifying clients, commonly referred to as "knowing your customer"—that the international standard explicitly prohibits anonymous accounts or the use of fictitious names.[4]

In particular, FATF encourages countries to require that financial institutions undertake customer due diligence measures under the following circumstances:

- When establishing a new business relationship
- When carrying out occasional transactions above $15,000
- When carrying out wire transfers above $1,000
- When there is a suspicion of money laundering or terrorism financing
- When the institution has doubts about the veracity or adequacy of previously obtained customer identification data

POLITICALLY EXPOSED PERSONS

One rule of thumb in implementing due diligence measures is to be cautious when dealing with well-known political figures who, by virtue of their office, might have become exposed to corruption. Such figures include, but are not limited to, senior politicians, senior civil servants, and senior military officers in every country of the world, as well as their families, colleagues, and advisors.[5] The "industry" term used to describe these individuals is "politically exposed persons" (PEPs).[6] They pose quite a challenge for banks, not only because of their sheer numbers, but also due to the ever-changing conditions brought on by new political appointments, family relationships, and business associations.[7]

In general, enhanced due diligence on PEPs should include:

- implementing customer identification measures
- seeking approval of senior management before opening accounts
- establishing and verifying the source of the funds
- conducting ongoing monitoring

CORRESPONDENT AND SHELL BANKS

Another prevalent approach that illicit actors use to access the formal financial system is by exploiting two particularly vulnerable types of institutions: correspondent banks and shell banks. FATF has issued guidance on how to deal with each situation.

When a bank does not have a branch in a foreign country, it often allows a local bank to supervise its financial affairs there and essentially act as its agent. The so-called correspondent bank is then empowered to provide credit, deposit, collection, clearing, and payment services to customers in the main bank's name. The potential for abuse in such relationships arises when the local jurisdiction or bank in question has weak AML/CFT controls.

Banks that decide to maintain this very common type of relationship should carry out a number of protective measures:

- Gather information about the correspondent bank's business practices, reputation, and supervisory capacity
- Determine whether the bank has been subject to a money laundering or terrorism financing investigation or regulatory action
- Ascertain the adequacy and effectiveness of the bank's AML/CFT controls
- Obtain approval from senior management before establishing new correspondent relationships
- Document the respective AML/CFT responsibilities of each institution
- When the relationship involves "payable-through accounts," the correspondent bank must carry out customer due diligence obligations as outlined by FATF and provide that information upon request[8]

In addition to urging extra caution regarding correspondent banks, the FATF standards explicitly state that institutions should not conduct business with shell banks because of their potential for abuse.[9] Shell banks are entities "that have no physical presence … in the country where they are incorporated and licensed, and are not affiliated [with] any financial services group that is subject to effective consolidated supervision."[10]

Using the same logic, FATF asks all financial institutions to implement enhanced due diligence measures for customers who do not physically visit the bank with which they are doing business. Given the growing number of people who do their banking remotely—i.e., via internet, phone, fax, or mail—such measures are necessary because of the obvious potential for abuse.[11] Although FATF has recognized the need for vigilance, to date it has not issued guidance on the exact steps institutions should take in

Case Study

Yassir Arafat: PEP Par Excellence

In 2002, Israeli intelligence claimed that Yassir Arafat, former head of the Palestine Liberation Organization (PLO) and chairman of the Palestinian Authority (PA), had amassed a personal fortune of $1.3 billion.[1] This was corroborated by a team of American accountants hired by the Palestinian Ministry of Interior to examine Arafat's finances. According to the chief investigator, "Although the money for the portfolio came from public funds like Palestinian taxes, virtually none of it was used for the Palestinian people; it was all controlled by Arafat. And none of these dealings were made public."[2] A September 2003 International Monetary Fund report on the Palestinian economy concurred with these findings, concluding that Arafat made numerous investments with tax money that he "diverted" from the Palestinian Ministry of Finance.[3]

Arafat, who died in 2004, reportedly used a variety of tools to amass his wealth, including a holding company to handle various ventures. For example, he invested $285 million in Egyptian mobile phone company Orascom Telecom Holding SAE and its affiliates. He also made some $30 million worth of private equity investments, mostly in the United States; these included $3.2 million in Virginia-based Simplexity Inc., which makes electronic-commerce software; $2.1 million in Vaultus Inc., a New York/Boston firm that makes software for wireless computers; $1.3 million in New York–based Strike Holdings LLC, whose assets include a trendy bowling alley just outside Washington, D.C.; and diverse amounts in companies as varied as a Coca Cola bottling plant in Ramallah, a cell phone company in Tunisia, and venture capital funds in the United States and Cayman Islands.[4]

Salam Fayad, who has served as Palestinian prime minister and finance minister and, before that, as an official with the World Bank, accused Arafat this regard—rather, it has left individual countries to determine the level of risk on their own.

RECORDKEEPING

The FATF standards call for banks to keep all transaction records, domestic and international, for a minimum of five years. These records are primarily intended to serve

of gouging his own people. In particular, he lamented the diversion of funds from an area as poverty-stricken as the Gaza Strip, calling the practice "totally unacceptable and immoral."[5] Such accusations were bolstered by reports that Arafat used several million dollars of aid money to buy weapons and support militant groups.[6]

Perhaps the most striking illustration of the lack of transparency and accountability in Palestinian finances was Arafat's "black book," a ledger in which he reportedly maintained sole possession of most, if not all, of his government's budgetary and banking information. The fragility and disastrous potential inherent in such a "system" came to the fore in April 1992, when Arafat's plane crashed in a sandstorm over the Libyan desert and he temporarily lost his account book.[7]

It is worth noting that Israel helped Arafat amass his wealth. Under the Oslo peace accords, Israeli authorities collected sales taxes on all goods purchased by Palestinians. After processing those funds, Israel eventually sent them to a personal account "maintained off-line" for Arafat by Tel Aviv's Bank Leumi, "no questions asked."[8] Israel hoped the funds would help Arafat establish control over the West Bank and Gaza, a task for which he needed "walking around money."

Arafat reportedly received additional large gifts from other parties over the course of his PLO chairmanship. Several noteworthy examples include a $50 million check from Saddam Hussein for supporting Iraq's cause in the 1991 Gulf War, as well as donations from Saudi Arabia and the KGB.[9]

Charges of money laundering have also extended to Arafat's family. In 2003, France's financial intelligence unit, Tracfin, alerted the government to a series of untaxed transfers totaling approximately $11.5 million, made from Switzerland to two Paris accounts belonging to Arafat's wife.[10] In addition, many Palestinian Authority sources have reported that Mrs. Arafat received a monthly stipend of $100,000 from the PA budget.

as a financial trail in case of a criminal investigation or prosecution.[12] Specifically, the following information should be recorded:

- Name of the customer and/or beneficiary

Case Study

Broadcasting Bank Accounts: Hizbollah's TV Station

Al-Manar, Arabic for "the beacon," is the official television station of Hizbollah. The terrorist organization uses al-Manar—which it calls the "station of resistance"—as an integral part of its overall operations. With a stated purpose of waging "psychological warfare,"[1] al-Manar is a potent instrument that has incited violence among viewers in Europe, the Middle East, Latin America, Asia, and elsewhere.

Although there are many mass communication media outlets owned by terrorist organizations, particularly on the internet, al-Manar is by far the most prominent, reaching 10 to 15 million viewers daily around the globe.[2] Hizbollah was the first terrorist group to establish its own television station and use it as "an operational weapon" to incite hatred and violence, recruit suicide bombers, and communicate with its soldiers in the field.[3] In fact, some of the station's employees are members of Hizbollah, and at least one has been known to engage in preoperational surveillance for the group using his al-Manar job as cover.[4]

Al-Manar's programming skillfully combines news, talk shows, propaganda music videos, and other elements in order to propagate an ideology of hate, terrorism, and militant Islam. Some of its more outrageous messages include:

- Calls for attacks against coalition soldiers in Iraq
- Efforts to recruit children to become suicide bombers
- "Blood libels" against the Jewish people, i.e., falsely accusing Jews of killing Christian children and using the blood to make unleavened bread for the Passover holiday
- Claims that the September 11 attacks were conducted by the U.S. government, Jews, and Mossad[5]

- Address
- Any other identifying information normally recorded
- Nature and date of the transaction

The station has also been known to solicit donations during commercial breaks, informing audiences worldwide how to contribute money to promote terrorism. Specifically, viewers have been directed to make deposits into accounts in four Lebanese banks: Beirut Riyad Bank, Banque Libanaise Pour Le Commerce SAL, Byblos Bank SAL, and Fransa Bank. These banks have reportedly received donations solicited for Hizbollah itself (under the name "The Organization for the Support of the Islamic Resistance in Lebanon"), as well as money gathered by Hizbollah funds such as "The Intifada in Occupied Palestine Fund," "The Palestine Uprising," "The Resistance Information Donation Fund," and "Support the Resistance Media al-Manar Television" (the latter fed by two accounts under the name of Nayef Abdel Hassan Krayem, al-Manar's general manager and chairman of its board of directors).[6] It is inconceivable that the Lebanese banks were unaware of this activity or its beneficiary, Hizbollah.

Al-Manar's other techniques for financing itself and Hizbollah include efforts to secure Western corporate sponsors. For example, past sponsors have included such prominent companies as Coke, Pepsi, Proctor & Gamble, and Western Union.[7]

To its credit, much of the international community has recognized the danger al-Manar poses. The U.S. State and Treasury Departments have both designated the station for serving as the media arm of Hizbollah and facilitating terrorist activity. And the European Union accused it of violating the Television Without Frontiers Directive, the legislation that governs all audiovisual law—specifically, al-Manar was found to be in breach of Article 22, which requires member states to "ensure that broadcasts do not contain any incitement to hatred on grounds of race, sex, religion or nationality."[8] In addition, countries around the world have barred al-Manar broadcasts—to date, the station has been removed from ten satellite providers in France, the Netherlands, Spain, Australia, China, Brazil, the United States, Barbados, and Thailand. Unfortunately, it is still being broadcast into Asia, Europe, and the Middle East by Saudi-owned Arabsat, Egyptian-owned Nilesat, and Indonesian-owned Palapa.[9]

- Type and amount of currency involved
- Type and identifying number of any account used

SUSPICIOUS ACTIVITY REPORTING

According to FATF's standards, if a financial institution "suspects or has reasonable grounds to suspect" that a given transaction includes proceeds of criminal or terrorist activity, it should file a Suspicious Transaction Report (STR)—known in the United States as a Suspicious Activity Report (SAR)—with its national financial intelligence unit (for a full discussion of these units, see chapter 3).[13] Situations that might warrant an SAR include complex, unusually large transactions (or unusual patterns of transactions) that have no apparent economic or lawful purpose. Filing an SAR does not mean that the customer in question is a criminal—the report is simply a red flag to law enforcement, to be investigated at a time of its choosing.

After an SAR is filed, a government agency might require the institution to take further action (e.g., providing records or monitoring accounts). In fact, FATF encourages such agencies—which include FIUs, banking supervisors, ministries of finance, and other entities—to work closely with their financial communities and provide them with red-flag indicators and case studies to help them detect suspicious activity.[14]

In Simple Terms

Financial institutions should file an SAR if a transaction is inconsistent with the normal activity that takes place in a given account or otherwise arouses suspicion. SARs alert the government to the possibility of activities involving money laundering or terrorism financing.

The international standard also warns banks not to "tip off" customers that an SAR has been filed on their account.[15] Doing so could potentially ruin any subsequent investigation or prosecution.

Finally, when financial institutions do their jobs properly, the international standard states that governments have the responsibility to protect them from criminal and civil liability. Safe harbor laws should therefore be issued to encourage institutions to comply with FATF's recommendations.[16]

CURRENCY TRANSACTION REPORTING

As described in chapters 1 and 2, many countries have enacted laws that require financial institutions to report any transaction above a certain amount—in the United States, for example, banks must file a Currency Transaction Report (CTR) with the government for every currency transaction over $10,000. FATF has strongly encouraged countries to put such measures in place, but it does not suggest a specific threshold.[17]

In each jurisdiction, the threshold amount should be low enough to uncover illicit transactions but also high enough to ensure legitimate banking is not obstructed. Many countries also grant exemptions for certain entities that either pose a low risk or are too burdensome to monitor; (e.g., vetted corporations; customers who make frequent large deposits for business reasons; government agencies). The international standard suggests that when exemptions are granted, they should be reviewed regularly.

CTRs also apply if multiple deposits are made on the same day and add up to more than the reporting requirement. As described in chapter 2, criminals often use this "smurfing" technique to avoid scrutiny by regulators or law enforcement, splitting large sums into small deposits made over several days while attempting to remain under a given threshold. Another form of smurfing is making a single deposit that is intentionally close to, but just under, the reporting requirement. For example, if a country's threshold amount is $10,000 and a deposit of $9,900 is made, there is a good chance a bank monitor would deem the transaction suspicious and file an SAR. Maintaining a CTR regime helps define what does and does not constitute suspicious behavior.

Some countries also use the CTR approach to regulate the cross-border movement of money. For example, one of the bread-and-butter tactics used by illicit actors is to transfer money across borders through the formal financial sector, often in the form of cash or other instruments such as money orders and travelers checks. FATF encourages countries to obligate their financial sectors to report any such transfers over USD/EUR 10,000. As with domestic banking transactions, institutions should carry out due diligence measures in these situations, such as recording the name, address, and unique account/reference number of the person originating the transaction.[18] Unusual or suspicious transfers under the threshold should also be reported to the relevant government agency.

U.S. DOMESTIC SYSTEM

The U.S. formal financial sector is considered large by any standard.[19] Banks are the cornerstone of this sector and range in size from global entities to small community institutions. Chartered at either the national or state level, they offer a full range of services for individuals, businesses, and governments, including:

- safeguarding money and valuables
- providing loans and credit
- providing payment services (i.e., checking accounts, money orders, and cashier's checks)
- exchanging and holding securities[20]

In light of these characteristics, U.S. banks are naturally on the front line in the war against money launderers and terror financiers. To safeguard this sector, Congress has legally obligated financial institutions to provide information on a wide assortment of transactions. Law enforcement agencies regularly use this information in both investigating and prosecuting those who abuse the financial system. The regulatory foundation of the financial sector's obligations rests in two key pieces of legislation: the Bank Secrecy Act and the USA PATRIOT Act.

The Bank Secrecy Act—commonly referred to as the BSA, and officially known as the Currency and Foreign Transactions Reporting Act—was initially passed by Congress in 1970. Since then, it has been amended eight times. In short, the BSA requires financial institutions to file reports of currency transactions exceeding $10,000 (including linked smurfing/structuring transactions that surpass that sum), to keep records of cash purchases of negotiable instruments such as travelers checks and money orders, and to report suspicious activities that "have a high degree of usefulness in criminal, tax and regulatory investigations and proceedings."[21]

Congress most recently amended the BSA in 2001, when it passed the PATRIOT Act. Drafted in response to the September 11 attacks, the act contains provisions on international AML efforts, the BSA, as well as currency crimes and protection.

Overview: PATRIOT Act

According to sections 312, 314, 326, and 352 of the PATRIOT Act, financial institutions are required to take the following measures:

- Information sharing with government agencies (voluntary information sharing among financial institutions is recommended as well)
- Procedures for verifying customer identity
- Enhanced due diligence programs
- Comprehensive AML programs

At a minimum, AML/CFT programs must include the development of internal control and compliance procedures, all requiring strict recordkeeping over and above the filing of SARs and CTRs. Financial institutions must also designate a compliance officer, conduct an ongoing employee training program, and maintain an independent audit function to test programs.

GOVERNMENT OVERSIGHT

There are two primary oversight arms for America's formal financial sector: banking regulators and the Financial Crimes Enforcement Network (FinCEN). The government has delegated responsibility for examining compliance with the BSA to the banking regulators. FinCEN, the official U.S. financial intelligence unit, serves as the central data collection and analysis bureau, processing BSA-mandated reports from across the country.

There are five primary federal regulators and 50 state regulatory bodies charged with ensuring that banks maintain effective BSA/AML compliance programs. The five federal bodies are: (1) the Office of the Comptroller of the Currency (OCC), (2) the Federal Reserve, (3) the Federal Deposit Insurance Corporation (FDIC), (4) the Office of Thrift Supervision (OTS), and (5) the National Credit Union Administration (NCUA). More than 98 percent of all depository institutions, holding well over 99 percent of all deposits, are regulated by these five bodies.[22] The regulators conduct safety and soundness examinations to ensure that banks are carrying out their BSA and AML/CFT compliance programs, and that these programs are commensurate with the institutions' business activities and risk profiles.[23]

If regulators find violations or deficiencies, they may take informal or formal action. Informal actions are rarely publicized and may include letters or memoranda of understanding. Formal enforcement actions are considered severe, and they are made public. They include cease-and-desist orders, formal agreements requiring the institution to take corrective action, and penalties such as civil fines or suspension from participating in the banking industry.[24] Some of the more prominent examples of such fines include a $25 million penalty against Riggs Bank (a case discussed at length in chapter 9), $10 million against AmSouth Bank of Birmingham in 2004, $80 million against ABN AMRO in 2005, and $10 million against Bank Atlantic in 2006.

FINCEN—A FAILED AGENCY

The Financial Crimes Enforcement Network was created to act as a control tower of sorts. Originally, it was intended to support law enforcement by maintaining financial paper trails.[25] Its mission changed over time, however, and today it has effectively become another regulatory agency. According to its website, FinCEN's primary mission is to "safeguard the financial system from the abuses of financial crime, including terrorist financing, money laundering, and other illicit activity."[26] Like other FIUs around the world, it is responsible for collecting and analyzing financial information and ensuring that this data is useful to criminal investigations and prosecutions. In addition, FinCEN acts as an intermediary between law enforcement authorities and financial institutions when the former need additional financial information.

Sadly, however, this mission has been compromised by the organization's "revolving door" staff situation, with directors, managers, money laundering experts, and analysts being replaced on a regular basis. Most notably, three agency directors came and went between 2003 and 2007—with a fourth named in March 2007. And in 2006–2007,

FinCEN lost its chief counsel and associate director for regulatory policy. According to Mitchell Feldman, president of bank compliance recruiting firm A. E. Feldman, this brain drain is a result of understaffing and overworked employees. For example, a job satisfaction survey conducted in 2007 found that FinCEN ranked among the worst places to work in the U.S. government, with particular weaknesses in teamwork and effective leadership.[27]

FinCEN has three primary flaws that prevent it from fulfilling its mission. First, it fails to systematically analyze the approximately 18 million financial intelligence reports it receives annually (which include CTRs and SARs). The U.S. financial industry spends a significant amount of money to comply with government-mandated reporting requirements, and institutions would no doubt be "shocked to learn the true extent of the under utilization of their reports."[28] If the government wishes to better combat illicit money, FinCEN must be better equipped to properly examine the data in its possession.

Banking AML Guidance

To inform banks of their responsibilities, both the federal regulators and the Federal Financial Institutions Examination Council (FFIEC) have issued important guidance to the industry, including letters, bulletins, and advisories that are all available on the web. And in June 2005, the FFIEC published an essential manual that outlines the prerequisites for an effective AML regime (the manual was updated as recently as 2007).[1]

Second, FinCEN reportedly dedicates only a small number of analysts to scrutinizing SARs. Moreover, these analysts are instructed to focus solely on instances of suspected terrorism financing. Many critics argue that FinCEN employees are not adequately trained to spot terror financing trends. In addition, FinCEN is notorious for not informing law enforcement when it uncovers actual criminal activity during a terrorism-related investigation.[29]

Third, and perhaps most serious, FinCEN has never managed to create an effective data mining tool. The agency has wasted millions of dollars and valuable time on failed schemes dubbed "Artificial Intelligence," "Component Analytical System," and "BSA Direct"—time that should have been spent following illicit actors' money. Moreover, FinCEN allows only limited access to its financial data, constraining the number of law enforcement authorities who can mine the material.

On the positive side, FinCEN does provide some valuable services to the financial community. It publishes *SAR Activity Review—Trends, Tips and Issues* (and its companion piece, *SARs by the Numbers*) to inform institutions of the latest suspicious activity trends.[30] It has also created a terrorism hotline that institutions can call if they have important information to report or questions to ask.[31] In addition, it issues advisories and bulletins on specific money laundering and terrorism financing schemes, on deficient AML/CFT jurisdictions and institutions, and on individuals who may be engaged in fraudulent activities or are otherwise deemed high risk.

U.S. DUE DILIGENCE EFFORTS

The U.S. banking system has implemented many of the measures outlined in FATF's international standards regarding customer due diligence.[32] At the most basic level, the government requires banks to have stringent customer identification programs. Section 326 of the PATRIOT Act outlines the standards for verifying customer identification when accounts are first opened.[33] Banks must then maintain records of this information, including customer name, address, and so forth.[34] They must also consult lists of known or suspected terrorists to ensure that the person opening the account does not appear.

U.S. banks are required to conduct enhanced due diligence measures when dealing with potentially high-risk customers. Section 312 of the PATRIOT Act specifically targets PEPs, instructing banks to ensure that money laundering is not taking place. In 2001, in an attempt to help banks deal with this problem, the government issued *Guidance on Enhanced Scrutiny for Transactions that May Involve the Proceeds of Foreign Official Corruption.*[35]

Also in accordance with the international standard, U.S. banks are barred from maintaining correspondent accounts with foreign shell banks.[36] And institutions must take measures to ensure that the correspondent accounts they do maintain do not provide services to shell banks.

In Simple Terms

How Has the U.S. Government Helped Banks Reduce Risk?

- By requiring them to have stringent customer identification and due diligence programs
- By issuing guidance on politically exposed persons
- By prohibiting them from maintaining correspondent accounts with shell banks
- By identifying high-risk jurisdictions in which they must conduct additional due diligence.
- By requiring them to implement detailed risk assessments and incorporate higher standards based on increased risk.

Finally, the U.S. government has identified high-risk geographical areas and advised financial institutions to carry out additional due diligence measures when conducting business there. These areas include:

- Countries under U.S. sanctions (list administered by the Treasury Department)[37]
- Countries identified as supporting international terrorism (list administered by State Department)[38]
- Jurisdictions deemed to be of "primary money laundering concern" (list administered by FinCEN)[39]
- Jurisdictions identified on FATF's NCCT list (see chapter 3)[40]
- Jurisdictions identified in the State Department's annual International Narcotics Control Strategy Report (INSCR)[41]
- Identified offshore financial centers

Case Study

Citibank: Laundering through "Private Banking"

U.S.-based Citibank is one of the largest financial institutions in the world, with approximately 180,000 employees in more than 100 countries. As of this writing, it holds $700 billion in known assets and more than $100 billion in "private banking" assets.[1] Private banking is a sector of the industry that caters to extremely wealthy clients, generally those with $1 million or more in deposits. The practice is particularly vulnerable to illicit activity, however—a fact demonstrated most notoriously in the case of Citibank client Paul Salinas, brother of former Mexican president Carlos Salinas. According to the U.S. General Accountability Office (GAO), from 1992 to 1994, Citibank helped Salinas funnel more than $100 million in illicit money out of his country and eventually into Swiss bank accounts.[2]

The Salinas case centered on abuses of Citibank's correspondent relationships with "private banks" and "private investment corporations." Given their wealthy clientele, private banks often use practices that emphasize secrecy, such as using codenames for accounts, commingling bank funds with client

Banks can also red-flag countries on their own if prior experiences, transaction histories, or other factors lead them to conclude that a given jurisdiction poses a high risk.

U.S. TRANSACTION REPORTING

Whenever a currency transaction takes place above $10,000, U.S. banks are required to file a Currency Transaction Report with FinCEN[42] and maintain sufficiently identifying records for five years afterward.[43] The CTR is then inputted into a BSA database that is available to federal banking regulators and the law enforcement community.[44] Banks must also file with FinCEN and maintain records when customers purchase bank checks, drafts, cashier's checks, money orders, and travelers checks in excess of $3,000.

In addition to regular reporting, banks must file Suspicious Activity Reports with FinCEN if they know or suspect that a transaction (1) involves funds derived from or intended for illegal activities, (2) is part of a plan to evade laws or reporting requirements (e.g., smurfing/structuring), (3) has no apparent business or lawful purpose, or

funds (which effectively disguises the movement of the latter), and using offshore private investment corporations in countries with strict secrecy laws.

In order to move Salinas's money, Citibank set up a shell investment company in the Cayman Islands, in addition to bank accounts in London and Switzerland. According to a GAO report on the matter, Citibank accepted millions of dollars from Salinas but never asked for standard information on his financial background or verified the source of his money.[3]

After Salinas's 1995 arrest for murder and financial corruption, Citibank lawyers began to monitor his accounts. The bank continued to behave irresponsibly, however. For example, Salinas' Citibank account manager in New York advised his wife to move the money elsewhere. And although the bank did eventually inform federal officials about his suspicious transactions, it did not tell them about the network of foreign shell companies and offshore accounts it had set up to shield the Salinas fortune. During a Senate hearing, the Citibank manager responsible for Salinas's account confirmed that all of this information "was known...on the very top," and that she and other lower-level employees were "little pawns in this whole thing."[4]

Shortly before the GAO report was issued, Swiss authorities confiscated $114 million from Salinas's account, and Mexican officials froze an additional $119 million.[5]

Case Study

SWIFT and the Terrorist Finance Tracking Program

In 2006, it came to light that the U.S. Treasury Department had issued a subpoena to SWIFT—a Belgium-based company with U.S. offices that operates a worldwide messaging system used to transmit bank transaction data—seeking information on suspected international terrorists. According to press and Treasury reports, authorities with the department's Terrorist Finance Tracking Program had reviewed SWIFT data as part of specific investigations of organizations such as al-Qaeda, Hamas, and Hizbollah. The U.S. government claimed that "following the money" in this manner enabled authorities to "identify and locate operatives and their financiers, chart terrorist networks, and help keep money out of their hands."[1]

Some policymakers have argued that organizations like al-Qaeda typically avoid the international financial system.[2] Yet, the revelation that Treasury has devoted an entire tracking program to the problem clearly shows that terror financiers use the formal banking system to move their money.

Nevertheless, European officials were outraged when they discovered that Treasury was using a European company's data without consulting European government officials. In June 2007, the department agreed to appoint an "eminent European" to conduct annual oversight regarding the handling, use, and dissemination of such data, ensuring that controls and safeguards were in place. Treasury also committed to a set of "Representations" describing EU data protection concerns, which were published in the Official Journal of the European Union in July 2007 and in the U.S. *Federal Register* in October 2007.[3]

(4) is not the sort of transaction in which the particular customer would normally be expected to engage.[45]

In 2006, FinCEN received approximately 16 million CTRs and 1 million SARs.[46] This is far more than the agency is capable of actually going through in an effective manner. As mentioned previously, however, the reports provide a paper trail for law enforcement should the need arise over the course of an investigation.

SUSPICIOUS ACTIVITY LOOPHOLE

In what FATF has determined to be a loophole in the U.S. system—one that is certainly abused by money launderers—American banks are not required to file SARs for suspicious transactions under $5,000.[47] Although banks may file below the threshold voluntarily, FATF has correctly characterized the regulation as a "weakness" that hampers U.S. efforts to detect "terrorist financing related transactions," given that terrorists require relatively little money to carry out their activities.[48] Moreover, smurfing/structuring continues to be the leading suspicious activity filed, making the case even stronger for lowering the threshold to zero.[49]

To its credit, the U.S. government has mandated that bank employees who file SARs above or below the threshold be given safe harbor, without fear of liability if they performed their actions in good faith. The government has also implemented the international standard prohibiting banks from tipping off clients when an SAR is filed.[50]

WIRE TRANSFER TROUBLE

U.S. banks are required to obtain and retain records when a wire transfer is above $3,000. The records must include the originator's name and address, along with other information such as amount, date, payment instructions from the originator, and the identity of the beneficiary institution.[51] In cases where originators are not established customers, banks must also verify their identity before agreeing to carry out the

In Simple Terms

- U.S. banks must file a Currency Transaction Report with FinCEN every time a currency transaction exceeds $10,000
- U.S. banks must file a Suspicious Activity Report with FinCEN if a transaction is unusual in any way or inconsistent with normal activity in the account
- U.S. banks must file with FinCEN when customers purchase bank checks, drafts, cashier's checks, money orders, or traveler's checks in excess of $3,000
- U.S. banks are required to obtain and retain records for wire transfers above $3,000, but not to file them with FinCEN
- U.S. banks are not required to keep records or even ask for customer identification for wire transfers under $3,000—a major deficiency in the system

transaction, collecting information such as social security numbers, alien identification numbers, or passport numbers.

In general, these regulations are compliant with the international standard. Yet, they contain three serious deficiencies that leave the U.S. banking system open to money launderers and terror financiers.

First, although banks must create and keep the above-described records for transfers over $3,000, they are not required to file them with FinCEN. Second, the U.S. threshold is significantly higher than the international standard of $1,000. FATF believes this negatively impacts the U.S. financial system due to "the risks identified with low value wire transfers."[52] In practical terms, anyone can walk into a U.S. bank and transfer money below $3,000 without even being asked for identification. Third, banks are not required to keep even basic records of transactions under this threshold—a major deficiency that is certainly abused by illicit actors.

CONCLUSION

The fundamental premise of judiciously applying a strong AML regime in the formal financial sector is that banks become less vulnerable to abuse when their transactions are held to greater accountability and transparency. In other words, the international and domestic system is better equipped to fight financial criminals when there is a higher level of due diligence and suspicious activity reporting.

There is no panacea for the problem of money laundering and terrorism financing in the formal financial sector—using banks to move illicit money and obscure one's tracks will always be possible to some degree. Government authorities can hope to accomplish two major goals, however: (1) make it more difficult and costly for those who wish to move illicit funds (which often drives these actors to the informal sector), and (2) maintain good financial records of all transactions so that this information can be used in prosecutions.

Former Treasury Department general counsel David Aufhauser encapsulated the situation well in his 2003 testimony before the Senate Committee on Banking, Housing, and Urban Affairs:

> Money is the fuel for the enterprise of terror. It may also be its Achilles' heel. It can leave a signature, an audit trail, which, once discovered, might well prove the best single means of identification and capture of terrorists and pinpointing their donors. Financial records are literally the diaries of terror. Stopping the flow of money to terrorists may be one of the very best ways we have of stopping terror altogether.[53]

Chapter 5

No Questions Asked: Hawala and the Informal Financial Sector

In this chapter:

- Advantages of hawala
- Country of concern: United Arab Emirates, the mecca of illicit finance
- Ideal types of government oversight
- U.S. legal requirements
- Shortfalls in the system

It is estimated that hundreds of billions of dollars are transferred each year using the informal financial sector.[1] According to the World Bank, for example, the amount of money sent back home by migrants working abroad—only a portion of total informal transfers—has doubled since 2002, reaching as high as $350 billion per year.[2] At the same time, security and intelligence agencies have become increasingly aware that some informal transactions are linked to money laundering and terrorism financing. The Financial Action Task Force (FATF), for example, believes that informal networks are widely used by terror financiers. Although terrorist groups require longer-term funding to support their overall activities, the direct operational costs of major attacks (e.g., the Madrid bombings of 2004 or the London bombings of 2005) can be as little $10,000–12,000—a sum easily transferred informally.[3]

Following the September 11 attacks, analysts and policymakers focused an immense amount of attention on an ancient system of moving money—hawala. As described in chapter 2, hawala is essentially a simple broker system based on trust. Many different cultures use hawala-like systems. The most commonly known are often connected to ethnic groups or to specific geographic regions, and some will sound familiar to Washington policymakers: hawala/hundi (meaning "trust" in Urdu and Hindi; indigenous to Southeast Asia), fei chien (meaning "flying money system"; indigenous to China), padala (meaning "to send" in Tagalog; indigenous to the Philippines), and phoe kuan (meaning "message houses"; indigenous to Thailand).[4]

In Simple Terms

Experts commonly refer to hawala networks as "value transfer systems," "alternative remittance systems," or "underground banking." All such systems have the same features in common:

- They allow funds to be sent anonymously, often with few or no records of the people sending and receiving the money
- When records are kept, they are often inaccessible to government authorities
- Criminals are adept at using and abusing them

The case of "Sanjay and Sanya" in chapter 2 illustrated the defining trait common to all of these systems: transferring money or value without physically moving it. That is, a broker on one side of the transaction accepts money from a customer who wishes to send funds to someone. The first broker then communicates with a second broker who distributes the desired amount to the intended recipient. The brokers profit from customer fees, and they have a variety of methods for settling up with each other.[5] For

Country of Concern

United Arab Emirates—The Mecca of Illicit Finance

In 2008, the U.S. State Department issued a report warning that the United Arab Emirates (UAE)—a Persian Gulf federation encompassing Abu Dhabi, Ajman, Dubai, Fujairah, Ras al-Khaimah, Sharjah, and Umm al-Quwain—was "particularly susceptible" to money laundering.[1] Indeed, the emirates are known as the region's criminal hub, serving elements as disparate as mob figures, arms dealers, drug traffickers, diamond traders, underground money brokers, and jihadis. All of these illicit actors have been known to engage in laundering, and the UAE's law enforcement community is notorious for looking the other way.

The UAE possesses an advanced, but lightly regulated, financial services sector. Each of the emirates has an abundance of informal financial networks, known as hawaladars. Moreover, the UAE is a cash-based society and a heavy the same reasons given in chapter 2, "hawala" will be used as a catchall term for these sorts of transactions throughout the following sections.

It is important to keep in mind that most people who use hawala are not criminals—they are simply trying to move legitimately earned money for legitimate purposes (even if hawala happens to be illegal in their country, as it is in Egypt, for example). Nevertheless, a significant amount of hawala transactions are conducted by criminals who wish to move their money cheaply and without transparency.[6] Research suggests that these criminals get their money from a wide assortment of illicit activities, including drug trafficking, arms dealing, human smuggling, corruption, and tax evasion.[7] Even if their transactions constituted only a minute percentage of total hawala transfers, they would still add up to an enormous amount of money.

ADVANTAGES OF THE INFORMAL SECTOR

There are many advantages to using hawala—for both the remitter/recipient and the operator—over the formal banking system. In addition to greater convenience and reliability, the cost of sending money via hawala is almost always much cheaper than wiring it through a bank or similar institution. Hawaladars offer better prices because they do not have to follow official exchange rates. Moreover, they often have

trader of precious metal, especially gold. Illicit actors exploit each of these traits, using gold and hawalas to move their money around the world with few, if any, obstacles. They also exploit the country's seemingly permissive attitude toward smuggling—a phenomenon witnessed most conspicuously in Dubai. There, dhows—wooden boats that have been used for centuries to move goods in this part of the world—are rarely inspected and often dock in an aptly named location, "Smugglers Creek."[2]

Perhaps most disturbing, the UAE played a central role in the financing of the September 11 attacks:

- Before the attack, al-Qaeda moved money freely around the world using the al-Barakat hawala network, which had one of its headquarters in the UAE (see separate case study for a full discussion of al-Barakat)[3]

- A UAE money changer transferred funds to Marwan al-Shehhi, a citizen of the emirates who flew United Airlines Flight 175 into the World Trade Center[4]

(continued)

- According to the U.S. government, two of Usama bin Laden's sisters used the UAE to smuggle cash to him in Afghanistan[5]
- One of bin Laden's financial chiefs, Shaykh Said, also known as Mustafah Muhammad Ahmed, lived in Dubai and wired money to three of the terrorists before the attack. The funds were traced back to the al-Ansari Exchange branch in Abu Dhabi[6]

Even before September 11, the UAE served as a haven for some of the most notorious examples of terrorism financing and money laundering:

- Al-Qaeda used the Dubai Islamic Bank to send funds that were used in the 1998 attacks on the U.S. embassies in Kenya and Tanzania[7]
- Russian arms merchant Victor Bout, implicated in black market sales to Rwanda, Sierra Leone, and Angola, lived in and operated his business out of the UAE for many years (see chapter 10 for a full case study on Bout)[8]

Ironically, the UAE's leadership claims to have implemented an excellent

representatives in isolated or remote areas with few or no banks, so they can charge far lower fees when sending money to such locations. Another advantage is speed—in many cases, a hawala transaction can be completed within 24 hours, including direct delivery to the recipient. In contrast, transnational bank transactions can take a week or longer, particularly in remote parts of the world that lack banks or established correspondent relationships. Finally, illiterate people are often disinclined to go to a bank where they have to read and sign forms—they naturally prefer hawala, where that is not required.[8]

For those who wish to conduct illicit business, hawala protects their confidentiality. Hawaladars maintain very few records, offering customers near anonymity. They generally keep only simple debt logs, and even these are often discarded after operators settle up with one another. This means the paper trail is limited or nonexistent, making transactions very difficult to track. Even when proper records are kept, they are often in a foreign language or shorthand, making them difficult to decipher for Western or even local authorities without the hawaladar's help. Conducting criminal investigations under such circumstances is a major challenge.

There are also clear advantages for the hawala operator. Hawalas are often run in tandem with another business, ranging from the grocery store set-up described in regime to counter money laundering. To its credit, the country has cooperated with international anti–money laundering/combating the financing of terrorism (AML/CFT) investigations, but it has done little to deter this type of activity from actually taking place—the well-meaning regulations it has enacted are not well enforced.[9]

In 2008, for example, the UAE adopted a set of measures to register hawaladars. By April of that year, more than 240 of them had been registered, prompting Abdulrahim Mohamed al-Awadi, head of the UAE Central Bank's AML unit, to boast, "We know who they are."[10] What al-Awadi failed to mention is that registration is voluntary—no official in the UAE government can reliably estimate how many additional hawaladars operate in the country.[11] Other officials have exposed similar contradictions. In 2005, Interior Minister Sheik Saif bin Zayed al-Nahyan stated that the UAE had made great progress against money laundering: "Give us the evidence, and we will do something about it."[12] In the same breath, however, he called the UAE a "neutral country, like Switzerland." Reading between the lines, and examining the country's recent track record, one can see that the UAE has little actual interest in pursuing illicit actors.

chapter 2 to restaurants, clothing stores, import/export businesses, souvenir stores, and most any other type of establishment. Money made from hawala fees reduces overall operating costs and is easily integrated into normal business activities. Some operators have also used their hawala businesses to play the currency market, seeking to profit from exchange rate speculation.[9]

INTERNATIONAL STANDARDS

With the understanding that hawala networks and other informal brokers traditionally operate outside the formal financial sector, FATF has developed standards geared toward helping authorities reduce the likelihood of abuse. The agency also encourages countries to establish compliance programs that are "flexible, effective and proportional" to the risk presented.[10] In other words, government oversight should not be so burdensome that it forces these types of services to go underground, making it even more difficult to detect illicit activity.

FATF's Special Recommendation VI outlines three measures for meeting the challenges presented by the informal sector:

1. Countries should license or register informal operators[11]

2. Countries should hold operators to all FATF standards
3. Countries should take punitive action against operators who continue to provide services illegally, including administrative, civil, or criminal sanctions[12]

The first step in this process is to place a competent government agency in charge of the licensing/registration process. This agency should conduct ongoing due diligence to ensure that informal financial networks are not engaged in criminal behavior, including background checks on agents, owners, directors, and shareholders. In addition, FATF recommends that owners be required to submit a list of all the addresses at which they operate, as well as all the bank account numbers they use to run their business.

Once these initial processes are complete, the international standard recommends that countries compel informal networks to carry out many of the same measures as the formal financial sector, including:

Case Study

Al-Barakat: Informal Terrorism Financing Network

In 1986, a group of companies in Somalia formed the al-Barakat network of hawalas. By 2001, the network—also known as the al-Barakat Bank—operated in 40 countries (including headquarters in the UAE), transferred an estimated $140 million per year, offered phone and internet services, and had become Somalia's largest private employer. Given the country's nonexistent economy and nonfunctioning formal banking system, receiving remittances from abroad become the lifeline of many Somalis. And al-Barakat was the perfect outlet to facilitate those transactions.[1]

Al-Barakat came under heavy scrutiny after the September 11 attacks for its suspected role in helping al-Qaeda and other terrorist organizations transfer money. In November 2001, the U.S. Treasury Department placed the network on the Specially Designated Global Terrorist list, accusing its officers of funneling $15 million per year to al-Qaeda and calling them "the quartermasters of terror."[2] With remittances representing approximately 25 to 40 percent of Somalia's gross national product, the al-Barakat designation had a considerable effect on the Somali economy.

- Maintaining proper records on customers and transactions
- Reporting suspicious activity
- Requiring customers whose transactions exceed a certain threshold to provide appropriate identification; if the operator cannot properly identify the customer, the transaction should not be processed[13]
- Keeping records for at least five years[14]

If an operator violates these requirements, authorities are encouraged to employ penalties in line with the severity of the offense. As mentioned above, however, it may be unwise to overburden informal networks with regulations. In light of this concern, governments tend to seek a middle ground between the current unregulated conditions and FATF's ideal (i.e., placing the same stringent requirements on the formal and informal sectors).

Between 1997 and November 2001, Somali refugee Abdirahman Sheikh-Ali Isse operated a hawala business in Alexandria, Virginia. His nephew Abdi joined the business in 2000. Calling themselves "Rage Associates," they served as agents of al-Barakat, eventually moving their operation from Isse's home to al-Barakat's offices in Alexandria.[3] They did not obtain the necessary license as required by federal and Virginia law.

In June 2002, both men were charged with money laundering. Specifically, they had "smurfed"/structured $4,244,499 in cash from individuals wishing to transmit money to Somalia, Ethiopia, Kenya, and Sudan.[4] Using methods described in previous chapters, they would make multiple small deposits of cash in different Northern Virginia banks (including First Union, Bank of America, and Chevy Chase), keeping the amounts under $10,000 to avoid triggering the government's currency transaction reporting requirements.[5]

For each customer transfer, Isse and Abdi normally charged a 4 percent fee. They retained 1 percent and remitted the other 3 percent to al-Barakat. Al-Barakat would then give 1 percent to the agent in the receiving country.[6] By 2001, the network had collected $6 million in fees from this one branch alone.[7]

Although the U.S. government acknowledged that the two men had no knowledge of al-Barakat's alleged ties to al-Qaeda or other terrorist groups, both were convicted of money laundering and operating an unregistered hawala business. Isse was sentenced to 18 months in prison, and Abdi to 37 months.[8]

Licensing or Registering?

FATF defines licensing and registering in Interpretive Note to Special Recommendation VI:

Licensing would require informal networks to "obtain permission from a designated competent authority" in order to carry out their services legally.

Registration would require informal networks to "register with or declare [their existence] to a designated competent authority" in order to operate legally.

FATF recognizes that registration is likely the most cost-effective approach "when compared to the significant resources required for licensing."[1]

U.S. DOMESTIC SYSTEM

Hawala and other informal financial networks—legally referred to as "money services businesses" (MSBs)[15] in the United States—pose a considerable investigative and regulatory challenge to the U.S. government. Part of the problem is that these networks are "expanding at a rapid rate, often operate without supervision, and transact business with overseas counterparts that are largely unregulated."[16] The problem is compounded by the fact that a significant number of U.S. residents remain poor and illiterate, leaving them unable or unwilling to use the more expensive and complex formal banking sector. Such individuals naturally gravitate toward the informal sector to move their money.

Accordingly, the U.S. government has proceeded along a dual track. On the one hand, it has encouraged MSBs to comply with regulations that promote financial transparency. On the other hand, it has encouraged individuals who do not use the banking sector to do so, helping them understand the various means of sending legitimate funds abroad using the formal sector.[17] To meet these goals, it has employed a multifaceted approach that includes:

U.S. Government Agencies and Hawala

To meet the challenges posed by the informal sector, the United States has introduced both a regulatory and an oversight system:

- Registration is overseen by the Financial Crimes Enforcement Network (FinCEN; see chapter 4 for a discussion of this agency)
- Oversight is administered by the Internal Revenue Service (IRS)

- clarifying legal requirements;
- outreach and education programs to both MSBs and people who do not use the banking sector;
- targeted compliance examinations; and
- civil and criminal enforcement against those operators who do not follow the rules.

The government has allocated significant resources to inform MSBs of their legal requirements. For a number of reasons, these operators have traditionally been reluctant to follow the law. First, their businesses are often small, and the requirements would be expensive to implement. Second, they are accustomed to operating without standard recordkeeping practices and mixing their informal transactions with their other business activities. Third, many of these operators do not speak English.

U.S. LEGAL REQUIREMENTS

To run an MSB in the United States, operators must comply with a number of legal obligations, including registering with the government, maintaining records, carrying out customer due diligence procedures, and complying with other regulatory controls mandated by the Bank Secrecy Act (BSA). First, each MSB owner must register both the business itself and all of its agents with FinCEN.[18] Failure to register is against

Hawala and AML/CFT

The U.S. government requires that all hawaladars and other MSBs implement AML/CFT programs in order to prevent abuse. These programs must include the following measures:

1. Maintaining records of domestic and international transactions for five years[1]
2. Verifying customer identity for every transaction over $3,000[2]
3. Filing Currency Transaction Reports for transfers over $10,000[3]
4. Creating and keeping records if a customer purchases money orders or travelers checks over $3,000[4]

MSBs must formally describe their programs in writing and make this document available to FinCEN and the IRS upon request.

the law.[19] Although the current number of MSBs is not known, in 1997 there were an estimated 200,000 nationwide. As of December 2008, however, only some 40,000 were registered, meaning that the majority of MSBs in the United States are in breach of the BSA.[20]

In addition, 46 states require MSBs to apply for a license. Unfortunately, not all states have adopted the same licensing requirements, making it difficult for MSBs to operate across state lines.[21]

As with the banking sector, the government also requires MSBs to file Suspicious Activity Reports (SARs) if they suspect that:

1. the transaction involves funds derived from illegal activity
2. the transaction is designed to evade any BSA regulation
3. the transaction is believed to facilitate criminal activity

Case Study

Beacon on the Hill

In February 2004, the Manhattan district attorney announced a huge victory against an MSB that conducted billions of dollars worth of illegal offshore transactions in the Caribbean, Middle East, and South America. The New York City–based Beacon Hill Corporation, which operated from 1994 to 2003, was convicted of money laundering and operating without a license.[1] Law enforcement officials also determined that the corporation had cheated the city, state, and federal government out of tens of millions of dollars in taxes—one of the largest schemes of its kind ever uncovered.[2] Through a forfeiture action, authorities were able to freeze more than $13 million in the firm's corporate accounts.

Beacon Hill's services included transmitting funds from individuals, shell corporations, and "casas de cambio" (exchange houses) in South America. According to court documents, its 12 employees transferred money to and from the corporation by wire and check deposits.[3] In total, the firm made more than $6.5 billion worth of illegal wire transfers alone using its 40 corporate accounts at a major New York Bank.[4] Manhattan district attorney Robert Morgenthau stated, "I had no idea we were going to find this much money.... There's nothing this size anywhere. The magnitude really shocked me."[5] He

4. the transaction has no apparent business or lawful purpose or is not the sort in which the customer would normally be expected to engage[22]

If MSBs do not uphold their regulatory obligations, they could face civil and/or criminal enforcement by the Justice Department or other law enforcement agencies.[23] For example, MSBs must renew their registration every two years, and failure to do so is punishable by a civil penalty of up to $5,000 for each day the violation continues and/or a criminal penalty of up to five years imprisonment.[24] Similarly, failure to have an adequate AML/CFT program is finable up to $25,000 per day.[25]

LAW ENFORCEMENT OVERSIGHT

In addition to introducing a federal registration and regulatory regime, the United States has also instituted an oversight system for the informal sector. The primary

also admitted that the city had not begun investigating Beacon Hill until it stumbled across an internet ad that read, "You want an account in a secrecy jurisdiction, come to us!"

As a result of the corporation's almost nonexistent recordkeeping practices, law enforcement found it very difficult to identify the real parties behind the transactions or to trace all the money that passed through the accounts. Those records that were recovered showed that Beacon Hill had transmitted more than $31.5 million to accounts in Pakistan, Lebanon, Jordan, Dubai, Saudi Arabia, and elsewhere in the Middle East.[6]

Beacon Hill conducted some of its transactions via Hudson United Bank. After the Beacon investigation, officials determined that Hudson's AML program needed serious reform. For example, from 1997 to 2003, the bank's 90 Broad Street branch in Manhattan alone had conducted $65 million in transactions either originating or terminating in the so-called Tri-Border Area of South America—a region that is notorious for money laundering and terrorism financing (see chapter 9 for a full discussion of this area).[7] Hudson agreed to pay a total of $5 million to the city of New York for its role in this activity.[8]

Beacon Hill also held three dozen accounts with J. P. Morgan Chase, through which it made wire transfers totaling more than $9 billion.[9] Morgan Chase was not charged with any crime, but it has stopped dealing with wholesale money transmitters.

agency responsible for MSBs is the IRS.[26] Specifically, the IRS is charged with examining MSB policies, procedures, records, and currency transactions to ensure that the proper forms are being filed. In addition, the agency ensures that MSBs register with FinCEN and conducts compliance examinations.

Although the IRS is the lead agency in this regard, it is important to underscore that all law enforcement agencies can and have pursued financial crime cases involving MSB violations of money laundering laws, the BSA, and terrorism financing laws. In recent years, law enforcement has been increasingly successful in pursuing both unlicensed and criminal MSB operators. The only publicly available statistics on such cases originate from the Bureau of Immigration and Customs Enforcement (ICE), today a part of the Department of Homeland Security. From 1992 to 2005, ICE initiated more than 260 investigations and executed more than 100 search warrants in connection with MSBs. The bureau also made roughly 120 arrests and 130 indictments, seizing $23 million.[27]

A Significant Vulnerability

In the informal financial sector, the U.S. government threshold for filing an SAR is $2,000. In other words, if an MSB operator suspects that a client is sending money to Usama bin Laden in an amount under $2,000, he is not legally required to file a report or take any other action.

This is a dangerous loophole in the U.S. system—FATF has strongly encouraged the United States to impose a zero threshold for reporting suspicious activity, in line with the international standard.

Even with such help from other agencies, FATF has questioned the IRS's ability to properly oversee a sector as large in scope as the American MSB industry. According to the 2006 National Money Laundering Threat Assessment, U.S. law enforcement investigations have demonstrated that a large portion of MSB transactions involve members of the Somali, Yemeni, Pakistani, Afghani, Filipino, Indonesian, Chinese, African, Indian, and Latino communities remitting money to areas "with non-existent, unaffordable, or untrustworthy financial institutions."[28] Destinations that receive a significant amount of suspicious funds from U.S. remitters include Russia, Colombia, the Dominican Republic, and various parts of Central and South America and Mexico. In addition, increased money laundering investigations are taking place in Middle Eastern communities that remit funds to Egypt, Sudan, and other parts of the Middle East.[29] FATF has determined that the sheer size of the problem "poses a major challenge to the authorities in implementing an effective oversight system." [30] And IRS resources, it concludes, are "wholly inadequate" to the task.

Adding resources alone will not solve the problem, however. According to FATF, two additional barriers stand in the way of effective compliance. First, American MSB operators do not exercise sufficient control over their agents. Second, the IRS cannot possibly succeed in its efforts until all 50 states standardize their procedures for licensing and other issues.

OUTREACH AND EDUCATION

The U.S. government has tasked FinCEN with carrying out an awareness campaign that includes industry training, public presentations, issuance of guidelines, and a list of registered MSBs. FinCEN has also developed a special website devoted solely to the MSB sector (www.msb.gov). In addition to the MSB list, relevant posted information includes:

Case Study

Manhattan Foreign Exchange

On March 20, 2003, law enforcement agents in New York arrested four individuals in connection with a Pakistani MSB called Manhattan Foreign Exchange. Run from the basement of a Kashmiri restaurant in midtown Manhattan,[1] this business was one of New York's largest remitters to Pakistan, transferring more than $33 million to the country during a three-year period, mostly in drug proceeds.[2] It also sold fake U.S., Pakistani, Canadian, and British passports and travel documents.[3]

Shaheen Khalid Butt, the business's Kashmiri owner, was charged with money laundering, currency reporting violations, conspiracy, and immigration fraud charges.[4] He had been arrested on similar charges in 1994 and sentenced to five years probation.

Over the course of the investigation, law enforcement bugged the basement of the Kashmiri restaurant and videotaped couriers dropping off bags of cash. In the recorded conversations, there was open talk about "powder" and "kilos," and couriers often carried bundles of cash in paper bags.[5] According to U.S. Attorney James Comey, authorities used this and other electronic surveillance to show that Butt and his unlicensed business "received frequent cash deliveries, tens of thousands of dollars at a time, from various people."[6]

- A quick reference guide to BSA requirements
- What AML/CFT programs should include
- Requirements on how to conduct business with foreign agents and counterparts
- Guide to money laundering prevention

IRS Coming Up Short

To date, the IRS has been unable to conduct exhaustive assessments of MSBs in the United States or compel them to register. This constitutes a major weaknesses in the U.S. AML/CFT regime.

- Letter rulings and frequently asked questions
- Information on how to obtain and maintain banking services
- Multilingual videos and CD-ROMs that include case studies designed to educate MSB employees about BSA obligations
- Information for MSB customers on why operators must ask for personal information
- "High-Risk Indicators" to aid banks when providing services to MSBs

CONCLUSIONS

Efficiency, anonymity, and lack of paper trails explain the attractiveness of hawala and other informal networks for those who use them. Although the vast majority of transactions conducted through these networks are legitimate, it is clear that hawala also attracts individuals and groups engaged in criminal activities such as money laundering, drug trafficking, smuggling, and terrorism financing. Moving illicit funds through this sector is very easy, posing a huge challenge to international law enforcement agencies. Robert Looney, a noted professor of economics at the U.S. Naval Postgraduate School, summarized this challenge well:

> Given its size and semi-legitimate status... it is not hard for terrorists to transfer money using Hawala channels. They are labyrinths replete with pseudonyms, middlemen and dead-ends. Wealthy Arab patrons in the Middle East likely send funds to al Qaeda through Hawala organizations, as do myriad Arab charities acting as fund-raising fronts. The smaller the value of the transfer the less attention it is likely to attract, but it is still easy to transfer large amounts of money without raising questions.[31]

Unless governments are willing to spend a tremendous amount of resources to successfully regulate this sector, illicit actors will continue to have a free hand in moving their tainted money.

Chapter 6

Hide-and-Seek Through Cash Smuggling

In this chapter:

- What is cash smuggling?
- Region of concern: Southeast Asia
- Disclosure/declaration
- U.S. government efforts to counter bulk cash smuggling
- Bright spots

One of the oldest ways of moving money has witnessed a resurgence in recent years. Intelligence gathered from captured terrorist suspects and other sources indicates "a trend toward bulk-cash smuggling and use of cash couriers," according to U.S. Treasury undersecretary for terrorism and financial intelligence Stuart Levey.[1] It is virtually impossible to stop this type of smuggling entirely. In fact, intelligence and law enforcement agencies around the globe report that it is one of the primary methods used by terror financiers, money launderers, and organized crime to move their money.[2]

Reliance on physical money is a mixed blessing for illicit actors. On the one hand, it has made it more difficult for terror financiers to raise money from donors or

Terrorist Organizations and Cash Smuggling

As described in chapter 5, terrorist operations are relatively inexpensive compared with conventional military operations, and small sums can finance very damaging attacks. Cash smuggling has played a significant role in the international flow of terrorist money. The list of organizations that employ this tactic is long, including groups such as Hizbollah, Hamas, the Tamil Tigers, and the Revolutionary Armed Forces of Colombia (FARC), just to name a few.

charities—transferring cash is much more of a hassle than writing a check or wiring funds. On the other hand, physically moving money is difficult for law enforcement to track and offers near-total anonymity.

As described in chapter 2, cash smugglers have a wide variety of tactics for remaining undetected, concealing their cash in automobiles, commercial shipments, express packages, luggage, private aircraft, boats, and elsewhere. They frequently use clandestine roads, unpatrolled waterways, and other avenues to circumvent official border

Region of Concern

Southeast Asia

Two of the most notorious terrorist attacks in Southeast Asia were funded almost entirely by cash couriers. Jemaah Islamiah (JI), an affiliate of al-Qaeda, carried out both the 2002 Bali bombings and the 2003 South Jakarta bombing with less than $60,000. JI's head of operations, Riduan bin Isomuddin (also known as Hambali), was hiding in Thailand at the time of both attacks. Before the Bali bombings, he hired several cash couriers to move money to the perpetrators. Specifically, he transferred $30,000 in two batches via couriers who took several weeks to complete the runs.[1]

The Bali attack killed 202 people and injured 209. It was a sophisticated operation, coordinated by JI member Imam Samudra and involving logistics specialists, bomb makers, a support team, and suicide bombers.[2] Three bombs were detonated—two in popular nightclubs and the third outside the U.S. consulate in Denpasar. Indonesia tried and successfully convicted various members of the organization, sentencing three of them to death.

Hambali also provided the funding for the JW Marriott Hotel bombing in Jakarta. Again, he sent a total of $30,000 in al-Qaeda funds from Thailand to Indonesia in April 2003 through a string of couriers.[3] On August 5, the perpetrators detonated a suicide car bomb outside the hotel lobby, killing 12 people and injuring 150. Although no suspects have been brought to justice for the attack, all of the evidence overwhelmingly points to JI as the organization responsible, and to Hambali as the financier.[4]

crossing points. Most couriers prefer a more mundane option, however: commercial airlines. Plane travel requires little preplanning and allows couriers to reach foreign destinations quickly and easily. Most important, it allows them to stay close to their money. For their part, customs authorities have limited resources for preventing such activities, particularly given the fact that smugglers can swallow money pellets or use other bodily means to avoid discovery.

Although cash couriers can be used to move any amount of money for legitimate or illicit reasons, the phenomenon of "bulk cash smuggling"—in the United States, defined as attempting the cross-border transport of $10,000 or more—is almost always associated with criminal activity. This type of smuggling—which often involves containerized cargo shipments—is a staple of criminal schemes that generate large amounts of profit.

International efforts to halt cash smuggling have been slow, particularly in parts of the world that rely on cash-based economies. The areas of greatest concern include Africa, the Middle East, and Latin America.

Customs officers and border security officials are the gatekeepers to each country and therefore the most important tool for detecting cash smugglers. Unfortunately, many customs bureaus around the world lack the funding, training, and equipment needed to spot this threat.[3] In general, detection has improved in recent years thanks to international guidance from the Financial Action Task Force (FATF) and other bodies. Yet, in order to redress their vulnerabilities, countries will need to take more vigorous action on several fronts, including international information sharing, coordinated targeting efforts, implementation of regulatory regimes, and enforcement operations.

INTERNATIONAL STANDARD

FATF issued Special Recommendation IX in 2004 with the objective of curtailing criminals' ability to "finance their activities or launder the proceeds of their crimes through the physical cross-border transportation of currency and bearer negotiable instruments."[4] The recommendation specifically aims to help countries implement five important measures:

1. Detecting the physical cross-border movement of currency

2. Stopping or restraining currency related to terrorism financing or money laundering

3. Stopping or restraining falsely declared or disclosed currency

4. Applying appropriate sanctions for false declarations or disclosures

5. Confiscating currency related to terrorism financing or money laundering[5]

FATF has made clear that this recommendation was in no way intended as a restriction on trade payments between countries or as a currency control measure.

To meet the recommendation, FATF encourages countries to implement either a "declaration" or a "disclosure" system for incoming and outgoing money. Countries need not use the same system for both situations.

Customs officials strongly prefer the declaration model, in large part because of the paper trails it creates. In a declaration system, individuals transporting currency or bearer negotiable instruments are required to submit a declaration form to the relevant government agency if the amount exceeds a certain threshold. FATF has encouraged countries to implement a threshold of USD/EUR 15,000 or less.

Case Study

Al-Qaeda Funds Attacks in Turkey

In November 2003, al-Qaeda partially funded two sets of attacks in Istanbul using cash couriers. Authorities believe that Usama bin Laden himself approved the operation.[1]

The first attack targeted two Jewish synagogues on November 15. The explosions killed 27 people and injured over 300, mostly Turkish Muslims.[2] Al-Qaeda struck again five days later when two suicide truck bombs exploded outside an HSBC bank and the British embassy, killing 30 and wounding more than 400. Although the attack killed several Britons, including consul-general Roger Short, most of the casualties were Turkish Muslims.[3]

In December 2003, Adnan Ersoz, a member of al-Qaeda in Turkey, confessed that he helped organize the attack. He also admitted that al-Qaeda gave militants in Turkey $150,000 to carry it out. Ersoz received $100,000 from the head of al-Qaeda in Turkey, Habip Aktas, and another $50,000 via an Iranian courier.[4] Authorities believe that the $100,000 was delivered by one of the al-Qaeda operatives charged in the case, Louai Sakka, a Syrian national who reportedly smuggled the money rolled in a sock.[5]

Turkey charged 74 people with involvement in the bombings. In February 2007, a Turkish court handed down life sentences to seven al-Qaeda associates.[6]

In a disclosure system, individuals do not need to declare any funds they are carrying unless asked to do so by the authorities. According to FATF, countries that choose this system should ensure that they empower authorities to make such inquiries based on "intelligence, suspicion or on a random basis."[6] In practice, however, disclosure systems are simply not effective.

> **Declaration or Disclosure?**
>
> **Declaration System:** All persons transporting funds exceeding USD/EUR 15,000 are required to submit a declaration form.
>
> **Disclosure System:** All persons transporting funds exceeding USD/EUR 15,000 are required to disclose that information upon request of the competent authorities.
>
> Customs officials have strongly advocated the declaration system because it creates a paper trail. Many governments have opted for only inbound or outbound currency declarations. To be effective, however, a country needs both.

Regardless of the system chosen, if customs officers or border agents determine that there has been a false declaration or disclosure, FATF recommends they be given the authority to request more information from the traveler regarding the origin and intended use of the money. This information—along with the amount of currency involved and the customer's identity—should be made available to the country's financial intelligence unit on a timely basis. Countries are also encouraged to consider imposing a reverse burden of proof if they uncover a false declaration/disclosure or have "reasonable grounds for suspicion of money laundering or terrorist financing."[7] That is, if travelers who are questioned under these circumstances are unable to demonstrate that their funds are legitimate, authorities should be empowered to confiscate the money on the spot, without having to wait for a criminal conviction or similar measure. With or without immediate confiscation, FATF emphasizes that such individuals should be subject to "effective, proportionate and dissuasive sanctions," whether criminal or administrative.[8]

In addition, governments should proactively target smugglers using risk assessments, identifying specific routes, flights, ships, and concealment methods that have been linked to terrorism or illicit finance. Potential targets should also be checked against known watch lists, including the various UN lists and other law enforcement databases. FATF has determined that access to intelligence reports, seizure analysis, and historical data is essential in identifying common tactics used by cash smugglers.[9] It is explicitly prohibited, however, to profile based on race, ethnicity, religion, or sex.

Best Practices: Use of Technology and Profiling?

In addition to making full use of intelligence, analysis, and threat assessments, FATF has determined that one of the best ways to capture smugglers is to enhance countries' technical capabilities. This could include the use of canine units trained to spot currency, X-ray machines, scanners, and similar measures.

FATF also encourages countries to establish passenger screening systems to analyze the behavior, appearance, and communications (verbal and nonverbal) of potential cash smugglers. Some have interpreted this as "profiling," but that is not the case—FATF's standard focuses on behavioral criteria that could indicate illicit activity, not on supposed racial, ethnic, or other traits usually associated with profiling.

U.S. DOMESTIC SYSTEM

As the United States strengthens its formal and informal financial sectors and creates greater transparency, many illicit actors are being forced to launder their money elsewhere, taking it to jurisdictions with lax or even complicit financial institutions. Cash smuggling is one of their many tactics for moving money out of the country.

The United States has 317 official land, sea, and air points of entry/exit, and numerous "unofficial" points as well. Authorities believe that both types of routes are regularly used by cash smugglers. The country's 3,987-mile border with Canada and 1,933-mile border with Mexico provide ample opportunities for such movement in both directions. For example, law enforcement has discovered that some smugglers use tunnels along the Mexican border; from 1990 to 2005, authorities found 33 such passageways.[10] The cash smuggled through all of these routes is derived from a wide array of criminal activity, including drug trafficking, human smuggling, bribery, contraband smuggling, extortion, fraud, illegal gambling, kidnapping, prostitution, and tax evasion.[11]

The United States regularly conducts joint investigations with Mexican authorities to determine what happens to smuggled cash once it crosses the border. Their findings include the following:

- In many cases, cash is deposited into Mexican banks or "casas de cambio" (exchange houses) and subsequently wired back to the United States.
- Some of these complicit Mexican financial institutions physically transport the cash back to the United States via couriers or armored cars, depositing it into correspondent bank accounts.

- Some smugglers move the cash further south to Costa Rica, Panama, Venezuela, or other Latin American countries, where it is used to pay for goods on the black market.
- In other cases, individuals move the funds to offshore jurisdictions with lax controls.[12]

Although U.S. law enforcement agencies are aware of the threat posed by these problems, they are also constrained by limited resources. As a result, border authorities are forced to concentrate on screening inbound, rather than outbound, travelers and cargo. This vulnerability will eventually have to be addressed.

U.S. DECLARATION/DISCLOSURE SYSTEM

The United States has implemented a declaration system for all individuals moving bulk cash or other monetary instruments into or out of the country. With the passage of the Bank Secrecy Act in 1970, Title 31, section 5316 of the U.S. Code made it illegal to physically transport more than $10,000 (or its foreign equivalent) across U.S. borders without filing a Report of International Transportation of Currency or Monetary Instruments (CMIR).[13] The USA PATRIOT Act made bulk cash smuggling a criminal offense as well.[14]

There are, however, different laws for inbound and outbound travelers. All individuals entering the United States must fill out a customs declaration form indicating whether they are carrying more than $10,000.[15] If the answer is "yes," they must also fill out a CMIR. Outbound travelers are required to fill out paperwork only when they are carrying more than $10,000, in which case they must complete a customs declaration form.

If border agents ascertain that a false declaration/disclosure has taken place, or if they suspect that a

Who Is Responsible for Stopping Smugglers?

Two U.S. agencies have been given primary responsibility for investigating cash smuggling and making seizures: Customs and Border Protection (CBP) and the Bureau of Immigration and Customs Enforcement (ICE). These agencies—part of the Department of Homeland Security—are the designated "competent authorities" vested with the power to stop, search, seize, compel forfeiture, and make arrests related to cross-border crimes, with or without a search warrant. This power extends to "any vehicle, vessel, aircraft, or other conveyance, any envelope or other container, and any person" entering or departing the United States via any point.[1]

traveler's funds are tied to money laundering or terrorism financing, they are empowered to arrest the traveler and seize the money, which is then subject to forfeiture. Once CBP/ICE carry out such an arrest, an investigation ensues to verify any criminal or terrorist links.[16]

Whenever a traveler fills out a CMIR, this information is collected by the Financial Crimes Enforcement Network (FinCEN; see chapter 4 for a discussion of this agency). Similarly, when border agents discover a false declaration, they electronically record the amount involved, the traveler's identification data, and any other relevant information into a computer database and forward it to FinCEN.[17] This data is a vital resource—FinCEN shares it with the appropriate federal, state, local, and foreign regulatory law enforcement agencies, who then use it in criminal, tax, and regulatory investigations.

Case Study

Operation Dragon: Largest Single Drug-Money Seizure in History

The law enforcement community hit the jackpot on March 16, 2007, when "Operation Dragon" netted more than $207 million in seized drug proceeds in Mexico City.[1] The U.S. government called it "the largest single drug cash seizure the world has ever seen."[2]

Surprisingly, the money did not belong to a Mexican drug cartel, nor did it represent profits from traditional drug sales such as Colombian cocaine, Mexican marijuana, or black-tar heroin. Rather, Mexican police and U.S. Drug Enforcement Administration agents seized the money from a broker who supplied chemicals to Mexican cartels specializing in methamphetamine—most of which was destined for the United States. According to law enforcement officials, many drug traffickers believe that "meth," as it is called on the street, has major advantages over drugs like cocaine—it is a highly addictive, it can be made at home and smuggled easily, and it can produce huge profits.[3]

Zhenli Ye Gon, a naturalized Mexican citizen from Shanghai, China, ran a pharmaceuticals front company responsible for one of the Western Hemisphere's largest pseudoephedrine networks, the primary ingredient in meth.[4] The Operation Dragon bust took place at his home in Lomas de Chapultepec, one of Mexico City's most exclusive neighborhoods. Along with the cash (mostly $100 bills hidden in walls, closets, and suitcases), American agents

SANCTIONS

Civil and criminal sanctions await individuals who fail to file a CMIR when required, or who file a form that misrepresents the amount of money they are carrying. Penalties include imprisonment of up to ten years and, under certain circumstances, an administrative fine up to $500,000. Prosecutors must prove that the defendant knowingly intended to avoid the reporting requirement. If money laundering or terrorism financing are involved, the potential maximum prison sentence increases to twenty years.[18] Even if the U.S. Attorney's Office declines to prosecute, customs can still seize and keep the money.[19]

Finally, the United States has implemented a reverse burden of proof on travelers carrying money, as called for by FATF. That is, authorities can seize the money

seized eight luxury vehicles, seven weapons, and a machine to make pills. Seven people were arrested—but not Gon himself.[5] He was not captured until July 2007, in a suburb of Washington, D.C.[6]

In the U.S. district court affidavit, federal authorities alleged that between December 2005 and August 2006, Gon's company Unimed Pharm Chem de Mexico illegally imported 86 metric tons of restricted chemicals into Mexico "for the express purpose of manufacturing pseudoephedrine/ephedrine." The affidavit claimed that the imported chemicals were enough to produce 36,568 kilograms of meth, with a street value of approximately $724 million.[7]

The case received tremendous media attention in Mexico, in part because Gon claimed that most of the seized money was not his. By his account, Mexican president Felipe Calderón had forced him to safeguard $150 million to serve as part of a "slush fund" for the Mexican National Action Party's 2006 presidential campaign. In the event Calderón lost the election, Gon claimed, the money would have been used to carry out "terrorist" activities. Mexican officials have called the allegations preposterous, with President Calderón personally dismissing them as "pure fiction."[8]

Gon continues to proclaim that he is an innocent pharmaceuticals executive. As of this writing, he is still awaiting trial in Washington, where he faces charges of violating U.S. drug laws by selling chemicals to American buyers. Mexican officials have filed for extradition, but Gon's lawyers have said that he intends to apply for political asylum in the United States.[9] In the meantime, Mexico has charged eleven people, including several of Gon's relatives, with drug trafficking and organized crime.[10]

if the traveler is unable to demonstrate a legitimate origin and destination for the funds.

IMPRESSIVE RESULTS

In its 2006 Mutual Evaluation Report, FATF found the United States fully compliant with the recommendations on cash smuggling. To make its case, U.S. authorities had presented FATF with impressive statistics. From 2001 through February 2005, ICE and CBP seized a combined total of more than $107 million from bulk cash smugglers. In addition, border agents arrested more than 260 individuals on bulk cash smuggling violations. For the fiscal years 2003–2005, the Justice Department prosecuted 248 bulk cash smuggling cases and successfully convicted 207 criminals.[20]

Despite these numbers, FATF proposed several ways the United States could improve its anti–money laundering/combating the financing of terrorism regime. In

Case Study

American Contractor in Iraq Busted for Cash Smuggling

In 2008, construction contractor David Ricardo Ramirez was indicted on smuggling charges for sending $150,000 in cash from Iraq to Texas and "structuring" bank transactions to avoid reporting requirements. Ramirez worked in Iraq for one year, planning sites for new construction at Balad Air Base. His employer—Readiness Management Support (RMS), a U.S.-based company—supports air force operations overseas.[1]

Court documents reveal that Ramirez sent cash to his sister in San Antonio, often via Fed Ex packages that contained gifts such as jewelry, kites, and T-shirts.[2] In 2007, law enforcement intercepted a package containing $14,800 in sequentially numbered $50 and $100 bills, all concealed inside a wooden humidor. Authorities then followed Ramirez's sister to see what she did with the money. According to court documents, she deposited most of it in a night deposit box and drive-up windows so she would not have to answer questions from tellers. She made these deposits over several days and in small amounts to avoid the $10,000 reporting threshold (see chapters 2 and 4).[3]

Ramirez's lawyer claimed that he might have gotten the money by particular, FATF recommended investing more resources in the detection and investigation of outbound cash smuggling.[21] As mentioned previously, CBP/ICE places greater emphasis on examining potential inbound smugglers due to resource limitations. Yet, given the fact that drug traffickers and other criminals move a significant amount of their earnings out of the country using cash couriers and bulk smuggling, Washington should find a means of bolstering CBP/ICE's capabilities and reach.[22]

CONCLUSIONS

Bulk cash smuggling is a well-established practice for terrorism financiers, money launderers, and organized crime figures looking to move their funds across borders. Although their other financial tactics have grown more sophisticated over the years, they are also increasingly resorting to old-fashioned, informal methods of moving cash in order to evade the tighter formal financial controls implemented since the

doing side jobs for other contractors, which would have been "inappropriate but not illegal."[4] The lawyer also stated that Ramirez was unaware of the U.S. cash reporting requirements. Although federal authorities have not disclosed how Ramirez obtained the smuggled money, several factors belie his lawyer's claims and point to illegal activity. Aside from the implausibility of making $150,000 from a year's worth of "side jobs," one report stated explicitly that the cash came from bribes offered by other contractors (though again, authorities have not disclosed what Ramirez may have done in exchange for these bribes).[5] Ramirez's "long criminal record" casts further doubt on any notions that the money was clean—prior to accepting the job in Iraq, he had faced charges on a number of different offenses over the years, including "theft by check, robbery, drug possession, drunken driving, and unlawfully carrying a weapon."[6] In fact, he was on probation for a drug conviction when RMS hired him—a stunning revelation highlighting the government's oft-criticized failure to conduct or mandate simple background checks on contractors responsible for handling billions of taxpayer dollars in Iraq.

In October 2008, Ramirez pled guilty to the charges and was sentenced to 50 months in prison. He was also forced to forfeit everything he had bought, including a condominium in Austin worth $95,000, a real-estate plot in Val Verde County worth $25,000, a Ducati motorcycle worth $33,000, and a 1989 Lamborghini worth $80,000.[7]

September 11 attacks. Schemes involving cash couriers have distinct advantages—they are easy to carry out but difficult to detect and interdict. At the same time, however, bulk cash is often heavy and cumbersome, creating additional opportunities for law enforcement to spot smugglers.

In the end, it is impossible to eliminate bulk cash smuggling operations entirely. The only way to reduce this threat is for countries to establish appropriate intelligence networks and regularly conduct interdiction operations.

Chapter 7

Trade-Based Money Laundering

In this chapter:

- Defining trade-based money laundering
- Region of concern: terrorist groups and Latin America's Black Market Peso Exchange
- Use of gold and diamonds
- U.S. government system
- Sharing data through Trade Transparency Units

Trade-based money laundering (TBML)—or "the use of trade to legitimize, conceal, transfer, and convert large quantities of illicit cash into less conspicuous assets or commodities"—has reached "staggering" proportions in recent years.[1] In perhaps the most serious example of the danger posed by this practice, intelligence reports indicate that terrorist groups are heavily abusing commodities—including precious gems, gold, and other untraceable goods—to move their money. It is an open secret that Hizbollah, Hamas, al-Qaeda, and other organizations operate in parts of the world with little or no government control, allowing them to engage in TBML and a host of other illegal activities.[2] As mentioned previously, some of the more prominent of these "grey areas" include the Tri-Border Area where Argentina, Brazil, and Paraguay intersect (see below and chapter 9); West African countries that are involved in conflict diamonds; and Dubai, the mecca of illicit traders.

Typically, TBML schemes involve invoice fraud and trade manipulation, principally via the "misrepresentation of price, quantity or quality of imports or exports."[3] As demonstrated in chapter 2, specific tactics include over-invoicing, under-invoicing, double-invoicing, and false invoicing. With these methods, illicit actors are able to move large amounts of money while successfully avoiding taxes, tariffs, and customs duties. And when combined with smuggling, drug trafficking, and the formal and informal financial sectors, TBML greatly complicates law enforcement efforts to follow the financial trail.

Criminals who abuse trade are assisted by a number of factors:

1. The massive amount of global trade that takes place daily
2. Financial diversity (i.e., diverse financial controls in different countries, diverse financial arrangements between governments, and—last but certainly not least—the innumerable different types of financial deals found in the business world)
3. The commingling of legitimate and illicit funds
4. The low risk of detection
5. Limited government resources to detect suspicious trade transactions (e.g., most customs agencies inspect less than 5 percent of all inbound and outbound cargo)[4]

Region of Concern

Terrorist Groups and Latin America's Black Market Peso Exchange

As described in chapter 2, the largest money laundering scheme in the Western Hemisphere is the Black Market Peso Exchange (BMPE). U.S. authorities estimate that Colombian drug cartels alone launder $5 billion each year from drug sales in the United States.[1]

In some cases, the drug traffickers that use the BMPE are also U.S.-designated terrorist organizations. These groups include but are certainly not limited to al-Qaeda, Hizbollah, the Revolutionary Armed Forces of Colombia (FARC), the National Liberation Army (ELN), the United Self-Defense Groups of Colombia (AUC), and the Shining Path (Sendero Luminoso, or SL).[2] Indeed, there is a natural synergy between narco-traffickers and terrorists. As former U.S. ambassador-at-large for counterterrorism Francis Taylor put it:

> Drug traffickers benefit from the terrorists' military skills, weapons supply, and access to clandestine organizations. Terrorists gain a source of revenue and expertise in illicit transfer and laundering of proceeds from illicit transactions. Both groups bring corrupt officials whose services provide mutual benefits, such as greater access to fraudulent documents, including passports and customs papers. Drug traffickers may also gain considerable freedom of movement when they operate in conjunction with terrorists who control large amounts of territory.[3]

TBML is also a vital component of many informal financial schemes, including "black" hawala (see chapter 5) and the Black Market Peso Exchange (see case study). In such contexts, illicit actors often use trade to balance their books or, in more technical terms, provide "counter-valuation."[5]

GOLD AND DIAMONDS

Besides narcotics, many terrorists and money launderers use gold, diamonds, and other precious stones to conduct their business. These commodities are among the most compressed form of wealth in the world today—as a result, they are quite popular with illicit actors.[6] In fact, some experts believe that the gold trade has become "the money laundering mechanism of choice."[7] According to internal law enforcement

A recent sting operation targeting a Latin American drug trafficking and TBML ring merits special mention in light of its links to Hizbollah. In late April 2009, a Dutch-led team of authorities from seven nations arrested 17 suspects on Curacao, the largest of the Netherlands Antilles islands off the coast of Venezuela. The suspects—who hailed from Colombia, Lebanon, Cuba, Venezuela, and Curacao—were charged with running an international drug ring that used shipping containers and couriers to smuggle cocaine to the Netherlands, Belgium, Spain, and Jordan. They laundered the proceeds of these crimes by purchasing property in Colombia, Venezuela, Lebanon, and the Dominican Republic, and by investing in companies on Curacao. According to Dutch authorities, the drug ring also had "international contacts with other criminal networks that financially supported Hizbullah in the Middle East. Large sums of drug money flooded into Lebanon, from where orders were placed for weapons that were to have been delivered from South America."[4]

Of course, Latin American TBML schemes—whether tied to the BMPE or not—are only one of many such networks currently in operation around the globe. For example, the "Afghan Transit Trade" scheme, which takes in the golden triangle between Afghanistan, Pakistan, and the United Arab Emirates, is a similar network of the same proportions. Using trading networks, smuggling, corruption, hawala, and invoice manipulation, this operation has its own distinct South Asian and Arabian flavor. And like the BMPE, it facilitates terrorism financing as readily as money laundering.

reports, it is used to wash huge amounts of dirty cash. For example, authorities have tied the movement of billions of dollars worth of gold to deals by Latin American drug cartels, leading them to believe that the commodity is joining the U.S. dollar as the standard currency of the drug trade.[8]

Gold and diamonds have been a haven for wealth since antiquity. Expert John Cassara described what this means for criminals in practical terms:

> Gold is a readily acceptable medium of exchange—it acts as both a commodity and a de facto bearer instrument, there is a ready market for it worldwide, its quality is easily verified, and it offers easy anonymity. Diamonds are the most compressed form of physical wealth in the world and are easily smuggled. Their quality and price are often subjective, however; gold offers greater price stability and certainty.[9]

In part because of these traits, law enforcement agencies find it difficult to investigate gold and diamond cases. For example, illicit actors can easily manipulate gold by smelting it, turning it into bars, scrap, or jewelry. They can also easily manipulate diamonds, which can be mined in one part of the world, cut and polished in another, and sold in a completely different market. To complicate matters, it is extremely difficult to develop expertise on the complexities of the international gold and diamond trades. Finally, money launderers have the advantage that both gold and diamonds are often mined in remote parts of the world and are virtually untraceable to their original source.[10]

International standard-setters have yet to effectively counter the use of gold and diamonds in the money laundering process. The only countermeasure that has come close is the Kimberly Process—a joint government, industry, and civil society initiative to stem the flow of conflict diamonds. But this regime was set up to combat the trafficking of one commodity from one part of the world, not to fight money laundering and terrorism financing writ

Popularity of Gold and Diamonds

Over the past half-century, law enforcement agencies have conducted many money laundering investigations relating to diamonds and gold. Illicit actors like these two commodities in particular because they are easy to use in schemes involving (1) over-invoicing, under-invoicing, or false invoicing (e.g., substituting scrap for real gold, or declaring a low-quality diamond but shipping an extremely valuable one), and (2) tax fraud (e.g., obtaining a tax export credit by falsely declaring commodities). Like cash, smugglers can take gold and diamonds across borders via couriers, containers, or vehicles of any kind.

large.[11] Accordingly, it might be time, as John Cassara put it, to "start rethinking the definition" of what constitutes a blood diamond.[12] The same holds true for gold and other precious gems.

U.S. EFFORTS AGAINST TBML

U.S. policymakers have begun to pay more attention to TBML. Although the problem is difficult to quantify precisely, some experts believe as much as 67 percent of U.S. money being laundered abroad is moved out of the country via undervalued exports.[13] In light of this astounding number, the United States has become one of the few countries to crack down on the abuse of trade by drug lords, gangsters, and terror financiers.

The Bureau of Immigration and Customs Enforcement (ICE) is the primary agency responsible for investigating the problem. This is only natural given that (1) TBML is customs fraud, and (2) the bureau has primary access to trade information as well as unique statutory authority over, and expertise relating to, commercial trade fraud and financial investigations.[14] In light of its leading role, ICE has taken the important step of creating special units to share trade data with its international counterparts (see the section below on data sharing between countries).

In Simple Terms: The U.S. Government and TBML

A number of U.S. agencies play a crucial role in combating trade-based money laundering. The Bureau of Immigrations and Customs Enforcement (ICE) has taken the leading role, given its unique capabilities and powers. The Drug Enforcement Administration (DEA), Internal Revenue Service–Criminal Investigations (IRS-CI), Customs and Border Protection (CBP), and Financial Crimes Enforcement Network (FinCEN) play key supporting roles.

The Drug Enforcement Administration (DEA) has sole responsibility for coordinating and pursuing narcotics investigations abroad. Given the strong interconnections between drug trafficking and TBML, the agency aggressively investigates the Black Market Peso Exchange in the Americas. In addition, it has agents worldwide who investigate BMPE-like schemes, all of which rely on trade to launder illicit funds.[15]

Numerous other federal agencies play a role in cases involving the abuse of trade. FinCEN addresses TBML by collecting and analyzing Suspicious Activity Reports (SARs) from the formal financial sector.[16] Similarly, Customs and Border Protection and the Department of Commerce are charged with collecting and maintaining records of all U.S. imports and exports.[17] And the Internal Revenue Service–Criminal

Case Study

Al-Qaeda Uses Gold to Move Value

As coalition troops invaded Afghanistan in 2001, the Taliban and members of al-Qaeda made sure to smuggle as much of their money as possible out of the country via Pakistan. One of their main means of doing so was to use couriers laden with bars of gold. The couriers carried the gold over the border and eventually to Karachi. There, they used hawala brokers to transfer the gold's value to Dubai, where other brokers converted it to gold bullion. Authorities estimate that during one three-week period in late November to early December 2001, al-Qaeda transferred $10 million in cash and gold out of Afghanistan.[1] That same December, British troops located an al-Qaeda manual in Afghanistan that included material on how to smuggle gold on small boats or conceal it on one's body.[2]

Terrorists likely prefer to hold their assets in gold because its value is easy to determine and remains relatively consistent over time. Moreover, gold holds cultural significance in many areas of the world, including Southeast Asia, South and Central Asia, the Arabian Peninsula, and North Africa.[3] It is also relatively easy to buy and sell gold all over the globe, since many major cities have gold exchange markets known as "bourses."

Investigations (IRS-CI) is responsible for collecting and analyzing Currency Transaction Reports (CTRs) from businesses that conduct transfers involving more than $10,000 in cash or other negotiable instruments.[18]

U.S. REGULATION OF PRECIOUS METALS, STONES, AND JEWELS

The United States has made very slow progress on this front. To its credit, the government has taken an initial good step in mandating that dealers in these commodities establish anti–money laundering programs per the Bank Secrecy Act. In 2005, FinCEN announced a binding "interim final rule"[19] describing the four mandatory elements for such programs:

1. "Policies, procedures and internal controls, based on the dealer's assessment of the money laundering and terrorist financing risk associated with its business"

2. "A compliance officer who is responsible for ensuring that the program is implemented effectively"

3. "Ongoing training of appropriate persons concerning their responsibilities under the program"

4. "Independent testing to monitor and maintain an adequate program"[20]

The IRS has been placed in charge of monitoring dealer compliance with this rule. As mentioned in chapter 5, however, the IRS has already been tasked with overseeing compliance in the informal financial sector—something it has failed to do because of a lack of funding. This same shortcoming would almost certainly prevent the agency from countering abuses in the precious metals/stones sector as well.

Another problem with FinCEN's rule lies in the fact that dealers are not required to file Suspicious Activity Reports.[21] Even if this deficiency were addressed, most dealers would no doubt ignore the requirement—there is no government agency forcing them to do otherwise, and they have yet to comply with other mandatory aspects of FinCEN's regulations.

SHARING AND ANALYZING TRADE DATA

Customs and law enforcement investigations have demonstrated that one of the most effective ways of combating TBML is to actively monitor imports and exports between countries. In this regard, the United States has been very well organized.[22]

Every country has a customs authority and collects trade data. Although there are differences in the way governments gather and store their data, enough similarities exist to conduct effective TBML investigations. Such investigations require three basic elements:

1. Access to import and export data as well as transaction reports like those mandated by the Bank Secrecy Act in the United States

2. Expertise in analyzing and investigating this type of data

3. Sharing and receiving this type of data with and from other countries

In the first formal international effort to combat TBML, the United States has worked with Argentina, Brazil, Paraguay, Columbia, and Mexico to create Trade Transparency Units (TTUs).[23] Intended to serve as "effective gateways for the prompt exchange of trade data and information between foreign counterparts," TTUs use this shared data to help detect money laundering and other illicit activity.[24] Moreover, by creating these units in Argentina, Paraguay, and Brazil, Washington has signaled that its initial target is the previously mentioned Tri-Border Area, where a large illicit economy thrives. According to ICE, this region is "a source of fundraising for radical Islamic

Case Study

Operation White Dollar

In May 2004, American, Colombian, Canadian, and British authorities dismantled a far-reaching BMPE network that had laundered millions of dollars in drug proceeds. "Operation White Dollar" was the culmination of a two-year investigation that eventually led to the indictment of 34 individuals and companies in Colombia, the United States, and Canada.[1]

The indictment targeted all parties associated with the scheme, including:

- five alleged "first-tier peso brokers," i.e., those who make contracts directly with drug trafficking organizations;
- two alleged "second-tier peso brokers," i.e., those who concentrate on arranging for the pickup of street-level drug proceeds and placing those funds into the banking system; and
- nine alleged "third-tier peso brokers," i.e., those who make contracts directly with the Colombian dollar purchasers.[2]

In addition, law enforcement agencies froze more than $20 million in drug proceeds in bank accounts around the world.[3]

During the course of the operation, undercover officers successfully posed as money launderers in the United States and Canada, offering to clean vast sums of drug money and deposit them into the U.S. banking system.[4] These transactions enabled investigators to trace funds to bank accounts in England and the Cayman Islands.[5]

Many agencies throughout the U.S. government participated in the operation, including the Organized Crime Drug Enforcement Task Force (OCDETF), the U.S. Attorney's Office for the Southern District of New York, the DEA, the New York City Police Department, the IRS, the Office of the Special Narcotics Prosecutor for the City of New York, the Manhattan District Attorney's Office, and the South Florida Money Laundering Strike Force in Miami.[6]

groups, including Hezbollah and Hamas." It is also considered "South America's busiest contraband and smuggling center, where billions of dollars annually are generated from arms trafficking, drug smuggling, counterfeiting, intellectual property-rights violations, and other crimes."[25]

Case Study

Operation Deluge

In the short time that TTUs have been up and running, they have already scored some big victories. In August 2006, "Operation Deluge" targeted a scheme that had undervalued U.S. exports to Brazil in order to evade more than $200 million in Brazilian customs duties between 2001 and 2006.[1] In a huge bust, 950 Brazilian Federal Police officers and 350 customs agents executed search warrants at 238 locations in the states of Parana, Santa Catarina, Sao Paulo, Bahio, Rio de Janeiro, Pernambuco, Ceara, and Espirito Santo.[2] They also executed 128 arrest warrants that netted both government officials and the directors and owners of several large Brazilian companies. Nine of the detainees were employees of Brazil's Internal Revenue Service.[3] For their part, U.S. ICE agents in Miami seized approximately $500,000 in goods slated for export to Brazil.[4]

The United States and Brazil accused the criminals of tax evasion, document fraud, public corruption, and undervaluation of exports. The commodities in question included a motley assortment of goods: "electronics equipment, computer and telecommunications equipment, tires, orthopedic equipment, surgical gloves, fruits, plastic bottles, fabric and clothes, batteries, vehicles and motorcycles, vitamins and dietary supplements, and perfumes."[5]

According to Brazilian authorities, the leader of the ring was Marco Antonio Mansur, arrested with his son Marco Antonio Mansur Filho in their apartment in the Paraíso neighborhood of southern Sao Paulo. A wealthy businessman who once lived in Paraguay, Mansur named his company after his initials: MAM.[6] Police accused him of creating dozens of front companies in order to carry out his undervaluation scheme; these companies were registered in Uruguay, Panama, the British Virgin Islands, and the U.S. state of Delaware.[7]

TTUs are charged with monitoring systemic vulnerabilities in financial, commercial, trade, and transportation sectors that are most susceptible to exploitation by criminal and terrorist organizations. In order to carry out this mission, the American TTU—administratively part of ICE—uses the latest technology to analyze massive amounts of trade data. It also shares this technology with its South American partners. Armed with advanced data-mining software that examines numerical relationships, TTU investigators sift through information looking for anomalies that might indicate illicit activity.[26] Specifically, this computer program—a commercially available product called Data Analysis and Research for Trade Transparency (DARTT)—is "designed to detect and track money laundering, contraband smuggling and trade fraud."[27] According to Charles Allen, deputy head of the U.S. TTU, DARTT has already generated leads in cases involving the "smuggling of gold, computer parts and other commodities in and out of the US."[28]

Other countries around the world are beginning to understand the importance of sharing trade data, and ICE has received numerous additional requests to help start TTUs. For example, Panama, India, and the Philippines have publicly expressed their interest.[29] One of the primary reasons for this interest is governments' desire to target tax and duty evaders. When illicit actors move and launder money effectively, that means a potentially massive loss of tax revenue that should end up in national coffers.

Ultimately, the goal of the TTU project is to create a global network of such units, patterned after the international network of financial intelligence units described in chapter 3.[30] The U.S. government envisions that such a network would "provide a forum for the open exchange of trade data between all participating countries ... in the effort to thwart money laundering and transnational crime."[31] Indeed, if this vision does become reality, it would significantly reduce the threat posed by TBML.

CONCLUSIONS

Despite their extensive knowledge of how criminals operate outside the formal financial sector, policymakers are only recently coming to the realization that manipulating international trade remains one of the easiest ways to transfer value. It is not difficult to manipulate invoices, and law enforcement has struggled to find and prosecute those engaging in this type of activity. Meanwhile, international standard-setters such as FATF have yet to issue concrete standards on fighting trade-based money laundering. This constitutes a major liability in the international financial system.

Cooperative mechanisms capable of detecting trade anomalies will be instrumental to countering this problem. The law enforcement community has come to the conclusion that the only practicable and effective way of combating TBML is to actively monitor imports and exports between countries and share trade information. Yet, until more countries sign up to share this type of information regularly, criminal and terrorist organizations will have a free hand to abuse the trade sector.

Chapter 8

Donor Beware: Terrorists and the Charitable Sector

In this chapter:
- Country of concern: Saudi Arabia
- International concerns
- Outreach and risk assessments
- Supervision/monitoring
- Information-gathering and investigations
- Sanctions

Although it is impossible to determine exactly how much money terrorist organizations have at their disposal, what is certain is that they rely on charities to raise and move a great deal of it. Groups like al-Qaeda, Hizbollah, and Hamas can readily exploit charities because many countries around the world are reluctant to rigorously scrutinize this sector and ensure transparency.

Islamic Charities

Islamic law stipulates that it is a religious obligation to make charitable donations, or *zakat* in Arabic. Therefore, individual donors transfer large sums of money each year to charities, usually out of a genuine desire to help those in need. As a result of traditionally lax (or completely absent) oversight, illicit actors are in an ideal position to exploit this goodwill for terrorism financing or other purposes.

Any criminal organization can abuse a charity, but terrorist groups are uniquely suited to doing so because of their ideological leanings. For example, many politicians in the Arab world and Europe cloud the issue by recognizing two separate "wings" of terrorist organizations: one military, the other sociopolitical and often dedicated to charitable activity. The military wing may well be targeted by all of the usual counterterrorism machinery at a state's disposal, but the "charitable" wing is often deemed exempt. This distinction is both damaging and inaccurate. It is a fact that designated terrorist groups have used mosques, Islamic schools, relief projects, sports organizations, and other legitimate entities to fund or directly facilitate their violent "military" operations. The United States has taken the position that such groups are radioactive—that is, their terrorist acts inevitably infect even their most

Country of Concern

Saudi Arabia

Saudi Arabia is often the first country mentioned in discussions related to combating the financing of terrorism (CFT), particularly in the context of charities. Since the September 11 attacks, however, the U.S. government has sent out mixed messages regarding accusations that the kingdom facilitates rather than curbs such financing. On the one hand, Stuart Levey, the Treasury Department's undersecretary for terrorism and financial intelligence, described the flow of illicit money coming from the kingdom best: "If I could somehow snap my fingers and cut off the funding from one country, it would be Saudi Arabia....No one identified by the United States and the United Nations as a terror financier has been prosecuted by the Saudis."[1] Other officials have focused more on the positive aspects of the relationship with Saudi Arabia, pointing to "excellent progress" in Riyadh's CFT efforts.[2]

These apparent contradictions are evident in the government's internal deliberations and legislative measures as well. In 2007, for example, Congress concluded that Saudi Arabia has an "uneven record in the fight against terrorism, especially with respect to terrorist financing."[3] And a State Department report released only months later argued that "Saudi donors and unregulated charities have been a major source of financing to extremist and terrorist groups over the past 25 years."[4] Similarly, the 9/11 Commission Report concluded that Saudi Arabia may have diverted funding to al-Qaeda, describing the kingdom as "a place where al-Qaeda raised money directly from individuals and through charities."[5] Yet, according to this same report, the commission had "found no evidence that the Saudi government as an institution or senior Saudi officials individually" had funded al-Qaeda.

Mixed messages from Washington aside, sentiment has generally been critical of the kingdom in the wake of September 11. Many in the benign activities, in ways both subtle and salient. Accordingly, U.S. terrorist lists do not distinguish between wings.

The benefits of abusing charities are clear: through them, terrorists can use all of the previously described methods for moving their money quickly and surreptitiously, including the formal and informal financial sectors, bulk cash smuggling, and trade-based

international community accused the Saudi government and prominent Saudi citizens of taking a lax stance against terrorists. In addition, some analysts believe the connections that Saudi officials and nationals share with Usama bin Laden (an exiled Saudi whose citizenship was revoked in 1994) and members of al-Qaeda demonstrate which side of the war on terror the kingdom supports.

For their part, Saudi leaders publicly emphasize that the kingdom has been victimized by terrorist attacks as well, and that it has been very cooperative with the United States and the international community regarding CFT issues. As evidence of this support, they point to numerous decrees and institutions designed to constrain the flow of illicit funds. And while they acknowledge that the kingdom provides financial support to Islamic and Palestinian organizations, they insist that "No official Saudi support goes to any terrorist organizations."[6] Yet, critics suggest that some of the massive royal family's 5,000 members have acted independently and supported terrorist groups through various charities and relief organizations.[7]

Lax Oversight of Charities. Saudi nationals contribute a reported 2.5 percent of their annual income to charitable causes such as hospitals, educational programs, nursing homes, and development projects. Some experts, including former U.S. State Department official Jonathan Winer, estimate charitable donations in the kingdom at $3–4 billion annually, of which $300–400 million is sent abroad.[8]

Saudi oversight of this large charitable sector has been lax. The government did not take its first step toward redressing that deficiency until December 2002, when it announced the creation of the High Commission for Oversight of Charities.[9] According to Riyadh, this agency was established to reform the way in which charities operated and increase their transparency. Shortly after the commission's creation, the government *(continued)* claimed that it had audited all charities in the kingdom. It has yet to publicly release the results, however.[10]

Despite the audit, Riyadh continued to face increasing pressure from Washington to scrutinize all money sent abroad and ensure that it did not end up in the hands of terrorists. In response, the Saudis introduced new banking regulations in 2003 that barred private charities from transmitting funds abroad until new rules could be implemented.[11] And in 2004, King Fahd announced the establishment of the Saudi Non-Governmental Commission on Relief and Charity Work Abroad,[12] which was intended to serve as the "sole vehicle" through which all private donations marked for international distribution would eventually flow.[13] Once the commission was in place, the overseas operations of all Saudi charities would either be consolidated under its control or dissolved altogether. Yet, it was not until October 2006 that the Saudi Interior Ministry submitted plans to the Consultative Council for actually creating the commission, and as of early 2009, it is not yet operational.

In the meantime, U.S. officials remain concerned that "wealthy donors in Saudi Arabia are still funding violent extremists around the world, from Europe to North Africa, from Iraq to Southeast Asia."[14] Riyadh has taken action against very few suspect charities, and only once has it has completely closed one down. In 2004, after sustained U.S. pressure, the kingdom shuttered the al-Haramain Islamic Foundation—a charity that was closely linked to the royal family—for its involvement in terrorism financing. At the same time, the U.S. Treasury Department designated al-Haramain, describing it as "one of the principal Islamic NGOs providing support for the al-Qaeda network and promoting militant Islamic doctrine worldwide."[15] For example, one of the foundation's own employees was involved in the 1998 bombing of the U.S. embassy in Tanzania.[16] To its credit, Saudi Arabia partnered with Washington in asking the United Nations to designate the charity internationally through the Security Council's "1267 Committee" (see chapter 3 for a discussion of this body).

money laundering. Islamist terrorists in particular favor charities for several reasons. First, Islamic charities have a presence wherever there are Muslims and thus serve as an excellent means for both radicalizing constituents and moving money. Such charities also enjoy the public trust and have access to considerable funds. Muslims give billions of dollars annually to charities, providing illicit actors with many opportunities to siphon

Funding for Palestinian Organizations. The Saudi government provides significant aid to Palestinian organizations and causes, including the Palestine Liberation Organization (PLO) and the Palestinian Authority (PA). According to American and Israeli reports, Riyadh has also directly or indirectly supported Palestinian terrorist organizations, including Hamas, which in the past reportedly maintained a large fundraising infrastructure in the kingdom (see the separate section below on Hamas).

In 2002, Riyadh announced that Saudi government and private aid to the Palestinians totaled $2.61 billion.[17] Annual contributions include $80–100 million to the PA, which the kingdom pledged to continue even after Hamas won a majority of the votes in the January 2006 parliamentary elections.

Riyadh permits only two Saudi charities to deliver aid to Palestinian institutions:

1. *Saudi Committee for the Support of the al-Quds Intifada (renamed the Saudi Committee for the Relief of the Palestinian People):* This charity, established by royal decree in October 2000, serves as the main source of Saudi funding to the Palestinians. In December 2003, the Saudi embassy in Washington issued a report stating that the charity's 31 relief programs had provided close to $200 million in aid since its inception.[18] In addition to monetary donations, the committee provides goods such as food, blankets, medicine, and ambulances. It also supports programs related to healthcare, education, and basic social services. In September 2006, the committee announced plans to provide $6.3 million to finance the construction of 100 housing units in Hebron in cooperation with UN-HABITAT.[19]
2. *The Saudi Popular Committee for Assisting the Palestinian Mujahideen:* From October 2002 through April 2003, this committee's reports indicate that it provided approximately $8.8 million to the PLO. *(continued)*

off funds undetected. Moreover, depending on the jurisdiction, a charity may be subject to little or no oversight (i.e., registration, recordkeeping, and monitoring). In addition, although the majority of Muslims believe they are giving money to support just causes, the CIA estimates that one-third of charities "support terrorist groups or employ individuals who are suspected of having terrorist connections."[1] To be sure, some charities

Money for Families of Suicide Bombers. In May 2002, Israeli officials alleged that the Saudi Committee for the Support of the al-Quds Intifada had "transferred large sums of money to families of Palestinians who died in violent events, including notorious terrorists."[20] Saudi officials called the allegations "baseless and false" and stated "unequivocally that Saudi Arabia does not provide financial support to suicide bombers or their families."[21] Yet, the committee's own records belie this denial.

For example, the committee website once contained more than 40,000 transaction records featuring the names of individual beneficiaries. Among these records were 1,300 submitted by a committee program tasked with supporting "Palestinian families whose primary breadwinners were killed by Israeli forces or under other violent circumstances"; these records included the names of the deceased individuals and the circumstances of their death.[22] Upon examining these records, analysts found that sixty of the names matched or closely resembled the names of militants who had carried out attacks from October 2000 to March 2002. Some of the records even listed the cause of death as either "martyrdom" or "martyrdom operation." The committee removed all records from its website in early 2005.

During a May 2002 interview, Saudi government spokesman Adel al-Jubeir was asked point blank about the issue. Although he avoided addressing the question in full, he effectively admitted that money had gone to families of suicide bombers in the past: "If some money went to those families, it's to help them in their need. But it didn't go to encourage [violence]."[23]

Support for Hamas. In 2003, spokesman al-Jubeir stated that "no Saudi government money goes to Hamas, directly or indirectly."[24] But he did admit that it is "very likely" that "some Saudi individuals" have provided financial support to the group.[25]

The U.S. government has released a number of reports that corroborate private Saudi assistance to Hamas at times in the past. In the 2001 *Patterns*

are unwitting victims of terrorist abuse, but the most significant threat has been posed by charities that knowingly funnel donor money to terrorist groups, often without the knowledge of the donors themselves. Finally, it is very difficult to confirm or control the ultimate recipient of a charitable donation. Given all of these factors, it is no wonder that the charitable sector poses a major challenge to the law enforcement community.

of Global Terrorism report, the State Department concluded that Hamas received money from "private benefactors in Saudi Arabia and other moderate Arab states."[26] And the department's 2005 Country Reports for Terrorism stated that these Saudi and Arab benefactors remained a primary source of funding for Hamas.[27]

Saudi support for Hamas appears to have changed sometime in mid-2004, however. U.S. intelligence officials have admitted that since then, "Saudi funding for Hamas has been curtailed and replaced by other regional sponsors," including major financial support from Iran. In testimony before the Senate Governmental Affairs Committee, former Treasury general counsel David Aufhauser quoted "informed intelligence sources" as saying that "for whatever reason, the money going to Hamas from Saudi Arabia has substantially dried up." Aufhauser indicated that Saudi support "has been supplemented by money from Iran and Syria flowing through even more dangerous rejectionist groups in the West Bank."[28]

Support for Iraqi Insurgents. In 2005, Treasury official Stuart Levey testified before Congress that Saudi individuals may be "a significant source" of financing for the Iraqi insurgency.[29] The 2006 *Iraq Study Group Report* concurred: "Funding for the Sunni insurgency comes from private individuals within Saudi Arabia and the Gulf States."[30] In addition, various news reports from Iraq have quoted insurgents stating that Saudi fighters are valued for their ability to provide for their own expenses and even finance operations. As one insurgent put it, "The Saudis go with enough money to support themselves and their Iraqi brothers."[31]

Saudi officials have vigorously denied these claims and appeal to U.S. officials for concrete information so that they can investigate and prosecute those involved. For their part, Iraqi officials have called on Saudi Arabia and other neighboring countries to do whatever they can to restrict the financial networks operating on their soil in support of insurgents.[32]

THE NEED FOR U.S. PARTNERS

The extent to which terrorists have abused charities is evident by the number of investigations, prosecutions, designations, and closures that have taken place since September 2001. Yet, many of these actions have been conducted unilaterally by the United States. Moreover, the U.S. Treasury Department has designated only a fraction of the hundreds of charities suspected of directly supporting or otherwise assisting terrorist groups.[2]

This abuse will continue until the United States, the European Union, and other countries around the world adopt a "common set of anti-terrorist policies, including similar regulatory frameworks, scope of groups targeted, and responses and penalties."[3] Without a shared international position on the issue and joint efforts to impose transparency on the charitable sector, current U.S. efforts to designate and freeze the funds of bad charities will have a "marginal impact at best in reducing the flow of funds

Case Study

Foundation of Terror: Benevolence International

The Benevolence International Foundation (BIF) was formed in 1992 with the purported mission of "helping those afflicted by wars" with "short-term relief such as emergency food distribution," as well as providing "education and self-sufficiency to children, widowed refugees, injured and staff of vital governmental institutions."[1] Its actions were diametrically opposed to this mission, however.

BIF was a merger of two organizations: Benevolence International and the Islamic Benevolence Committee.[2] Based in the Philippines, Benevolence International was founded by Usama bin Laden's brother-in-law Mohammed Jamal Khalifa. Its mission was to fund Abu Sayyaf, an al-Qaeda affiliate dedicated to spreading the group's Islamist ideology throughout Southeast Asia. Founded in Pakistan and Saudi Arabia, the Islamic Benevolence Committee raised money for the jihadis fighting against the Russians in Afghanistan throughout the 1990s.[3]

In 1993, the recently united BIF opened an office in Plantation, Florida, and a second office in Chicago soon thereafter. Both offices actively raised funds for conflicts in Chechnya and the Philippines.[4] And according to law enforcement, BIF's registered agent in Florida, Adham Amin Hassoun, was very close to Jose Padilla, a terrorist suspect arrested in Chicago in 2002 for allegedly plotting to detonate a "dirty bomb."[5]

At its height, BIF operated in Afghanistan, Azerbaijan, Bangladesh, Bosnia and Herzegovina, Canada, China, Croatia, Georgia, the Netherlands, Pakistan, the Palestinian territories, territories under Russian suzerainty (Chechnya, toward terrorist organizations."[4] Given this reality, terrorists will naturally look for the least stringent jurisdictions to conduct their financial affairs.

CURRENT INTERNATIONAL STANDARDS

The international community has recognized that terrorists' abuse of charities—often referred to with the more general term "nonprofit organizations" (NPOs)—poses a major vulnerability in the global struggle to stop terrorism financing at its

Dagestan, Ingushetia), Saudi Arabia, Sudan, Tajikistan, the United Kingdom, the United States, and Yemen.[6] But in 2002, the Treasury Department designated the charity and shut down its operations in the United States, accusing it of "providing material support to organizations, including al-Qaeda, that are engaged in violent activities."[7] The United Nations also took action—in November 2002, the Security Council's 1267 Committee designated the foundation for its affiliation with al-Qaeda. As a result, all UN members were required to ensure that BIF did not operate in their territories.

The U.S. and UN crackdowns brought a great deal of evidence to light regarding BIF's connections with al-Qaeda. Just before the Treasury designation, for example, authorities raided BIF's offices in Bosnia. There, they found one of the most important founding al-Qaeda documents—a list of the organization's 20 main financiers, composed by Usama bin Laden in 1988. Bin Laden referred to this list as the "Golden Chain."[8]

In addition, the U.S. government argued that BIF executive officer Enaam Arnaout, a Syrian-born U.S. citizen, had maintained a close relationship with bin Laden since the mid-1980s. Arnaout reportedly worked with al-Qaeda members to "purchase rockets, mortars, rifles and offensive and defensive bombs, and to distribute them to various Mujahideen camps."[9] Authorities also claimed that they had a handwritten letter in which bin Laden indicated that Arnaout was authorized to sign on his behalf.[10]

The government pressed charges against Arnaout, but a U.S. district judge told prosecutors they had "failed to connect the dots" on one key accusation: that he had "identified with or supported" terrorism.[11] As part of a plea bargain, the government dropped all charges related to his association with al-Qaeda, and Arnaout pled guilty to racketeering. He began serving a ten-year sentence in 2003 but has publicly denied any link to al-Qaeda.[12]

source. This problem has drawn the attention of international organizations such as the Financial Action Task Force (FATF; see chapter 3 for a full discussion of this agency), the Group of Seven (G7), and the United Nations, as well as governments around the globe. Unfortunately, many national authorities either do not subject their charities to government oversight or do not do so effectively. For example, many charities are not required to register, keep proper records, report their activities to a central authority, or perform background checks on their employees. As a result, terrorist organizations are readily able to abuse the charitable sector in support of their activities.

To address these abuses, FATF encourages countries to establish effective measures to protect all organizations that "engage in raising or disbursing funds for charitable, religious, cultural, educational, social or fraternal purposes, or for the carrying out of other types of 'good works' from being misused or exploited by the financiers of terrorism."[5] At the same time, the agency recognizes the importance of striking the right balance to prevent overregulation. Controls should not be so burdensome that they discourage legitimate charitable activities.[6] The goal is to promote transparency that will "engender greater confidence in the sector, across the donor community and with the general public that charitable funds and services reach intended legitimate beneficiaries."[7]

To achieve this goal, FATF recommends both a defensive and offensive approach that rests on four pillars:

Outreach and Risk Assessments: The first step countries must undertake is a review of the sector to get a good picture of what abuses may be taking place. Governments should determine the size and scope of the charitable sector, its activities, and any other information deemed relevant.[8] In addition, they should review their laws and ensure that they are adequate to prevent abuse. If these reviews uncover any charities that are actively supporting terrorist organizations, governments should take the offensive against them.

FATF also encourages countries to conduct robust private sector outreach programs that promote transparency and integrity. Governments should raise awareness about the vulnerabilities charities face and publish best practices and actual requirements for the charitable sector's reference.

Supervision/Monitoring: Countries cannot take serious action against bad charities unless they empower authorities to effectively supervise the sector. FATF has determined that the first step in supervision should be to force charities into registering or applying for a license in order to operate. Governments should also ask charities to maintain (and provide upon request) the following:

- A description of their objectives and activities
- A list of their owners and managers, including senior officers, board members, and trustees
- Financial statements with itemized data on income and expenditures
- A detailed overview of the controls they have implemented to ensure that all funds are spent appropriately and in line with the organization's stated purpose
- Archived records extending back for a minimum of five years.[9]

The global charitable sector collects hundreds of billions of dollars annually from donors. Transparency, therefore, is in the interest of donors, as well as the charities themselves and national authorities. Charities should also follow a variation of the axiom that guides banks and other formal financial institutions: "know your beneficiaries and associates." That is, charities must make the best effort possible to "confirm the identity, credentials and good standing of their beneficiaries and associate NPOs," as well as "the identity of their significant donors" (while respecting donor confidentiality concerns).[10]

Information Gathering and Investigations: FATF maintains that governments should be responsible for monitoring charities' compliance on an ongoing basis. Authorities should investigate noncompliant organizations and apply sanctions against those found to be acting illegally.

Sanctions: For those charities identified as terrorism financiers or supporters of terrorist activity, FATF encourages countries to employ a range of sanctions such as "freezing of accounts, removal of trustees, fines, de-certification, delicensing and de-registration."[11] Government action should also include parallel "civil,

More Than One Approach to Charities

In FATF's view, there is no one correct approach to achieving transparency in the charitable sector—different jurisdictions will use different methods to achieve this goal. Some choose independent charity commissions, while others choose existing government ministries. In either case, it is worth remembering that governments typically recruit multiple agencies in the fight against terrorism, including intelligence and law enforcement officials, bank regulators, and others. Curbing the threat of terror financing in the charitable sector will require a similar level of cooperation between multiple players.

U.S. Legal Requirements for Charities

Under U.S. law, any person or group may set up a charity and apply to the IRS for tax-exempt status provided they meet the requirements of section 501(c)(3) of the Internal Revenue Code. These requirements include the following:

- Charities cannot distribute their income to private donors.
- A charity's founding documents, mission statement, and similar materials must assert clearly that the organization has charitable intentions.
- If the organization were to dissolve, all of its assets must be earmarked for charitable donation.
- A charity's operations must be for public and not private objectives.
- Charities cannot intervene in political campaigns and may engage in only a limited amount of lobbying.
- Charities are required to operate exclusively for specific purposes that include charitable, religious, scientific, and educational activities.

administrative or criminal proceedings with respect to NPOs or persons acting on their behalf where appropriate."

THE U.S. CHARITABLE SECTOR

American charities play a vital role in providing global comfort and support to people in need. To safeguard this mission, the U.S. government has developed a unique approach to preventing terrorist abuse of the sector. The primary goal of this approach is to ensure that aid reaches those in need and that charities are both transparent and accountable. Other important goals include effectively investigating cases of abuse and enlisting the sector's support by raising awareness and conducting outreach initiatives.[12] Toward these ends, the government has sought to pool the resources of federal agencies, state regulators, private sector watchdogs, and law enforcement agencies, in addition to employing various judicial and administrative powers and private sector initiatives.

Charities are part of the wider U.S. community of tax-exempt NPOs, which also include state and local governments, Indian tribal governments, and employee benefit plans. Collectively, these organizations play a critical role in the U.S. economy, employing one out of every four workers.[13]

The charitable sector comprises both public charities and private foundations. The former receive most of their funding from the general public, while the latter are typically endowments created and operated by a small group.[14] (For the purposes of this book, both types fall under the label "charities.") Today, nearly one million such organizations file for tax-exempt status with the Internal Revenue Service (IRS), which estimates that they control more than $3 trillion in assets.[15]

OVERSIGHT

Overseeing the charitable sector is a three-level process that includes the federal government, state authorities, and the private sector. At the federal level, the IRS is the primary oversight agency. At the state level, a number of agencies monitor charities that raise money in their state. Additionally, several private sector bodies act as self-regulating watchdogs.

Charities must file annual documentation with the IRS that includes financial statements.[16] Unlike most tax returns, which are confidential, these filings must be made available to the public by law. They include the charity's gross income, expenses, assets, liabilities, net worth, total contributions for the year, names and addresses of all substantial donors, and names and salaries of all "highly compensated employees." Charities must keep these records on file for at least five years.

For its part, the IRS reviews and verifies the information, conducts audits, and imposes sanctions for noncompliance. As part of this process, the agency also cross-checks information against the Treasury Department's "Specially Designated Nationals" (SDN) list to ensure that charities are not conducting business with illicit actors such as terrorism financiers (see chapter 10 for more on this list).

At the state level, authorities exercise oversight in several different ways. Some of the larger states have separate agencies or special officials whose primary responsibility is to oversee charities; in other states, the office of the attorney general assumes the role along with its other duties. Additionally, 39 states require registration and exercise regulatory oversight over any money raised in their territory.[17]

In the private sector, numerous watchdog organizations—such as Independent Sector and the Council on Foundations—help ensure that the charitable sector remains transparent.[18] One of their methods for doing so is to emphasize compliance with U.S. tax laws mandating that all financial information be readily available to the public. This allows donors to make informed decisions about where to make their charitable contributions.

OUTREACH

Governments cannot protect the charitable sector from terrorist abuse without the active support of the charities themselves. Accordingly, the U.S. government works with communities and individual charities to raise awareness of their obligations. It also issues "best practices" describing how to operate effectively and offers creative methods for reporting suspicious activity (e.g., through a telephone hotline or the internet).

In 2002, the Treasury Department released the "Anti-Terrorist Financing Guidelines: Voluntary Best Practices for U.S.-Based Charities." It updated these guidelines in late 2005, after the government formed a working group with members of the NPO community to ensure that proper input was taken into consideration.[19] These guidelines encourage NPOs to:

- practice sound governance and fiscal policies;
- implement proper recordkeeping procedures;
- vet employees and potential grantees;
- work principally through the formal financial sector when possible (keeping in mind that "normal financial services may not always exist" when disbursing money); and

Case Study

International Pariah: Tamil Tigers and the Tamils Rehabilitation Organization

The Tamil Tigers, also known as the Liberation Tigers of Tamil Eelam (LTTE), are a militant nationalist organization that has waged a violent secessionist campaign against the Sri Lankan government since the 1970s. Their stated goal is the creation of a socialist Tamil state in the northern and eastern parts of the country. Toward this end, LTTE carries out suicide bombings, assassinations, and other attacks against military and civilian targets, including commuter trains and buses, farming villages, temples, mosques, policemen, and local politicians. The organization is notorious for inventing the suicide bomb jacket and was one of the pioneers in using female suicide bombers.[1] To date, 32 countries have designated LTTE as a terrorist group.[2]

In 1985, Tamil refugees established the Tamils Rehabilitation Organization (TRO) to provide relief for those who had fled to India. The organization quickly grew, moving its headquarters to Sri Lanka in 1987. Since then, TRO has offered valuable support to both Tamils and others. Following the

- provide guidance to employees regarding OFAC sanctions programs and how to direct inquiries and report suspicious activities to the appropriate government agency.

DESIGNATING BAD CHARITIES

After the September 11 attacks, the U.S. government concluded that one of the most critical elements in stopping widespread terrorist abuse of the charitable sector was to "name and shame" bad charities, publicizing their activities domestically and internationally. The United States also has a robust targeted economic sanctions regime to pursue charities that have supported or are otherwise involved in terrorist activity.

Regarding sanctions, the government may designate charities or associated individuals under the authority of both the Treasury Department and the State Department. Once an entity has been targeted, the government freezes its U.S.-based assets and prohibits all U.S. nationals—including other charities—from dealing with it in any way.[20]

December 2004 tsunami disaster, for example, TRO provided relief to all victims—including Tamils, Singhalese, and Muslims.

Yet, TRO has also been linked to the Tamil Tigers since its inception. This link was formally acknowledged in 2002, when TRO was granted official nongovernmental organization status after LTTE and the Sri Lankan government signed a ceasefire. Despite this concession, the international community has increasingly come to the conclusion that TRO, alongside its charitable activities, continues to funnel money to Tamil militants. Accordingly, the British Charity Commission stripped TRO of its charitable status in 2005 for being unable to "account satisfactorily for the application of funds."[3] And in 2006, the Sri Lankan government froze all TRO bank accounts in the country.[4]

The United States has followed suit: in November 2007, the Treasury Department designated TRO under Executive Order 13224 and froze all of its U.S. assets (for more on this Executive Order, see chapter 10). According to the Office of Foreign Assets Control (OFAC), "TRO passed off its operations as charitable, when in fact it was raising money for a designated terrorist group responsible for heinous acts of terrorism."[5] The government also accused TRO of facilitating LTTE procurement operations on U.S. soil, including "the purchase of munitions, equipment, communication devices, and other technology."

There are two significant impediments to effective CFT efforts in the American charitable sector:

1. **Inadequate resources.** Many have questioned whether the IRS can fulfill its mandate as the primary federal oversight agency for charities. As discussed in chapters 5 and 7, the IRS is also responsible for overseeing both the informal financial sector and the precious metals/stones sector, and most observers have argued that it is ill-suited to either task, whether due to inadequate funding, lack of manpower,

Case Study

Holy Land Foundation: Humanitarian Relief and Terrorism Financing

Before the U.S. government shut down the offices of the Holy Land Foundation for Relief and Development (HLF) in 2001, it was the largest Islamic charity in America.[1] Originally known as the Occupied Land Fund, the foundation began its work in California in 1989 but eventually grew to have offices in Texas, New Jersey, and Illinois, with representatives operating throughout the United States, the West Bank, and Gaza. By 2000, the organization was raising more than $13 million annually.[2]

HLF's work focused primarily on Palestinian refugees in Jordan, Lebanon, and the Palestinian territories. According to the Treasury Department, the foundation also directly transferred millions of dollars to Hamas offices and related Hamas charities in the West Bank and Gaza. Hamas used these funds to, among other things, support the families of suicide bombers and encourage children to become martyrs.[3]

In July 1995, U.S. authorities arrested one of HLF's founders—Mousa Mohammed Abu Marzuk, a Hamas political leader—in New York as he attempted to enter the United States after being expelled from Jordan. Previously, he had promoted HLF as Hamas's primary fundraising arm in the United States.[4] A month later, Treasury added Marzuk to its Specially Designated Terrorist list. After detaining him for nearly two years, the government deported him back to Jordan in 1997.[5] In December 2001, Treasury named HFL itself to the Specially Designated Global Terrorist list for its connections to Hamas.[6] The European Union eventually followed suit, freezing the foundation's assets in 2005.[7]

The U.S. government's actions against HLF and its associates have or insufficient qualifications on issues such as counterterrorism. These problems would only be compounded if the agency were asked to take on expanded efforts against terrorism-supporting charities.

2. **Limitations on publicly available information regarding terrorist activities.** The law enforcement and intelligence community actually has a wealth of information to support the government's domestic and international terrorist designations. Much of this evidence is classified, however, and therefore unavailable

extended to the courtroom as well. In 2004, a federal grand jury in Illinois indicted Marzuk in absentia for conspiracy to raise funds for terrorist attacks against Israel. That same year, in a case spurred by a private lawsuit, a federal judge in Chicago ruled that HLF, in addition to two other charities—the Islamic Association of Palestine and the Quranic Literacy Institute—were liable for $156 million for providing support to Hamas.

The most significant case, however, began when a federal grand jury in Dallas indicted HLF on 42 counts, including conspiracy, providing material support to a foreign terrorist organization, tax evasion, and money laundering. The 2004 indictment alleged that between 1995 and 2001, the foundation had provided Hamas and associated individuals with more than $12.4 million. The court also named seven HLF officers, including foundation president Shukri Abu Baker, chairman Ghassan Elashi, and executive director Haitham Maghawri. Five of the seven were arrested; the other two have never been found and are considered fugitives.[8]

At the time of the indictment, HLF denied all charges, claiming that the FBI had falsified evidence and "fabricated a case" to show that the foundation had financed Palestinian suicide bombers.[9] The case continued, however, with the criminal trial opening in July 2007. Three months later, in a major setback for the U.S. government, the judge declared a mistrial because the jurors were deadlocked on some of the charges and had acquitted HFL on others.[10]

In November 1008, the Justice Department retried the case on the deadlocked charges. In a dramatic turnaround, HLF and five of its former organizers were found guilty on 108 separate charges, including funneling more than $12 million to Hamas. According to Peter Margulies, a law professor who studies terrorism financing cases, "The government showed in a streamlined case that where special assistance to the families of terrorists is concerned, cash is the moral equivalent of a car bomb."[11]

for public dissemination—a major disadvantage for policymakers seeking to garner public and international support against terrorism financing in the charitable sector or elsewhere.

U.S. Authority to Designate Charities

The secretary of the Treasury may designate any charity that meets the criteria outlined in a relevant executive order (EO) issued by the president. In addition, the secretary of state may designate charities as Foreign Terrorist Organizations (FTOs) pursuant to the Antiterrorism and Effective Death Penalty Act of 1996 and the Immigration and Nationality Act.

As of May 2009, the United States had designated 58 domestic and international charities pursuant to EO 13224 and 12947.

CONCLUSIONS

Protecting the charitable sector from illicit actors and complicit organizations is one of the most critical components of any anti–money laundering regime. When criminals and terrorists abuse this sector, donors begin to question the integrity of individual charities. This, in turn, jeopardizes charitable giving. Because the sector provides such an invaluable service to people in need around the world, maintaining its integrity is crucial.

The number of charities designated by the United States in recent years reflects the degree to which terrorist groups have exploited the sector, whether to finance their members' activities, recruit new operatives, provide logistical support, or raise and move money. As long as the international community fails to establish adequate oversight and regulation, terrorists will always be able to abuse the weakest links in the CFT chain.

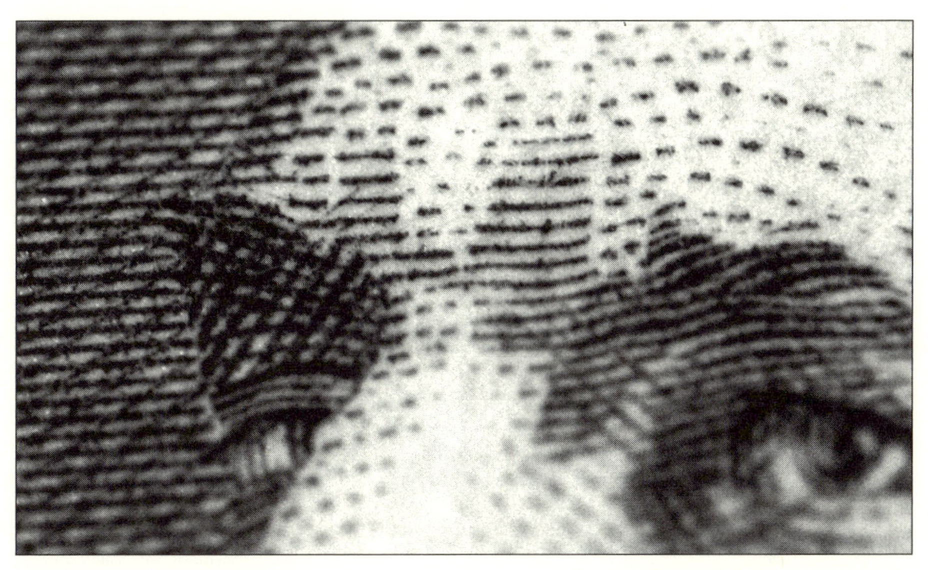

PART III
Enforcement

Chapter 9

Criminalization of Money Laundering and Terrorism Financing

In this chapter:

- Region of concern: the Tri-Border Area
- International conventions
- Campaigning for criminalization
- U.S. efforts and deficiencies

Countries cannot effectively pursue money launderers and terrorism financiers unless their activities are formally outlawed in as many jurisdictions as possible. Although the Financial Action Task Force (FATF) and other international standard-setters recognize that "no country is in a position to adopt specific laws that are identical to those of another country," all nations are obligated to criminalize laundering and terror financing in some fashion.[1]

Regions of the world that are largely devoid of government control—such as South America's Tri-Border Area—are particularly worrisome in this regard. Such hotspots serve as ideal fields of operation for launderers, terror financiers, and other criminal elements. Unless countries commit to (1) taking effective action against corruption, and (2) improving their judicial systems, law enforcement capabilities, and military resources, illicit activity in these areas will continue to thrive—thwarting U.S. and international anti–money laundering/combating the financing of terrorism regimes.

INTERNATIONAL CRIMINALIZATION OF MONEY LAUNDERING

The first item in FATF's "40 + 9 Recommendations" (see chapter 3) calls for the criminalization of money laundering.[2] The international standard stipulates that such action should be taken in accordance with two international agreements: the UN Convention against Illicit Traffic in Narcotic Drugs and Psychotropic Substances, commonly known as the Vienna Convention, and the UN Convention against Transnational Organized Crime, also referred to as the Palermo Convention.[3] To comply with this recommendation, countries cannot simply sign and ratify the conventions—FATF insists that they fully integrate the substance of these agreements into their legal structure.

The Vienna Convention—established in 1988 and initially designed to act as a drug-control instrument—was the first formal international effort against money laundering. Although it does not actually use the term "money laundering," the three

Region of Concern

Latin America's Tri-Border Area

As described in chapter 7, the Tri-Border Area (TBA) along the junction of Argentina, Brazil, and Paraguay—bounded by the key border towns of Puerto Iguazú, Foz do Iguaçu, and Ciudad del Este, respectively—is nearly devoid of governmental control. According to a U.S. Army report, this zone generates $6 billion in illicit money annually from activities such as terrorism financing, money laundering, arms trafficking, counterfeiting, drug trafficking, document falsification, and piracy.[1] Despite this rampant activity, Brazil and Paraguay have not yet criminalized terrorism financing, and Argentina did so only in 2007, after FATF threatened to revoke its membership in the organization.[2]

It is surprisingly easy to move across the borders of the TBA. People and motorbikes are reportedly permitted to cross without travel documents, and larger vehicles and smugglers can readily find ways to pass unnoticed.[3]

Given this combination of porous borders and known terrorist activity, the TBA has quietly become a top priority for U.S. policymakers since the September 11 attacks. According to former FBI director Louis Freeh, the area is a "free zone for significant criminal activity, including people who are organized to commit acts of terrorism."[4] Numerous intelligence and law enforcement agencies concur, calling the TBA a breeding ground for terrorist organizations. More specifically, authorities claim that many of the area's approximately 20,000 Muslim and Arab residents give financial support to groups such as Hizbollah, Hamas, Egyptian Islamic Jihad, and al-Qaeda.[5] According to Carlos Altemberger, chief of Paraguay's antiterrorist unit, "Terrorists partly finance their operations by remitting dollars from Ciudad del Este to the Middle East."[6] Other South American and U.S. officials have concluded that money raised in the TBA is used to finance "training camps, propaganda operations and bomb attacks in South America."[7]

categories of offenses included in the convention form the basis of what is now commonly referred to by that name:

1. Converting or transferring property with the knowledge that it is derived from a drug trafficking offense, or helping any person involved in such an offense to evade the law

Despite these admissions, the governments of all three TBA countries generally deny the problem, stating that they have not detected terrorist activity or cells in the region.[8] Counterterrorism officials from other countries disagree, with the United States and Israel reportedly going so far as to dispatch CIA and Mossad operatives to the region in order to neutralize what they believe could be an imminent terrorist threat.[9]

HIZBOLLAH IN THE TBA

Hizbollah is perhaps the most active terrorist group in the TBA, and its role there has been extensively documented. For example, a 2003 U.S. congressional report stated that the group "clearly derives a quite substantial amount of income from its various illicit activities in the TBA."[10] According to former State Department coordinator for counterterrorism Philip Wilcox, these activities have included narcotics, smuggling, and terrorism.[11] And former assistant Treasury secretary Patrick O'Brien acknowledged flatly that "Hezbollah has penetrated the area, and part of that smuggling money is used to finance terrorist attacks." He concluded, "We are worried."[12]

Hizbollah's most notorious activity in the TBA involved the planning and financing of two major terrorist attacks in Argentina during the early 1990s.[13] The repercussions of these attacks continue to be felt today, not only in relation to the still-lawless TBA, but also in light of the misconduct and complicity uncovered at the highest levels of the Argentinean and Iranian governments.

On March 17, 1992, Hizbollah detonated a car bomb outside the Israeli embassy in Buenos Aires, killing 29 and injuring more than 250. And on July 18, 1994, the group bombed the Asociación Mutual Israelita Argentina (AMIA) building, the city's main Jewish community center, killing 87 and injuring more than 100. Although Hizbollah denied responsibility for the attacks, a massive amount of evidence has accumulated against the group over the years.

(continued)

First, according to U.S. officials, the group that did claim responsibility for the bombings was actually a clandestine terrorist wing of Hizbollah.[14] Moreover, it was widely believed that Imad Mughaniya—the Hizbollah operations chief reportedly responsible for the deadly 1983 suicide bombing of the U.S. embassy in Beirut—masterminded both attacks. This accusation was later confirmed by an Iranian intelligence officer who defected to Germany.[15]

An investigation by Interpol and the FBI went a step further, arguing for Iranian involvement as well as Hizbollah culpability.[16] The Argentinean prosecutor's office concurred, asserting that then–Iranian president Ali Akbar Hashemi Rafsanjani ordered the AMIA attack and that Mughaniya oversaw it. Specifically, Rafsanjani was charged with "heading the intelligence office whose main function was to devise a preliminary plan to attack Argentina," while Mughaniya was charged with "overseeing the complex operations of Hizbollah overseas" and serving as "a specialist in recruiting soldiers for foreign operations, reporting to no one else but Iran."[17] Argentina issued warrants for both men; Rafsanjani's remains outstanding to this day, though Mughaniya was assassinated in 2008.

The investigation also found that Tehran transferred at least $152,812 to accounts controlled by Mohsen Rabbani, who at the time of the AMIA bombing served as the cultural attaché at the Iranian embassy in Buenos Aires and held diplomatic immunity. Authorities concluded that Rabbani oversaw the logistics of the AMIA attack, procuring the materials for the bombers.[18]

Perhaps the most definitive evidence of Iranian involvement came in 1998, when Argentinean authorities "uncovered records of phone calls between the Iranian embassy in Buenos Aires and suspected Hezbollah operatives" in the TBA.[19] Argentina immediately expelled six of the seven Iranian diplomats in the country.

Ironically, Argentina's persistent investigation of the bombings also uncovered shocking revelations about the government's own misconduct and

2. Concealing the true nature, source, location, disposition, movement, rights with respect to, or ownership of property with the knowledge that it was derived from drug trafficking

3. Acquiring, possessing, or using property with the knowledge that it was derived from a drug trafficking offense[4]

The convention requires countries to incorporate the first two categories into their incompetence. For example, many analysts now believe that former Argentinean president Carlos Saul Menem, a man of Syrian ancestry, accepted a bribe to conceal Iran and Hizbollah's role in the bombings.[20] And in July 2005, President Nestor Kirchner "issued a decree formally accepting a share of the blame for the failure of investigations into the AMIA attack"—a failure most notably illustrated by the removal of the federal judge presiding over the inquiry due to "serious irregularities."[21]

Meanwhile, efforts to uncover and target actual suspects in the bombings have progressed in recent years. In May 2003, Argentinean prosecutors linked Ciudad del Este and Foz do Iguacu to the AMIA bombing and issued arrest warrants for two Lebanese citizens residing in the former city. And in November 2005, Argentinean prosecutor Alberto Nisman named the suicide bomber who had conducted that attack: Hussein Berro, a 21-year-old Hizbollah member from Lebanon.[22]

The Argentina bombings and the ongoing lack of control in the TBA are even more troubling in light of Hizbollah's reported connection to al-Qaeda. The nature of this connection has been debated endlessly in policy circles, and counterterrorism agencies and other government authorities have been unable to declassify more than a few bits of information on the subject. Nevertheless, a 2003 congressional report asserted that the two groups are "probably cooperating in the [Tri-Border] region."[23]

Finally, the U.S. Treasury Department has taken action against the Hizbollah presence in the TBA twice in recent years. In 2004, it designated Assad Ahmad Barakat and two of his companies, calling him a "key terrorist financier in South America" and one of Hizbollah's "most prominent and influential members," in addition to citing his "close ties" with "numerous Islamic extremists and suspected Hizballah associates" in the TBA.[24] And in December 2006, Treasury designated nine individuals and two businesses in the region for providing financial and logistical support to Hizbollah.

domestic laws, while the third is subject to each country's "constitutional principles" and basic legal concepts."

As the international standard developed over time, perceptions changed regarding the underlying criminal activity that generates money for laundering—technically referred to as "predicate offenses." In 2000, the Palermo Convention expanded Vienna's nascent definition of money laundering, shifting the focus from drug trafficking to include the "widest range" of predicate offenses.[5] Today, the international standard encourages countries to categorize money laundering as an autonomous offense—in other words, to enable the prosecution of criminals simply by demonstrating that their assets have been obtained or handled illegally, without having to secure a conviction on the underlying criminal activity itself.

FATF's latest recommendations list 20 predicate offenses that can serve as grounds for a laundering prosecution, and the agency encourages countries to go beyond this minimum list in order to be as comprehensive as possible.[6] According to analyst Moses Naim, some of the most popular crimes from which money is laundered are arms trafficking (both conventional and unconventional), drug trafficking, human smuggling, and intellectual property rights violations.[7]

FATF also suggests several ways in which to criminalize money laundering:

1. The comprehensive approach—countries automatically prosecute the proceeds of any crime as money laundering

2. The predicate offense approach—countries list the crimes that can serve as the basis for a money laundering prosecution

3. A threshold approach—countries designate certain crimes as "serious offenses," e.g., any money-generating crime "with a maximum period of imprisonment exceeding one year (six months for countries applying minimum thresholds)."[8] In other words, for countries like the United States that use ranged sentencing guidelines (e.g., "6 to 18 months"), any crime whose maximum penalty is one year or more should be designated a serious crime, even if some criminals who commit it wind up receiving a lighter sentence. And in countries that use sentencing minimums rather than ranges, any crime whose penalty is at least six months imprisonment should be designated a serious crime. For countries that choose the threshold approach, any crime listed as a serious offense would also be automatically designated a money laundering offense. At minimum, FATF encourages countries to designate its 20 core predicate offenses as serious offenses.[9]

The extent to which countries implement these recommendations greatly affects their ability to exchange information and cooperate internationally. For example, many governments will not cooperate with foreign law enforcement authorities unless the activity being investigated is a crime in both countries—a phenomenon known as the "dual criminality" test. FATF therefore encourages countries to take the following steps:

1. Designate as wide a range of predicate offenses as possible

2. Take action against predicate offenses that occurred in another country but would have constituted an offense domestically as well

3. In cases where a foreign crime does not constitute a money laundering predicate offense domestically, authorities should still provide the greatest degree of assistance possible to ensure that justice is served[10]

INTERNATIONAL CRIMINALIZATION OF TERRORISM FINANCING

FATF's 9 Special Recommendations (see chapter 3) call for all countries to criminalize terrorism financing in accordance with the UN International Convention for the Suppression of the Financing of Terrorism.[11] This includes instituting the legal means to "prosecute and apply criminal sanctions" to all those who finance terrorism.[12]

FATF suggests a number of steps for achieving compliance with this standard:

1. Countries should criminalize all aspects of terrorism and terrorism financing, not just "aiding and abetting," "attempting," or "conspiracy." Legislation should cover any person who "willfully provides or collects funds" intended for terrorist uses—countries should not have to prove that the money actually funded terrorist acts.

2. Countries should empower authorities to prosecute terrorists and financiers whether their criminal acts took place domestically or elsewhere.

3. Countries should list terrorist activities as predicate offenses to money laundering.[13]

U.S. CRIMINALIZATION OF MONEY LAUNDERING

In 1986, the United States became the first country to make money laundering a crime when Congress passed the Money Laundering Control Act (MLCA).[14] The act was created in response to *United States v. Anzalone.* In this case, the defendant was accused of engaging in a practice now known as "structuring" (see chapters 2 and 4) in order to conceal a large transaction. Specifically, Anzalone purchased approximately $100,000 worth of cashier's checks from the same bank over a short period of time, keeping the individual checks below the $10,000 federal reporting requirement. The government charged him with failing to inform the bank of the structured nature of his transactions, arguing that he had carried out the scheme with the express purpose of avoiding detection, which in turn caused the bank to fail in its obligation to report his large transaction total. But the courts found that Anzalone had no duty to inform the bank of his structuring, and the indictment was dismissed. The Money Laundering Control Act rectified this legal gap, in addition to outlawing other activities in which individuals knowingly attempt to disguise the proceeds of crime.

Federal prosecutors have made the MLCA one of their favorite weapons against illicit actors because of its heavy penalties and broad reach. In addition to criminal

U.S. Efforts Recognized by FATF

During its last evaluation of America's anti–money laundering efforts, FATF concluded that "the system is working effectively overall," calling the set of U.S. laws dedicated to the issue "largely comprehensive." These laws are based on Title 18, sections 1956 and 1957 of the U.S. Code, which criminalize four categories of money laundering:

1. Basic money laundering
2. International money laundering
3. Money laundering in the context of an undercover "sting" case
4. Knowingly spending greater than $10,000 in criminal proceeds

A five-year statute of limitations applies to all cases involving these offenses.[1]

sanctions of up to 20 years in prison and $500,000 in fines, it permits civil penalty lawsuits by the government for the value of the assets involved in the criminal transaction. The U.S. track record on such prosecutions is impressive—from 2002 to 2005, for example, the government obtained 4,592 money laundering convictions at the federal level. Accordingly, FATF has recognized the United States as a country that "proactively investigates and prosecutes" money laundering.[15]

TOWARD FULL COMPLIANCE

As mentioned above, the Vienna and Palermo conventions explicitly require countries to criminalize a number of activities involving ill-gotten money, including the acquisition, possession, use, conversion, transfer, or concealment of such funds.[16] In its 2006 evaluation of the United States, FATF determined that Washington came close to fully complying with these requirements. The agency did point out one loophole: U.S. law does not sufficiently cover situations in which no transactions took place, i.e., when individuals acquire or possess tainted money without actually using or moving it. For example, if a criminal concealed the proceeds of a crime in a shoebox but did not carry out any transactions, a money laundering charge could not be successfully prosecuted.

Regarding predicate offenses, the United States adopts a list-based approach to defining which crimes may be tied to money laundering. To date, the government has designated approximately 300 such offenses.[17] This list does not include two of FATF's 20 recommended predicate offenses, however.[18]

In terms of jurisdiction, U.S. money laundering laws apply whether the crime took place domestically or internationally. For international crimes, U.S. authorities and prosecutors

Case Study

Riggs Bank: Laundering for a Dictator

In 2004, Riggs Bank—the Washington, D.C.–based institution that once billed itself as "the most important bank in the most important city in the world"—came under fire for laundering millions of dollars for former Chilean dictator Augusto Pinochet. During his reign (1973–1990), Pinochet was linked directly to corruption, illegal arms and drug trafficking, and the disappearance or murder of thousands of political opponents.

According to a 2005 U.S. Senate investigation, Riggs actively courted Pinochet as a client and afterward used a number of techniques to launder his money, including misleadingly named offshore accounts. Similarly, "in documents required by federal regulators…the bank referred to Pinochet not by name but as 'a retired professional' who held a 'high paying position in [the] public sector for many years.'"[1] Perhaps the most flagrant example of deception involved the top federal bank examiner in charge of supervising Riggs, who reportedly hid many of the details of the bank's relationship with Pinochet during his four years of service—and then joined Riggs as a senior executive after retiring from the government in 2002.[2]

In July 1996, Spain indicted Pinochet on charges of genocide, terrorism, and torture against Spanish citizens during his rule. After the indictment, a Riggs subsidiary in the Bahamas established two companies, Ashburton Co. Ltd. and Althorp Investment Co. Ltd., both putatively owned by trusts set up by Riggs. Although Pinochet and his family were the ultimate beneficiaries, his name did not appear anywhere on the trust or company documentation. Ashburton held the most Pinochet money, with a balance of $4.5 when it was closed in 2002.

In addition to the Pinochet debacle, which led to the eventual sale of Riggs, the bank also agreed to pay $25 million in civil penalties for violation of money laundering laws in its dealings with the embassies of Saudi Arabia and Equatorial Guinea.

have an extraterritorial reach if (1) a U.S. citizen committed the offense, or (2) at least part of the offense occurred on U.S. soil, whether the perpetrator is a citizen or not. As FATF pointed out, however, U.S. law regards only 12 of the agency's 20 recommended predicate offenses as grounds for money laundering charges if they take place on foreign soil.[19]

A number of policymakers have questioned the efficacy of the list approach. Justice Department officials indicated to FATF that "prosecuting offenses under sections 1956 and 1957 would be much easier if a threshold approach to categorizing predicate offenses (rather than the current list approach) was adopted."[20] The government has taken important steps to rectify this problem, including proposing a bill in Congress. On March 13, 2006, a group of senators introduced the Combating Money Laundering and Terrorist Financing Act of 2006. Among other provisions, this bill would institute a threshold

Case Study

Smuggling Ring Uses Commodities to Launder Money for Hizbollah

In 1996, an off-duty North Carolina deputy sheriff spotted a group of people loading thousands of dollars worth of cigarettes into cars with out-of-state license plates outside the JR Tobacco warehouse, a discount cigarette outlet. Each person was carrying a paper bag with enough cash to purchase 299 cartons of cigarettes—the maximum number per person allowable by law. This discovery led to a cigarette smuggling investigation dubbed "Operation Smokescreen," which yielded the arrest of eighteen individuals and the indictment of thirteen others in July 2000.[1]

The U.S. government charged the suspects with a number of crimes, including marriage, visa, and other types of immigration fraud; bribery and conspiracy offenses related to this fraud; conspiracy to smuggle contraband cigarettes; conspiracy to launder money; and terrorism-related offenses. In addition, authorities seized assets valued at about $1.5 million, consisting of cigarettes, real property, and currency.[2] In the previous year-and-a-half, investigators estimate that they were able to generate an estimated $7.9 million.[3]

The group's scheme involved smuggling cigarettes from North Carolina, where the state tax on tobacco sales is very low, to Michigan, where the tax is high, eventually profiting from the wide difference between the tax rates. The group then funneled some of the proceeds from this scheme to approach. As described previously, any illegal act that carries a penalty of one year's imprisonment or more would also be automatically designated a money laundering offense. In addition, the jurisdiction of U.S. authorities would be extended in money laundering cases to include any "activities outside of the United States that have an effect in the United States."[21] If Congress passes the bill, the United States would be in full compliance with this portion of the international standard.

U.S. CRIMINALIZATION OF TERRORISM FINANCING

There are four portions of the U.S. Code that deal directly with the financing of terrorism. These sections criminalize the following activities:

1. Providing material support for commission of certain terrorism-related offenses[22]

Hizbollah. They also used some of the money to purchase hi-tech equipment for Hizbollah (e.g., global positioning and night vision gear).[4]

Authorities examined Bank Secrecy Act data to identify accounts that the defendants used to hide and transfer funds.[5] Group members employed a number of tactics to launder the money, such as making charitable donations and purchasing homes, vehicles, and other property. They also used the banking sector and couriers to transfer money to Hizbollah in Lebanon.[6]

The entire operation was run by two brothers, Mohammed and Chawki Hammoud. Prosecutors linked Mohammed to Hizbollah through a variety of evidence: the FBI had wiretap recordings of him speaking by phone with Sheikh Abbas Harake, Hizbollah's military commander in Beirut; the raid on his house yielded a letter urging him to donate money to Hizbollah and suggesting that he had supported the group's military operations in the past; authorities also found a photo of him as a teenager at a Hizbollah training camp in Lebanon.[7] In addition, the smuggling ring often met at Mohammed's home to discuss Hizbollah activities and listen to speeches by its leaders.

In June 2002, Mohammed was convicted on a variety of charges, including funding a terrorist group from the proceeds of an interstate cigarette smuggling ring. U.S. District Court judge Graham Mullen sentenced him to 155 years in prison.[8] His brother was not found to have ties to Hizbollah, but he was convicted on other charges and sentenced to 51 months in prison. Seven other defendants pled guilty to a variety of charges, including conspiracy to provide material support to terrorists, cigarette smuggling, money laundering, and immigration violations.[9]

2. Providing material support or resources to designated Foreign Terrorist Organizations (FTOs)[23]

3. Providing or collecting terrorist funds[24]

4. Concealing or disguising either material support to FTOs or funds used or intended for terrorist acts[25]

These crimes are also predicate offenses for money laundering.[26]

U.S. law takes a very broad approach when specifying who can be prosecuted for these offenses. According to Title 18, section 2 of the U.S. Code, individuals can be punished as principals if they commit the crime in question, if they attempt or conspire to commit it, or if they aid, abet, counsel, command, induce, procure, or willfully cause it to be committed.[27] There is an eight-year statute of limitations for prosecuting these offenses, but this limit can be extended for certain terrorism offenses and is waived altogether in cases where the offense resulted in death.[28]

U.S. efforts to criminalize all aspects of terrorism financing were further bolstered by Executive Order 13224, signed by President Bush on September 23, 2001, pursuant to the International Emergency Economic Powers Act (IEEPA). This order prohibits the passing of funds to individuals or organizations categorized by the Treasury Department as "Specially Designated Global Terrorists" (see chapter 10). The government can prosecute violations of this order as terrorism financing offenses.[29]

Federal law enforcement agencies are responsible for investigating such violations, with the FBI holding primary jurisdiction in terror financing cases. The Justice Department is responsible for carrying out any subsequent criminal prosecutions. As of August 2006, the government had charged 126 individuals with terror financing offenses, with 54 either pleading guilty or being convicted.[30]

In its 2006 evaluation, FATF found the United States fully compliant with the international standards regarding terrorism financing. The agency did, however, note that certain provisions were difficult to follow and "unnecessarily complicated."

CONCLUSION

Enforcement is the cornerstone of any anti–money laundering/combating the financing of terrorism regime. Criminalization is therefore essential. Several international bodies have urged individual countries to do more in this regard, with FATF and the UN providing a blueprint for modifying legal systems in a way that helps prosecutors bring down terrorists, launderers, and terror financiers. These efforts have been echoed by leading nations such as the United States and its European allies. All of these parties have made clear that the only way to begin fighting the problem is to ensure that every country commits to criminalization.

Chapter 10

Targeted Economic Sanctions

In this chapter:

- What are targeted economic sanctions?
- Criminal vs. administrative/judicial procedures
- To list or not to list?
- U.S. Executive Orders
- Targeting process
- Bad banks and what to do about them
- Are U.S. sanctions lists fair?

For years, governments have used travel bans, diplomatic pressure, war, and other measures to influence or constrain the behavior of governments and individuals. When it comes to anti–money laundering/combating the financing of terrorism (AML/CFT) efforts, targeted economic sanctions—also commonly referred to as targeted financial sanctions—constitute the latest arrow in the quiver of finance ministries.[1]

The Watson Institute has aptly defined such sanctions: "These instruments are 'targeted' in that they are applied only to a subset of the population; they are 'financial' in that they involve the freezing or blocking of funds and other financial resources; and they are sanctions in that they are coercive measures applied to effect change."[2]

FREEZING AND CONFISCATING TERRORIST ASSETS

An effective targeted economic sanctions regime is critical in the war against illicit finance, particularly with regard to terrorists. Accordingly, the international community, through the UN, has instituted targeting programs that identify terrorists and their support networks. Under these programs, UN member states are required to apply a number of restrictions and prohibitions against designated entities. At the same time, states must balance these requirements with the more general mandate of respecting human rights and the rule of law, including the rights of innocent third parties.[3]

The first step in establishing an effective sanctions regime is for countries to implement the legal authorities necessary to freeze the funds of terrorists and their financiers—*without delay and without giving prior notice to those targeted.*[4] In most cases, this preventative step should be followed up with punitive measures such as confiscation.[5] Both steps deprive terrorists and their networks of the "means to conduct future terrorist activity and maintain their infrastructure and operations."[6]

Criminal vs. Administrative/Judicial Procedures. It is imperative to underscore that the targeting mechanism used in any sanctions regime must be separate from

Country of Concern

The U.S. Financial War against the Iranian Banking Community

The United States first targeted Iranian banks in earnest on June 29, 2005, when President Bush signed Executive Order (EO) 13382.[1] With this order, Washington sought to curb the spread of weapons of mass destruction by freezing the assets of proliferators and their supporters, and by isolating them from the U.S. financial and commercial systems. The Treasury Department also quietly warned foreign banks and companies that do business with Iran that they too could lose access to U.S. markets if they deal with entities connected to terrorism or the Islamic Republic's nuclear industry.[2]

The United States has maintained sanctions of one sort or another against Iran since 1987. Originally enacted in response to Tehran's sponsorship of terrorism, these sanctions prohibit U.S. citizens, companies, and foreign branches from conducting business with Iran.[3] But has this strategy yielded the desired effect of deterring the Islamic Republic from pursuing nuclear weapons, sponsoring terrorism, and other illicit objectives?

Sanctions have certainly had an impact in three areas, though the extent is difficult to determine. First, according to U.S. officials, sanctions may have slowed foreign investment in Iran's petroleum sector and hindered the regime's ability to acquire prohibited technology or fund terrorism-related activities. Second, officials believe that financial sanctions bar those Iranians involved in proliferation and terrorism from accessing the U.S. financial criminal liability proceedings.[7] Criminal procedures are considered too slow—FATF encourages countries to set up administrative or judicial procedures that can freeze terrorism-related funds quickly and efficiently.

FATF drafted its standards to complement international obligations such as UNSCRs 1267, 1373, and their successor resolutions, along with the Vienna and Palermo Conventions.[8] In order to carry out these obligations, FATF encourages countries to designate a "competent authority"—again, an administrative or judicial body such as a government agency or a court—to "issue, administer and enforce freezing and unfreezing actions under relevant mechanisms."[9] As for who should be targeted, FATF encourages countries to:

system, thereby complicating their support for such activities. Finally, sanctions provide a clear statement of U.S. concerns about Iran.[4]

Sanctions are not a silver bullet, however. Since 2003, the Iranian government has reportedly signed $20 billion worth of contracts with foreign firms to develop its energy resources—though it is uncertain whether these firms will actually carry out the contracts. In addition, Iranian banks have turned to non-U.S. financial institutions to fund their activities in currencies other than the U.S. dollar. Indeed, Iran's global trade ties and leading role in energy production make it difficult for Washington to isolate and pressure the regime. In 2006, for example, the growing worldwide demand for oil, coupled with high prices and Iran's extensive reserves, enabled the country to generate more than $50 billion in oil revenues.[5]

The latest iteration of the sanctions approach has focused on the Iranian banking system—specifically, on prohibiting U.S. institutions from dealing with suspect Iranian banks and convincing international institutions to sever ties as well. In March 2008, in an unprecedented move, the U.S. Financial Crimes Enforcement Network (FinCEN; see chapter 4) unilaterally published a list of 30 Iranian financial institutions that have "serious deficiencies" in the realm of money laundering and therefore pose a risk to the international system.[6] In addition, the Treasury Department has designated four major Iranian banks per EO 13382, charging them with the use of deceptive financial practices to support terrorist groups and the Iranian nuclear program.

Bank Sepah: This bank has provided a number of financial services to Iran's missile industry. It processed and arranged financing for dozens of multimillion-dollar transactions and reportedly used a range of *(continued)* deceptive practices to avoid detection. These methods included requesting that other institutions remove the bank's name from transactions.[7]

The missile firms in question—the Shahid Hemmat Industries Group (SHIG) and the Shahid Bakeri Industries Group (SBIG)—are key players in Iran's ballistic missile program. Sepah also provided services to their parent company, the Aerospace Industries Organization (AIO). The United States has designated AIO as well for its role in overseeing Iran's missile industry.[8]

Bank Saderat: According to the Treasury Department, Tehran has used Bank Saderat to channel funds to terrorist organizations, including Hizbollah, Hamas, the Popular Front for the Liberation of Palestine–General Command (PFLP-GC), and Palestinian Islamic Jihad. From 2001 to 2006, Saderat transferred $50 million to Hizbollah alone. In turn, Hizbollah used the bank to send millions of dollars to other terrorist organizations, including Hamas. As of early 2005, Hamas reportedly had substantial assets deposited in Bank Saderat.[9]

Bank Melli: Iran's largest bank, this institution reportedly provides services to other banks and firms involved in the country's nuclear and ballistic missile programs. This includes entities that have been designated by the UN for their involvement in those programs, such as Bank Sepah and its missile clients. According to the Treasury Department, following Sepah's designation under UN Security Council Resolution (UNSCR) 1747, Melli took special measures to avoid identifying the bank in transactions (e.g., removing its name from wire instructions). Treasury also disclosed that Bank Melli has helped facilitate the purchase of sensitive materials for Iran's nuclear and missile programs by "opening letters of credit and maintaining accounts."[10]

> ensure that their nationals or any persons and entities within their territories are prohibited from making any funds or other assets, economic resources or financial or other related services available, directly or indirectly, wholly or jointly, for the benefit of: designated persons, terrorists; those who finance terrorism; terrorist organizations; entities owned or controlled, directly or indirectly, by such persons or entities; and persons and entities acting on behalf of or at the direction of such persons or entities.[10]

Of course, banks, law enforcement agencies, and other bodies cannot effectively help their governments identify and freeze illicit money without easy access to

In addition, from 2002 to 2006, Tehran used Bank Melli to send at least \$100 million to the Quds Force, a special unit of Iran's Revolutionary Guard Corps whose mission is to organize, train, equip, and finance Islamist revolutionary movements around the globe. When handling transactions on behalf of the Revolutionary Guards, Bank Melli employed some of the same deceptive banking practices used to conceal transactions involving Bank Sepah.[11]

Bank Mellat: This bank reportedly provides services to two key Iranian nuclear entities: the Atomic Energy Organization of Iran (AEOI) and Novin Energy Company, both of which have been designated by the United States and the UN Security Council (under Resolutions 1737 and 1747). Since 2003 (and perhaps earlier), Mellat has facilitated the movement of millions of dollars for Iran's nuclear program.[12]

In targeting these and other Iranian institutions, the United States has worked in concert with the Financial Action Task Force (FATF—see chapter 3) and the UN. In October 2007, FATF stated that Iran's lack of a comprehensive AML/CFT regime represents a "significant vulnerability in the international financial system."[13] In response, Iran passed its first AML law in February 2008. That same month, however, FATF reiterated its concern about the country's continuing AML/CFT deficiencies.[14]

To date, the UN Security Council has passed three resolutions targeting Iran's nuclear activities. The most recent—UNSCR 1803, adopted March 3, 2008—calls on all countries to exercise vigilance over any institutions dealing with Iranian banks and their foreign subsidiaries.[15] The UN and FATF's actions illustrate the international community's increasing resolve to use the financial sector as a means of ensuring that Iran does not acquire nuclear weapons.

information about designated entities. The only way to ensure that they have such information is to publicly circulate a targeting list. Despite this obvious prerequisite, policymakers and analysts in America and abroad have debated endlessly whether designation lists are necessary. This situation is partially attributable to flaws in some of the international documents underlying domestic sanctions efforts. For example, UNSCR 1373 does not explicitly refer to domestic designation lists, but countries cannot implement the resolution's targeting requirements without creating such a list. The fact that the UN has not clarified this obligation is a clear demonstration of its inability to play a meaningful role against those engaged in illicit finance (see chapter 3 for more on the UN's role and limitations).

In addition, some countries insist on keeping their designation lists confidential, citing "human rights concerns." Keeping a list unpublished flies in the face of FATF and UN obligations, however, and compromises the transparency of these countries' financial systems. As for human rights concerns, it should be remembered that public lists play an important role in preserving rights, ensuring that individuals have a means of challenging their designation. FATF encourages countries

In Simple Terms

The UN, FATF, and other international standard-setters mandate that each country create its own targeted economic sanctions program that designates money launderers, terrorists, weapons proliferators, and other illicit actors.

Case Study

Victor Bout: The "Merchant of Death"

Arms dealer Victor Bout, arrested in 2008, was known as the "Merchant of Death" for his uncanny ability to deliver all kinds of illicit cargo—weapons in particular—anywhere in the world. Despite his capture, his case is a powerful demonstration of the flaws in domestic and international sanctions systems, highlighting the lack of interagency coordination in the U.S. government as well as the willingness of individual countries to flout international law enforcement efforts.

More than any other global arms trafficker, Bout was able to "exploit the anarchy of globalization to get goods...to market."[1] A fluent speaker of Russian, English, French, Portuguese, Uzbek, and several African languages, he held as many as five passports in various aliases.[2] Using a personal fleet of aircraft, he delivered both legal and illicit cargo—everything from surface-to-air missiles to fresh-cut flowers—often to rival sides of the same conflict. Bout was infamous for operating in Afghanistan (where he sold arms to both the Taliban and the Northern Alliance) and Angola (where he dealt with both the government and the National Union for the Total Independence of Angola, or UNITA). He also did business with Liberia's Charles Taylor, the Revolutionary United Front (RUF) in Sierra Leone, the Revolutionary Armed to establish delisting and unfreezing procedures "upon satisfaction of certain criteria consistent with international obligations and applicable legal principles."[11] This includes giving targeted individuals the opportunity to prove they are not the designated person in question. For those designated in accordance with UNSCR 1267, the UN publishes delisting criteria on its website.[12] It also requires governments to create a mechanism for giving designees limited access to frozen funds under certain circumstances (e.g., for basic or "extraordinary" expenses).[13]

Finally, governments should ensure that their banks have strong compliance programs. If a sanctions program is to be effective, funds must be frozen and transactions barred for potentially long periods of time. Banks must have the ability to sustain such measures as long as is mandated. For institutions that fail to comply with these and other regulations, FATF encourages countries to subject them to civil, administrative, or criminal sanctions.

Forces of Colombia (FARC), Libya's Muammar al-Qaddafi, American troops in Iraq and Afghanistan, Abu Sayyaf in the Philippines, Hizbollah in Lebanon, and various UN humanitarian missions around the globe.[3] Many of his known aircraft operated out of Sharjah, part of the United Arab Emirates.[4]

In Afghanistan, the Taliban reportedly paid Bout more than $50 million dollars before they were overthrown by the U.S.-led invasion in 2001. In addition to servicing the Taliban's national airline, Ariana Afghan Airways, Bout sold the group a fleet of military cargo planes that hauled arms, cash, operatives, and narcotics into and out of the country.[5]

In Angola, Bout made an estimated $14 million between 1997 and 1998, flying arms destined for the UNITA rebels. His cargo reportedly included 20,000 82-millimeter mortar bombs, 6,300 antitank rockets, 790 AK-47s, 1,000 rocket launchers, and 15 million rounds of ammunition.[6]

Bout's legitimate flying runs are just as famous. His TransAvia Export Cargo Company flew Belgian peacekeepers to Somalia in 1993 as part of Operation Restore Hope. In 1994, his aircraft flew 2,500 French troops into Rwanda. In 2000, when Abu Sayyaf held European tourists hostage, Bout flew negotiators to the Philippines. And in 2004, following the devastating Indian Ocean tsunami, his companies delivered humanitarian goods and services to Sri Lanka.[7]

Bout has been subject to legal action of varying types and from different sources. In 2002, the Belgian government issued an

(continued)

international arrest warrant for him on charges of laundering more than $325 million (the details of these charges have not been reported in the English-language press). Bout lived in Moscow at the time, however, and the Russian government refused to detain or extradite him. In February of that year, Bout conducted a two-hour radio interview pronouncing his innocence—a move clearly aimed at mocking the will of the international law enforcement community. For example, during the show, the host read aloud a news bulletin from the Russian bureau of Interpol in which spokesman Igor Tsiroulnikov had claimed "Today we can say with certainty that Victor Bout is not in Russian territory." In early March, the Russian Federal Security Service issued a telling "correction" of Tsiroulnikov's statement: "There is no reason to believe that this Russian citizen has committed any illegal actions."[8] In other words, Russia had no intention of handing over one of its own.

For its part, the United States moved against Bout in July 2004, adding him to the SDN list, freezing his assets, and imposing sanctions against him under EO 13348, which targets associates of Charles Taylor as part of the wider international effort against the former Liberian leader. In April 2005, OFAC added several of Bout's associates and companies to the SDN list under the same authority, freezing their assets as well.[9]

Yet, even as the Treasury Department was designating Bout, another branch of the government was doing business with him. During the postwar

U.S. TARGETING PROGRAM

The United States has the most robust targeted economic sanctions programs in the world. Since shortly after the September 11 attacks, the Treasury Department has maintained a blacklist of suspected terrorism financiers. This "Specially Designated Global Terrorist" (SDGT) list was established under Executive Order 13224, signed by President Bush on September 23, 2001. The SDGT list—along with the broader Specially Designated Nationals (SDN) list, described below—fulfills the UN and FATF standards for designating illicit actors.[14] Many foreign officials refer to these lists collectively as the "the Bush list."

The framework for the U.S. designation system was established in the 1990s, when President Clinton assumed wide-reaching authority to meet the threat of terrorism, including the power to impose targeted economic sanctions. The United Nations Participation Act of 1945,[15] the National Emergencies Act of 1976, and the International reconstruction of Iraq and Afghanistan, Bout's companies flew hundreds of missions for the Defense Department as a subcontractor for KBR and Federal Express.[10] These assignments reportedly included transporting personnel and delivering a wide variety of goods to U.S. troops, including tents, video players, armored cars, oil field equipment, and refurbished Kalashnikovs. In hiring an SDN, Washington's left hand clearly did not know what the right hand was doing.

One U.S. agency did manage to capture Bout, however. In March 2008, the Drug Enforcement Administration (DEA) and Thai authorities arrested him and his colleague Andrew Smulian in Bangkok. The DEA had become involved in the case due to Bout and Smulian's longstanding arms sales to FARC in Colombia. As described in chapter 7, FARC is both a U.S.-designated terrorist organization and a major drug trafficker. Between November 2007 and February 2008, Bout and Smulian attempted to arrange a deal with two DEA informants posing as FARC operatives; the sale would have involved millions of dollars worth of weapons and material, including surface-to-air missile systems, armor-piercing rocket launchers, and helicopters. After several meetings with Smulian in the Netherland Antilles, Denmark, and Romania, the DEA informants arranged a final meeting with Smulian and Bout in Thailand. There, the DEA and Thai police made the arrest; as of this writing, both men are still being held in Thailand and awaiting proceedings for possible deportation to the United States.[11]

Emergency Economic Powers Act[16] provided the legislative basis for this authority.[17] In January 1995, Clinton issued Executive Order 12947, which allowed Washington to sanction any group, individual, or government found "to have committed, or to pose a significant risk of committing, acts of violence that have the purpose or effect of disrupting the Middle East peace process."[18] Then, following the August 1998 terrorist attacks against the U.S. embassies in Dar es Salaam, Tanzania, and Nairobi, Kenya, Clinton issued EO 13099, which imposed sanctions on al-Qaeda, Usama bin Laden, and their associates.[19] In the wake of the September 11 attacks, President Bush used these same legal authorities to issue EO 13224, enabling the government to create a new targeting mechanism— the SDGT list—and to impose sanctions on entities that "support or otherwise associate" with designees.[20]

EO 13224 delegates the task of designating individuals to Treasury's Office of Foreign Assets Control (OFAC). In contrast to the UN's standard practice, OFAC provides a brief, public explanation on the internet as to why each designee is on the list. Although OFAC must demonstrate that it has acted with "reasonable cause" in issuing a designation, it need not prove guilt because it is not a judicial body. Those targeted are allowed to appeal their designation, either via OFAC or the judicial system.

As of January 2009, the U.S. government had used EO 13224 to designate 518 individuals and entities for activities related to terrorism and terror financing.[21] The designees include members of al-Qaeda, the Taliban, Hizbollah, and other terrorist organizations.

In addition, the State Department maintains the Foreign Terrorist Organization (FTO) list, which as of April 2008 included 44 designated groups. FTOs are designated by the secretary of state under the Antiterrorism and Effective Death Penalty Act of 1996, in consultation with the Treasury secretary and the attorney general.[22]

Finally, OFAC's overarching SDN list currently contains more than 6,000 suspected terrorists, drug traffickers, and other illicit actors.[23] It is worth noting, however, that FATF deems the SDN list incomplete because it omits some of the Taliban names maintained by the UN's "1267 Committee" (see chapter 3 for a discussion of this body). In its defense, the United States has pointed out that these names have neither a "statement of the case"—or, in less technical terms, a publicly released explanation—to prove that designation is warranted, nor sufficient information to match them with real suspects (i.e., listing a designee's name without a date or place of birth is insufficient information for the banking community to act on). Then again, as a permanent member of the Security Council, the United States allowed those names to be added to the 1267 list in the first place, so its arguments are somewhat contradictory. In any case, the U.S. targeting system is largely effective.

OFAC's Specially Designated Nationals List

The SDN list is a broad compilation of designated individuals and entities—a kind of "list of lists." It comprises not only SDGTs, but also those designated under other U.S. sanctions regimes, such as the counterproliferation and counternarcotics programs and various country-focused efforts. U.S. citizens are prohibited from providing services to or conducting transactions with an SDN.

FROZEN AND SEIZED ASSETS: U.S. STATISTICS

According to U.S. officials, one of the most important metrics for gauging success in the war on terror is the amount of terrorist money frozen or seized. In fact, when the 9/11 Commission's Public Discourse Project evaluated the state of America's counterterrorism capabilities, the government's CFT efforts received the highest grade, an "A-," in large part due to the statistics provided at the time.[24] In reality, however, the government's freezing/seizing efforts have been inconsistent at best. According to John Cassara, a former CIA case officer and Treasury special agent, Washington is "cooking the books" and "hiding behind the numbers."[25]

For example, in August 2005, the United States reported to FATF that it had frozen more than $300 million worth of assets belonging to the Taliban, al-Qaeda, and other terrorism-related entities.[26] Three years later, however, that estimate was mysteriously—and drastically—lowered, with Treasury undersecretary Stuart Levey telling the Senate Finance Committee that only "$20,736,920" in terrorism-related funds were blocked between September 2001 and December 2007.[27]

To be sure, either of these amounts are tiny compared to the amount of illicit money moving worldwide each day, a significant fraction of which is linked to terrorists. For example, Iran announced in June 2008 that it was withdrawing $75 *billion* in assets from European banks as a result of sanctions due to its nuclear program—a troubling prospect given the regime's known sponsorship of terrorism. It is worth mentioning that a great amount of this money was converted to gold, making it that much harder for any government to seize or freeze.[28] Another example of illicit money flows that dwarf U.S. counterterror seizures was Mexico's "Operation Dragon." As described in chapter 6, Mexican authorities seized approximately $207 million during a March 2007 operation against a methamphetamine ring.[29] In other words, a single drug bust yielded nearly ten times as much seized money in one day as U.S. CFT efforts did in six years, at least according to Undersecretary Levey's estimate before the Senate. Such numbers should be kept in mind whenever Washington talks about how much terrorist money has been seized.

THE U.S. TARGETING PROCESS

The targeting process begins when potential designees are chosen using the criteria set forth in EO 13224. Treasury analysts assemble an administrative record based on open-source and classified material regarding the subject. This record—known as an "evidentiary—serves as the factual basis underlying the decision to designate.[30] When the evidentiary is complete, lawyers from the Treasury and Justice Departments conduct a thorough review to determine whether there is sufficient legal basis for designation. This is done to ensure that the designation can withstand the scrutiny of U.S. courts and, in theory, international public opinion. Evidentiaries usually contain both classified and unclassified information, however, and not all of the classified material can be fully disclosed to the public due to national security sensitivities.[31] For example, information that can endanger the source of the classified material is never disclosed. (For more on this issue, see the section below on the PATRIOT Act.)

Designations are often linked to foreign countries—for example, a designee may reside in or be a national of another country. In such cases, the governments in question are usually notified in advance of the designation and encouraged to contribute information, including appropriate identifiers. Washington also encourages countries to co-designate in accordance with UNSCR 1373, assuming they have the legal measures in place to do so. In addition, the United States notifies the UN of the designation; if the target is linked to al-Qaeda, Usama bin Laden, or the Taliban, it is also submitted to the 1267 Committee for designation.[32]

Statement of the Case

As part of the designation process, the Treasury Department drafts and publicly releases an unclassified version of the evidentiary called a "Statement of the Case" (SOC). Among other elements, an SOC typically includes the basic identifying information that financial institutions need in order to carry out the sanctions (e.g., name, passport number, country of birth).

Following a designation, OFAC updates the SDN list and disseminates the new addition to the public using a variety of methods, including the internet. OFAC's downloadable SDN list is continuously updated in order to help banks, businesses, and other institutions take necessary action against a designee. In addition, OFAC maintains a listserv and sends out email notices—and, if requested, faxes—to all subscribers, including all domestic banks, banking regulatory agencies, and law enforcement agencies. Designations are also published in the *Federal Register,* which contains most routine publications and public notices of government agencies.[33]

USA PATRIOT ACT

The USA PATRIOT Act, passed in October 2001, amended the International Emergency Economic Powers Act and expanded America's targeted economic sanctions regime. Two portions of the act are particularly relevant in this regard: sections 106 and 311.

Section 106 "clarifies OFAC's authority" to take action "in aid of an investigation" prior to issuing a formal designation—namely, to block suspect entities' money beforehand if necessary in order to prevent asset flight.[34] Additionally, in cases where a designation is subject to judicial review, section 106 authorized submission of classified information to a court *ex parte* and *in camera*—that is, in private viewing with the presiding judge.[35] In other words, the government can use classified information from sensitive sources to support a designation without fear that it will be disclosed publicly or to those designated.

Section 311 is more far reaching. Under the title "Special Measures for Jurisdictions, Financial Institutions, or International Transactions of Primary Money Laundering Concern," this section empowers the government to designate a foreign jurisdiction, a foreign institution, a class of foreign transactions, or a foreign account if there are reasonable grounds to conclude that they are of "primary money laundering concern."[36] To date, the U.S. government has designated 16 jurisdictions and banks under this provision:[37]

- **December 2002:** Nauru and Ukraine were designated.[38] Ukraine was removed in April 2003 after making important changes to its AML laws.
- **November 2003:** Burma and two Burmese institutions (Myanmar Mayflower Bank and Asia Wealth Bank) were designated. Burma was listed due to serious deficiencies in its AML laws. The two banks were accused of facilitating financial transactions for drug trafficking organizations in Southeast Asia.[39]
- **May 2004:** The Commercial Bank of Syria and a subsidiary (Syrian Lebanese Commercial Bank) were designated for their links to terrorists, including Usama bin Laden.[40]
- **August 2004:** One Turkish Cypriot bank and one Belarusian bank were designated. The latter, a privately owned institution named Infobank, was designated for its involvement in laundering funds for Saddam Hussein's regime.[41]
- **April 2005:** Two Latvian financial institutions (Multibanka and VEF Bank) were designated.[42]
- **September 2005:** Macau-based Banco Delta Asia was designated for helping North Korean officials collect surreptitious multimillion-dollar cash deposits and for distributing counterfeit U.S. currency, among other offenses. Since the designation, North Korea has yet to find a replacement international banker. As Treasury undersecretary Stuart Levey observed, "What they [North Korea] really want is to re-establish banking relationships, but they can't do that until they persuade the world that they are a legitimate partner to have in the banking system."[43] (See chapter 4 for a full case study of this bank and the effects of the designation.)

COMPLIANCE

As mentioned previously, OFAC administers all sanctions programs in the United States. These programs apply to a broad range of actors, including

> all U.S. citizens and permanent resident aliens regardless of where they are located, all persons and entities within the United States, all U.S. incorporated entities and their

> foreign branches. In the cases of certain programs, such as those regarding Cuba and North Korea, all foreign subsidiaries owned or controlled by U.S. companies also must comply. Certain programs also require foreign persons in possession of U.S. origin goods to comply.[44]

Unless specifically exempted, all of these actors must block any property in which an SDN has an interest and report the action to OFAC. Blocked property may not be "transferred, withdrawn, exported, paid, or otherwise dealt in" without prior authorization from OFAC.[45] If OFAC believes that an individual or institution has violated the law, it has several options at its disposal, including cease-and-desist orders, civil penalties, suspension or revocation of licenses, and criminal charges.

It is up to each bank to assess its own susceptibility to money laundering and terrorism financing. As a general rule, banks should enhance their compliance procedures as the level of risk increases. In particular, the government recommends that all banks consider purchasing sophisticated screening software to help them identify suspicious transactions. In addition, the government has developed written guidance for banks to promote compliance.[46]

CIVIL LIBERTIES

Although the United States has gone to great lengths to protect the basic civil liberties of designated entities and individuals, many have claimed that the government has not done enough in this regard. Technically, all designees can request to have their designation rescinded if they meet one of three criteria:

1. They believe that the basis of the designation was false
2. They can demonstrate that the circumstances resulting in the designation are no longer relevant
3. They can propose remedial steps that would negate the basis for designation (e.g., by demonstrating a break from those who support terrorism)[47]

Delisting requests are typically submitted in writing to the director of OFAC. Designees also have the right to apply for special consideration if they need access to frozen funds in order to pay for basic expenses, including legal services, operating expenses, creditor payments, food, housing, medical treatment, and so forth.[48]

As of March 2008, OFAC had received 346 delisting requests.[49] Only 10 individuals had successfully lobbied for removal, however.[50] This track record, along with other factors, has led many designees and global human rights organizations to claim that the U.S. lists are unfair and even illegal. In addition to such accusations, there are many individuals whose lives have been made very difficult—for example, when they travel, shop, apply for home mortgages, and so forth—simply because their names are similar to those on the SDN list.

In May 2007, the Lawyers' Committee for Civil Rights filed suit against the Treasury Department, using the Freedom of Information Act to seek the following:

1. Disclosure of complaints the Treasury Department had received from consumers wrongly associated with the OFAC watch list.
2. The Department's policies and procedures to protect the privacy and civil rights of consumers.[51]

On February 14, 2008, a federal judge ordered the department to turn over documents that it had withheld, including letters, emails, and complaints regarding the watch list, as well as delisting petitions from individuals who had been erroneously listed. On March 17 the department released some, but not all, of the ordered documents—specifically, it refused to release "delisting" petitions.

CONCLUSIONS

After carrying out several comprehensive economic sanctions programs against countries such as Iraq and North Korea, the world has come to the conclusion that the cost of such an indiscriminate strategy—especially the severe humanitarian impact on civilian populations—is too high. For this reason, the UN, FATF, and other international bodies have embraced the use of smarter, targeted sanctions against illicit actors. The Watson Institute for International Studies aptly summarized the nature and purpose of this strategy:

> Targeted sanctions include financial, travel, aviation, arms and commodities restrictions on individuals or corporate entities with the objective of applying coercive pressure on transgressing parties, leaders and the network of elites and entities who support them. They aim to change behavior or prevent actions contrary to international peace and security.[52]

Despite this shift in focus, one of the biggest problems the international community will face in the coming years is that many countries are reluctant to devote resources to creating and enforcing these types of regimes. Meanwhile, the UN and the United States face serious problems in creating proper delisting procedures and informing the public about why certain individuals have been listed. These problems are in the process of being remedied, however. And it is a proven fact that targeted sanctions—when applied diligently and enforced by the international community—have had amazing success at stripping illicit actors of their ability to function. Indeed, sanctions have the potential to be one of our strongest tools in the AML/CFT toolbox.

Chapter 11

Global Assessment Regime

The need to develop mechanisms for evaluating international agreements is important, particularly with national security issues like money laundering and terrorism financing. The international community has turned to the Financial Action Task Force (FATF) "Mutual Evaluation" process in order to assess countries' progress. According to FATF and other bodies, these evaluations are the best means of not only monitoring compliance with international standards, but also spurring countries to work together while minimizing negative political influences on the process.

Specifically, all FATF members are committed to undergoing monitoring and peer review regularly to assess their compliance with FATF's "Forty Recommendations on Money Laundering" and "Nine Special Recommendations on Terrorist Financing." FATF—along with other institutions such as the International Monetary Fund (IMF) and World Bank—has relied on this Mutual Evaluation process as one of its primary instruments for measuring the effectiveness of a given country's anti–money laundering/combating the financing of terrorism (AML/CFT) regime.

OVERVIEW

Countries undergo Mutual Evaluations roughly every five to ten years and can choose the supervising international body—examples include FATF, a FATF-Style Regional Body (FSRB), the IMF/World Bank, and the Offshore Group of Banking Supervisors (OGBS).[1] This choice is given to avoid overwhelming any one international organization with evaluation requests. To ensure common processes and global consistency, each of these organizations has also agreed to use the same AML/CFT methodology when evaluating countries. In general, this methodology focuses on "whether the necessary laws, regulations or other measures required under the new standards are in force and effect, that there has been a full and proper implementation of all necessary measures, and that the system in place is effective."[2]

The process of undergoing a Mutual Evaluation is deceptively simple. A country begins by filling out a Mutual Evaluation Questionnaire (MEQ), which serves as the basis for determining the extent to which the 40 + 9 have been implemented. A team of financial, legal, and law enforcement experts from the evaluating body review the MEQ, then visit the country firsthand. There, they meet with government officials and members of the private sector to verify the accuracy of the material presented.[3]

This onsite evaluation can take anywhere from three days to two weeks. At the end of the process, the assessment team issues a Mutual Evaluation Report (MER) describing the country's AML/CFT regime and rating its effectiveness.

A BRIEF HISTORY

To date, FATF members have undergone three rounds of mutual evaluations. During the first round (1992–1996), the agency evaluated 28 jurisdictions for compliance with the original Forty Recommendations. Following this round, FATF revised the recommendations for two reasons: (1) to address member complaints that they were not specific enough, and (2) to significantly enhance them.

During the second round (1996–1998), the same 28 jurisdictions were evaluated. Afterward, FATF determined that not all countries were being assessed in the same manner, and that a comprehensive methodology was needed to ensure "fair, proper and consistent evaluations."[4] This need became even more pressing following the September 11 attacks. In the wake of that watershed event, the international community, European Union, and Group of Seven (G7) encouraged FATF to take the lead in coordinating efforts to prevent terrorist abuse of the international financial system. In October 2001, FATF issued the Nine Special Recommendations, which set new international standards for combating terrorism financing.

Prior to the attacks, international organizations such as the IMF and World Bank had typically conducted country assessments in a manner that echoed their institutional mandate. The resultant differences in style, approach, and focus meant that one organization's assessments were not automatically recognized by others. This changed after September 11. In summer 2002, the IMF and World Bank recognized FATF's recommendations as the international AML/CFT standard—thereafter, whenever they conducted an evaluation, they used FATF's standards as their benchmark.[5] That same year, FATF joined with other international standard-setters to issue a comprehensive AML/CFT assessment methodology.[6] This methodology offered guidance on the various measures that countries and financial institutions had to adopt in order to comply with the new standards, including financial intelligence units, appropriate legal frameworks, enhanced preventive procedures, and relevant UN Security Council Resolutions and international conventions.

To test the new methodology, FATF and the IMF/World Bank initiated a 12-month pilot program. During this period, the IMF/World Bank conducted 33 assessments while FATF and various FSRBs conducted eight.[7] All of these organizations agreed that the new methodology was a good first step, but that more work was needed.

In June 2003, after revising the Forty Recommendations for a third time, FATF—in cooperation with the IMF/World Bank, FSRBs, and other international institutions—decided to revise the assessment methodology to clarify the standards and make them as specific as possible.[8] FATF, the IMF, and the World Bank adopted this new methodology in 2004, and this is the version that has been used since to evaluate member compliance.[9]

Today, all international organizations that carry out AML/CFT assessments have agreed to use the FATF 2004 methodology and recognize each other's reports. This is important because it prevents duplication of efforts and ensures that all countries are being assessed the same way.

EVALUATION QUESTIONNAIRE

Typically, countries submit the MEQ questionnaires two months prior to an evaluation. MEQs must include the following information:

- A description of measures the country currently has in place for complying with each of the 40 + 9 Recommendations
- A description of measures the country plans to undertake to address any gaps
- Any other information the country believes would be helpful to the assessors

In addition, countries must submit a comprehensive list of their relevant AML/CFT laws and regulations. FATF's Assessors Handbook lists many examples of such materials:

- "the laws applicable to the offences of money laundering and financing of terrorism, ... the predicate offences and any other laws or regulations dealing with the criminalization of money laundering and terrorist financing"
- "the laws, regulations and procedures applicable to the confiscation, seizing and freezing of the proceeds of crime, and to freezing terrorist funds in accordance with relevant UNSCRs"
- if applicable, any AML/CFT reports filed in response to international obligations[10]

The most important information countries can provide are statistics regarding the effectiveness of their AML/CFT regime. This data should include the number of arrests and convictions made in connection with money laundering and terror financing charges. Such information is essential for assessors to deliver fair and accurate ratings.

ASSESSMENT TEAMS AND ONSITE VISITS

When assembling assessment teams for onsite country visits, FATF looks for technical experts who have relevant and practical experience in the legal, financial, and law enforcement sectors. Teams typically include four such experts—one legal, two financial, and one law enforcement—who come "from different countries, and whose expertise must cover all aspects of the fight against money laundering and the financing of terrorism."[11] The legal expert should be a judge, prosecutor, or justice ministry representative; the financial experts should be specialists in regulatory matters from a finance ministry, a central bank, or a regulatory authority; and the law enforcement expert should be drawn from operational services such as the police, customs, or a financial intelligence unit.[12] In addition, FATF sends a team leader from the FATF Secretariat to ensure that the trip goes smoothly.

During onsite visits, countries are required to organize meetings for the assessors with government ministries and agencies, as well as with relevant private sector groups.[13] In other words, the burden of proving compliance with the international standard ultimately rests on the assessed country.

MUTUAL EVALUATION REPORTS

The final step in the process, mutual evaluation reports provide an extensive assessment of a country's compliance with the international standard. MERs also provide general information on the country's AML/CFT regime (e.g., the government's general strategy, the structure of the country's financial sector, an outline of which agencies have oversight responsibilities).

Countries receive one of four ratings for their performance on each of the 40 + 9 Recommendations:

- **Compliant:** "The recommendation is fully observed with respect to all essential criteria."
- **Largely compliant:** "There are only minor shortcomings, with a large majority of the essential criteria being fully met."
- **Partially compliant:** "The country has taken some substantive action and complies with some of the essential criteria."
- **Non-compliant:** "There are major shortcomings, with a large majority of the essential criteria not being met."[14]

In February 2007, FATF adopted a new policy mandating the publication of every MER on the FATF website. Those jurisdictions found to be largely out of compliance with the 40 + 9 can also be placed on FATF blacklists. In addition, FATF carries out follow-up evaluations to monitor countries' progress.

MEASURING PROGRESS

Only by regularly evaluating countries can the international community determine whether it is making significant progress in the war against illicit finance. Knowing which countries are moving in the right direction and which are not is the first step in ensuring action in this regard.

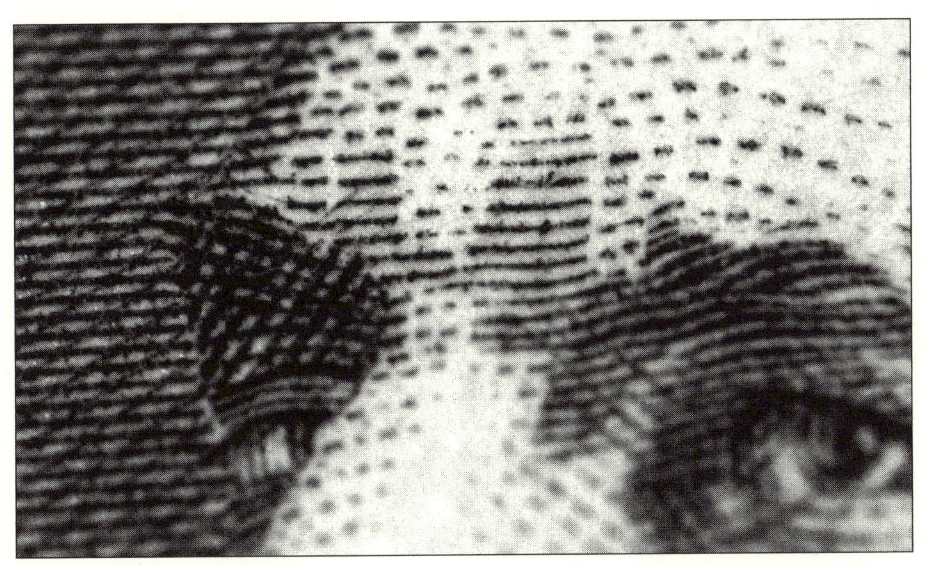

PART IV
Conclusions

Chapter 12

Turning the Tide: Implications and Policy Recommendations

Over the past fifteen years, a few members of the international community banded together to create a blueprint for fighting money laundering and terrorism financing. Unfortunately, many countries have refused to implement this blueprint. As a result, they lack the basic controls necessary to ensure that the international financial sector is not exploited by criminals, terrorists, and their support networks.

Just as the financial system has become global in nature, so too has the threat posed by tainted money. And in confronting this threat, the system is only as strong as its weakest link—as U.S. Treasury official Daniel Glaser put it, "Laxity in just a few jurisdictions undermines the efforts made by the rest."[1] Yet, most countries have yet to take even the most basic steps, such as criminalizing money laundering and terrorism financing, instituting controls in their formal and informal financial sectors, curbing the smuggling of cash, preventing abuse in the trade sector, and safeguarding the charitable sector.

Similarly, most countries have yet to implement a system of targeted economic sanctions programs against terrorists and their financiers—even though UN Security Council Resolution (UNSCR) 1373 obligates them to freeze without delay the assets of all terrorist organizations. In a post–September 11 world, failing to bar such actors from the financial system effectively gives them a free hand to conduct major attacks around the world.

The United States must encourage other countries to take action—not as a favor to Washington, but because it is their obligation under various UN resolutions and the international standard set forth by the Financial Action Task Force (FATF). Governments, banks, or other entities that do not take responsible action in this regard should be taken to task by the UN, FATF, and the United States alike.

FATF and the UN also have significant internal work to do. As many experts have pointed out, all anti–money laundering/combating the financing of terrorism (AML/CFT) regimes should be based on three principles: prevention, detection, and enforcement. It is not enough to implement regulations that prevent and detect financial crime—if investigations and prosecutions are not high on a country's priority list, then its AML/CFT regime will fail. Despite this fact, FATF and the UN have placed little emphasis on enforcement actions. They have even failed to take the fairly obvious step of assessing countries based on whether their regimes are actually effective.

Ultimately, countries must realize that it is in their own interest to make it harder and more expensive for illicit actors to operate. FATF and UN deliberations aside, each country should take the necessary individual steps to pursue those who have the ability to harm us all.

RECOMMENDATIONS FOR U.S. POLICY

The United States should make AML/CFT compliance one of the underpinning factors of its foreign policy. Below are several steps the government can take to help it—and willing partners in the international community—better curb the threat posed by money launderers and terror financiers.

The United States should strongly encourage countries to criminalize money laundering and terrorism financing and effectively pursue those who engage in such activities. Some countries fail to outlaw such behavior, while others have appropriate legislation in place but fail to enforce it. In either case, these countries are not helpful allies in the war on terror and should be publicly taken to task. Specifically, Congress should mandate the publication of an annual list of countries that have not criminalized money laundering and terrorism financing in accordance with FATF's international standards, or that have actively or passively allowed such activity to take place within their jurisdictions. Publicizing noncompliance in this manner could serve as a strong incentive for countries given the potential negative effects on foreign investment, tourism, and foreign aid.

The United States should actively encourage European Union members to maintain their own targeted economic sanctions programs aimed at freezing the funds of all terrorist organizations, and to keep these programs separate from the normal criminal process. Many EU member states have declared that they rely on the union's supernational authority on matters such as counterterrorism designations. Time and again, however, FATF has found that individual EU countries are out of compliance with its international standards, which mandate that each country have its own sanctions program. The EU's targeting mechanism does not work—the numerous member states rarely agree on a given designation because of their varying national interests. This must change if the international community is to effectively pursue illicit actors through sanctions.

The United States should strategically choose five allies and together build model AML/CFT regimes. "Strength in numbers" is a good way to ensure the health of the international financial system, and the U.S. government should dedicate significant resources to establishing a coalition of the willing. Doing so would both focus U.S. technical assistance resources and ensure that strategic allies are acting in unison. Currently, the United States bears a great deal of the responsibility for training countries on AML/CFT standards and obligations. If a core group of capable countries shared this responsibility, it would serve as a tremendous force multiplier in encouraging countries around the world to take action.

The U.S. government must strongly encourage FATF to issue international standards on trade-based money laundering. Most jurisdictions around the globe have done very little to counter this type of laundering, creating a major vulnerability in the international financial system. In addition to encouraging FATF, Congress should allocate significant resources to building up the Department of Homeland Security's "Trade Transparency Unit" initiative. Administered by the Bureau of Immigrations and Customs Enforcement (ICE), this initiative allows for prompt international exchange of key trade data and serves as a powerful analytical tool in pursuing those who manipulate the trade sector.

Congress should amend the PATRIOT Act to mandate that formal and informal financial institutions use a zero threshold for identifying customers and filing "Suspicious Activity Reports." As described in chapters 1 and 4, one of the biggest loopholes in the U.S. AML/CFT framework remains the unnecessarily high threshold amounts assigned to banking procedures in three areas: customer identification, recordkeeping, and suspicious activity reporting. Regarding wire transfers, for example, institutions are required to carry out such procedures only when the transaction exceeds $3,000. This means that multiple small deposits of illicit money—a practice known as "smurfing" or "structuring" (see chapters 2 and 4)—can be easily placed into the financial system.

Similarly, financial institutions are not required to report suspicious activity unless the transaction is above a certain amount: $5,000 in the case of the formal financial sector (see chapter 4), and $2,000 in the case of the informal financial sector (see chapter 5). These somewhat arbitrary thresholds effectively allow suspicious activity below these amounts to take place unhindered.

Of course, banks and other formal institutions have determined that it is in their own best interests to keep records and report suspicious activity below the government's thresholds, and to bar individuals who do not have accounts at a given institution from transacting business there. The most problematic loophole therefore lies not in the formal sector but in the informal sector. For example, even if every money services business (MSB)—i.e., non-bank institutions that conduct monetary transactions—in the country registered with the government and followed every regulation (most MSBs do neither), anyone could still walk in off the street and send money in amounts smaller than $3,000. Legally speaking, MSB operators are not required to keep records for such transactions, nor to report suspicious activity for amounts smaller than $2,000.

Although these vulnerabilities cannot be completely rectified due to cost, limited resources, and immigration issues, Congress can make it more difficult for criminals to abuse this system. *The best means of doing so is to abolish both the $3,000 threshold for requiring customer identification and the $2,000 and $5,000 thresholds for reporting suspicious transactions. This measure would enable all U.S. financial operators—from the largest bank to the smallest MSB—to better detect illicit activity.*

Congress should mandate that all 50 states standardize their procedures for dealing with the MSB sector. Currently, there are two major problems in this sector: (1) relatively few MSBs have registered with the government, in part due to the inordinate hassle of conducting interstate transactions, and (2) the IRS—the sector's main oversight agency—has had trouble effectively monitoring MSBs. One way to address both problems is to mandate that all states adopt the same laws and regulations regarding the sector, which would encourage operators to register and potentially simplify the IRS's mission. Whatever the case, swift, clear, and forceful legislative action will be needed to better curb the threat from this sector. Congress asked states to abolish the disparities in their licensing procedures as far back as 1994, in the Money Laundering Suppression Act. Given that state governments apparently ignored this recommendation, Congress should upgrade it to a legal requirement.

The U.S. government must reorganize the Financial Crimes Enforcement Network (FinCEN), making it an effective agency that truly supports the law enforcement community. FinCEN was originally created to support law enforcement by providing a financial paper trail for investigators. As described in chapter 4, however, the organization's mission has changed over time—today, FinCEN has effectively become another regulatory agency. To make matters worse, the organization is known for both its "revolving door" staff situation (with directors, managers, money laundering experts, and analysts being replaced on a regular basis) and its poor working conditions (a 2007 job satisfaction survey ranked FinCEN among the worst places to work in the U.S. government). Perhaps most serious, FinCEN fails to systematically analyze the approximately 18 million financial intelligence reports it receives annually, in part because it has never managed to create an effective data mining tool. Instead, the agency has wasted millions of dollars and valuable time on failed instruments—resources that should have been spent following illicit actors' money. Finally, FinCEN allows only limited access to its financial data, constraining the number of law enforcement authorities who can mine the material.

To address these problems, the government should dedicate significant funds to reorganizing FinCEN and ensuring that it is equipped to properly exploit financial data. The government should consider outsourcing the project of creating a data mining tool to a competent private sector company. In addition, Congress should mandate that FinCEN give law enforcement greater access to financial data.

The United States and FATF should strongly encourage all countries to publish the results of their AML/CFT mutual evaluations. When FATF member states undergo the thorough Mutual Evaluation process described in chapter 11, the agency's findings are readily available for public and private consumption, allowing financial institutions and governments alike to make informed decisions regarding their policies toward certain jurisdictions. For the hundreds of countries that are not FATF members, however, the evaluation process can be much more opaque. For example, some of these countries are assessed by FATF-Style Regional Bodies (FSRBs) and other organizations that do not necessarily mandate publication of evaluation reports. FATF does not have the power to obligate nonmembers to publish their reports. It does, however, have the responsibility to publicly call out countries that "insufficiently apply FATF recommendations."[2] Therefore, whenever a country chooses not to make its evaluation results public, FATF should place it on the International Cooperation Review Group (ICRG) designation list as described in chapter 3. In addition, for those FSRBs that become "Associate Members" of FATF, the organization should mandate that they require their members to publish the results of their evaluations.[3]

Congress should mandate that the State Department reorganize its annual International Narcotics Control Strategy Report (INSCR) to better reflect the structure of FATF's 40 + 9 Recommendations. Doing so will greatly assist those in the U.S. government and international community who use this resource most frequently. The INCSR, published each March, offers a country-by-country description of "efforts to attack all aspects of the international drug trade, chemical control, money laundering and financial crimes."[4] Not structuring the information according to FATF's international standards makes it much more difficult to use as an important reference guide.

The U.S. government should create a new office to conduct robust follow-up with financial institutions involved in terrorism financing cases, helping them develop the tools needed to curb this threat. This new office should be a joint Justice Department/FinCEN entity. Given the government's understandable reluctance to reveal information about ongoing investigations, the follow-up process should not begin until after a terrorism financing case has been adjudicated. At that point, the new office should review the proceedings in detail and determine if and when Suspicious Activity Reports were filed. If such reports should have been filed but were not, the office would then work collaboratively with the institutions in question to help them better recognize suspicious activity. Punitive action should only be taken if such institutions consistently fail to rectify deficiencies.

The United States should encourage FATF to designate diamond and gold smuggling as "predicate offenses" to money laundering. Both of these commodities are heavily used in money laundering and terrorism financing. In addition, conflict diamonds have played a major role in propagating civil wars in Africa, while gold is a standard currency in the drug trade. Both have the advantage of being mined in remote parts of the world and being virtually untraceable to their original source. They are also easily used in trade-based money laundering schemes involving over-invoicing, under-invoicing, false invoicing, and tax fraud.

By targeting these commodities and adding them to its list of predicate offenses, FATF would effectively force countries to pay special attention and take concrete action. Examples of such action might include providing customs agents with special training on different types of diamond and gold smuggling techniques; devoting extra resources to gathering intelligence on the movement of these commodities; and issuing special guidance to diamond and gold exchange houses and similar businesses regarding the risk of abuse by illicit actors.

The United States should actively pursue a UN Security Council Resolution that creates a targeted economic sanctions program against Hizbollah and Hamas. Currently, the UN plays a key role in the fight against terrorism financing by maintaining the primary international terrorist designation list. UNSCR 1267 requires all member states to take specific measures against entities associated with the Taliban, al-Qaeda, or Usama bin Laden; the "1267 Committee" maintains a publicly available list of these entities. Given the scale and nature of attacks committed by both Hizbollah and Hamas, as well as the threat they pose to both the international financial system and international order, the United States should put forth more effort toward securing UN designations for both groups.

There are two ways to pursue this objective. First, the UN could adopt a universal definition of terrorism. To date, the United States has not pursued this measure vigorously because there is no consensus that it is necessary or in accordance with U.S. foreign policy objectives. Even so, a universal definition would enable the international community to make tremendous progress against other terrorist organizations.

The second route is to pursue designation of Hizbollah and Hamas through a Security Council Resolution. Although certain member states would no doubt oppose this course of action, universal adoption would not be necessary—in the Security Council, a resolution passes once nine of the 15 members vote "yes," so long as none of the five permanent members vetoes the measure.[5] It is worth noting that the European Union has already designated Hamas at the super-national level, and there are a number of individual member states that would be supportive of such a designation.

Either route would require significant investments of political will and time, along with approval from the highest levels of the U.S. government. Failing that, the United States will continue to fight the battle against Hizbollah and Hamas without the international cover necessary to do so effectively.

The United States should allocate more resources to U.S. customs authorities and the IRS, enabling them to inspect more goods and people leaving the country and to better investigate unregistered "hawala" operators. In its 2006 evaluation of the United States, FATF determined that customs and the IRS needed more resources to effectively complete their missions. Due in part to budgetary limitations, customs authorities check goods and people entering the country more comprehensively than those leaving the country—a situation that creates greater opportunities for money launderers to abuse the U.S. financial system by manipulating trade transactions and smuggling cash. For its part, the IRS does not have the resources it needs to pursue "hawaladars" and other informal financial operators who have not registered or who continue to remit money abroad to criminals and terrorists.

The United States should also allocate more resources to the IRS for the purpose of monitoring charities. The IRS is the primary federal body in charge of monitoring the informal financial sector, the gold and precious stones sector, and the charitable sector. FATF and other observers have determined that the agency lacks the resources needed to effectively handle any one of these duties, let alone all three. Given the charitable sector's unique vulnerability to exploitation by terrorists, the government should give the IRS the resources it needs or task other agencies with helping to expand current monitoring and outreach efforts, as described in chapter 8.

Congress should pass the "Combating Money Laundering and Terrorist Financing Act of 2006" or similar legislation in order to change the U.S. treatment of predicate offenses from a "list" approach to a "threshold" approach. As described in chapter 9, countries can take various approaches to criminalizing money laundering, including:

1. The predicate offense approach—countries list the crimes that can serve as the basis for a money laundering prosecution

2. A threshold approach—countries designate certain crimes as "serious offenses," e.g., any money-generating crime "with a maximum period of imprisonment exceeding one year."[6] For countries like the United States that use ranged sentencing guidelines (e.g., "6 to 18 months," with the actual sentence at the judge's discretion), any crime whose maximum penalty is one year or more would be designated a serious crime, even if some criminals who commit it wind up receiving a lighter sentence. In addition, any crime listed as a serious offense would also be automatically designated a money laundering offense. At minimum, FATF encourages countries to designate its 20 core predicate offenses as serious offenses.[7]

The United States has chosen the list-based approach; to date, its list includes approximately 300 predicate offenses to money laundering.[8] A number of policymakers have questioned the wisdom of this approach, however, with Justice Department officials indicating to FATF that "prosecuting offenses under sections 1956 and 1957 would be much easier if a threshold approach to categorizing predicate offenses (rather than the current list approach) was adopted."[9] The government has taken important steps to rectify this problem, including proposing the Combating Money Laundering and Terrorist Financing Act.[10] Among other provisions, this bill would institute a threshold approach, bringing the United States into full compliance with the relevant FATF standard.

CONCLUSION

U.S. policymakers cannot overlook the importance of crafting a sound policy against money launderers, terrorism financiers, and the networks that support them. They must work closely with international allies to ensure that each country is doing all it can to keep illicit actors out of the financial system.

This task has taken on adaded urgency because of the threat posed by rogue states such as North Korea and Iran, and by terrorist organizations such as al-Qaeda, Hizbollah, and Hamas—all of whom have used tainted money to create chaos in parts of the world crucial to U.S. interests. Washington must therefore expand its targeting and pursuit efforts while urging other countries to do the same.

Glossary

40 + 9: The FATF-issued international standard for preventing, detecting, and suppressing both money laundering and terrorism financing, collectively known as the "Forty Recommendations on Money Laundering and Nine Special Recommendations on Terrorist Financing." Although they are technically just "recommendations," they carry the force of "mandates for action" throughout much of the international community and financial sector.

1267: UN Security Council Resolution 1267 and subsequent resolutions require all member states to take specific measures against individuals and entities associated with the Taliban, al-Qaeda, or Usama bin Laden. The "1267 Committee" maintains a public list of these individuals and entities, and countries are encouraged to submit potential names to the committee for designation.

1373: UN Security Council Resolution 1373 requires states to freeze without delay the assets of individuals and entities associated with any global terrorist organization. This is significant because it goes beyond the scope of Resolution 1267 and requires member states to impose sanctions against all terrorist entities, not just those tied to the Taliban, al-Qaeda, or Usama bin Laden.

AML/CFT—Anti–Money Laundering/Combating the Financing of Terrorism: Collective term used to describe the legal framework and obligations countries must implement. *See also "40 + 9."*

BMPE—Black Market Peso Exchange: One of the most pernicious money laundering schemes in the Western Hemisphere. It is also one of the largest, processing an estimated $5 billion worth of drug proceeds a year from Colombia alone via trade-based money laundering (TBML), "smurfing," cash smuggling, and other schemes.

BSA—Bank Secrecy Act: Officially known as the "Currency and Foreign Transactions Reporting Act," it requires financial institutions to help various government agencies detect and prevent money laundering. Specifically, the BSA requires banks and other financial institutions to file reports of currency transactions exceeding

$10,000, to keep records of cash purchases of negotiable instruments, and to report suspicious activity.

CBP—Customs and Border Protection: *See ICE.*

CMIR—Report of International Transportation of Currency or Monetary Instruments: The United States has established a declaration system that applies to all incoming and outgoing physical transportation of cash and other monetary instruments. It is illegal to transport more than $10,000 (or its foreign equivalent) in cash or other monetary instruments into or out of the country without filing a CMIR.

CTR—Currency Transaction Report: Financial institutions are required to file a CTR with FinCEN whenever they process a currency transaction exceeding $10,000. These reports include important identifying information about the transactions. Once FinCEN receives them, they are input into a BSA reporting database that is available to federal banking regulators and the law enforcement community.

Customer Due Diligence/Know Your Customer: The first step financial institutions must take to detect, deter, and prevent money laundering and terrorism financing, namely, maintaining adequate knowledge about customers and their financial activities.

Egmont Group: The international standard-setter for financial intelligence units. Created with the explicit purpose of serving as a center to overcome the obstacles preventing cross-border information sharing between FIUs.

EO—Executive Order: An EO is an edict issued by a U.S. president, loosely derived from the "executive power" granted to the office by the Constitution. EOs have the force of law when made pursuant to certain acts of Congress that give the president discretionary powers.

Evidentiary: When the U.S. government first targets an individual or organization for potential inclusion on a terrorist designation list, Treasury Department analysts assemble an administrative record based on open-source and classified material regarding the subject. This "evidentiary" serves as the factual basis underlying the decision to designate. In addition, the department eventually releases an unclassified version of this report (called a "Statement of the Case") to help financial institutions carry out sanctions against the designee.

FATF—Financial Action Task Force: Also known by the French name Groupe d'action financière sur le blanchiment de capitaux (GAFI), FATF was created by the G7 leaders in 1989 in order to address increased alarm about money laundering's threat to the international financial system. This intergovernmental policymaking task force was given the mandate of examining money laundering techniques and trends, reviewing domestic and international action, and setting the international standard for combating money laundering and terrorism financing.

FinCEN—Financial Crimes Enforcement Network: The U.S. financial intelligence unit. See "FIU" and "Egmont."

FIU—Financial Intelligence Unit: In many countries, a central national agency responsible for receiving, requesting, analyzing, and/or disseminating disclosures of financial information to the competent authorities, primarily concerning suspected proceeds of crime and potential financing of terrorism. An FIU's mandate is backed up by national legislation or regulation.

FSRB—FATF-Style Regional Body: These bodies—which are modeled on FATF and are granted certain rights by that organization—serve as regional centers for matters relating to AML/CFT. Their primary purpose is to promote a country's implementation of comprehensive AML/CFT regimes and implement the FATF 40 + 9.

FTO—Foreign Terrorist Organization: A terrorist organizations designated by the U.S. secretary of state in consultation with the secretary of the treasury and the attorney-general under the Antiterrorism and Effective Death Penalty Act. The State Department maintains a public list of designees.

G7—Group of Seven: The multinational group that established FATF in 1989. Includes Canada, France, Germany, Italy, Japan, the United Kingdom, and the United States.

Hawala: A very simple and centuries-old broker system based on trust, found throughout Southeast Asia and the Arab world. It allows customers and brokers (called "hawaladars") to transfer money or value without physically moving it, often in areas of the world where banks and other formal institutions have little or no presence. It is used by many different cultures, but under different names; "hawala" is often used as a catchall term for such systems in discussions of terrorism financing and related issues.

Hawaladar: A broker in a hawala or hawala-type network.

ICE—Immigration and Customs Enforcement: One of two agencies within the U.S. Department of Homeland Security vested with the authority to stop and search individuals, enforce asset seizures/forfeitures, and make arrests related to cross-border crimes. Both have the power to perform such actions toward "any vehicle, vessel, aircraft, or other conveyance, any envelope or other container, and any person" entering or departing the country, without a search warrant.

Integration: This is the last stage of the money laundering process. The laundered money is introduced into the economy so that it appears to be normal business earnings, making it very difficult for law enforcement to detect. Known methods of integration include real estate purchases, front companies, false loans, foreign bank complicity, and false import/export invoices. *See also "layering" and "placement."*

IRS—Internal Revenue Service: U.S. law enforcement agency tasked with overseeing the charitable sector and MSBs.

Layering: This is the second stage of the money laundering process. The purpose of this stage is to make it more difficult for law enforcement to detect or follow the trail of illegal proceeds. Methods include converting cash into monetary instruments, buying and selling material assets with cash, and moving money between bank accounts. *See also "integration" and "placement."*

MEQ—Mutual Evaluation Questionnaire: The process of undergoing a FATF "Mutual Evaluation" begins when countries fill out a Mutual Evaluation Questionnaire. This document serves as the underlying basis for assessing the extent to which a country has implemented the 40 + 9 Recommendations.

MER—Mutual Evaluation Report: At the end of the FATF mutual evaluation process, the assessment team issues a report that describes the country's AML/CFT regime and rates its effectiveness.

MSB—Money Services Business: Any individual or business that engages in accepting and transmitting funds by any means through a financial agency or institution. All informal financial operators in the United States, including hawaladars, are legally categorized as MSBs. Examples include currency dealers, check cashers, and issuers and sellers of travelers checks, money orders, or stored value.

Mutual Evaluation: All FATF members have committed to undergoing periodic multilateral monitoring and peer review to assess their compliance with the agency's

40 + 9 Recommendations. Mutual Evaluations are one of FATF's primary instruments for determining the effectiveness of a country's AML/CFT regime.

OFAC—Office of Foreign Assets Control: The U.S. Treasury Department office responsible for maintaining the SDN list, which compiles the names of individuals and organizations targeted by sanctions programs focusing on terrorism, weapons of mass destruction, narcotics, and other issues.

PATRIOT Act: Passed by Congress shortly after the September 11 attacks, the "Uniting and Strengthening America by Providing Appropriate Tools Required to Intercept and Obstruct Terrorism Act" (or USA PATRIOT Act) amends certain portions of the BSA and contains provisions on international anti–money laundering efforts as well as currency crimes and protection.

PEPs—Politically Exposed Persons: PEPs are individuals who, by virtue of their office, might have become exposed to corruption. They include, but are not limited to, senior politicians, senior civil servants, and senior military officers in every country in the world, as well as their close families, colleagues, and advisors. Financial institutions must conduct enhanced due diligence measures when conducting business with PEPs.

Placement: This is the first stage of the money laundering process. Illicit money is disguised or misrepresented, then placed into circulation through financial institutions, casinos, shops, and other businesses, both local and abroad. A variety of methods can be used for this purpose, including currency smuggling, bank complicity, currency exchanges, securities brokers, blending of funds, asset purchase, and so forth. *See also "integration" and "layering."*

SAR/STR—Suspicious Activity Report/Suspicious Transaction Report: If a financial institution suspects or has reasonable grounds to suspect that the funds involved in a given transaction derive from criminal or terrorist activity, it is obligated to file a report with its national FIU containing key information about the transaction. In the United States, SAR is the most common term for such a report, though STR is used in many other jurisdictions.

SDGT List—Specially Designated Global Terrorist List: Following the September 11 attacks, the U.S. government created this list as a storehouse of individuals and entities deemed to be supporting or engaging in acts of terrorism. More significantly, the government also began to impose sanctions on those who support or otherwise associate with any individual or organization on the list. These sanctions specifically target "all property and interests in property of designated individuals or entities that are in the United States or that come within the United States, or that come within the possession or control of U.S. persons."

SDN List—Specially Designated Nationals List: OFAC's SDN list is a broad compilation of designated individuals and entities—a kind of "list of lists." It comprises not only SDGTs, but also those designated under other U.S. sanctions regimes, such as the counterproliferation and counternarcotics programs and various country-focused efforts. U.S. citizens are prohibited from providing services to or conducting transactions with an SDN.

Shell Company: An incorporated company with no significant operations, established with the sole purpose of holding or transferring funds, often for money laundering purposes. As the name implies, shell companies have only a name, address, and bank accounts; clever money launderers often attempt to make them look more like real businesses by maintaining fake financial records and other elements.

SOC—Statement of the Case: When a U.S. terrorist designation is made public, the Treasury Department drafts and releases an unclassified version of the "evidentiary" called a "Statement of the Case" (SOC). Among other elements, an SOC typically includes the basic identifying information that financial institutions need in order to carry out sanctions against the designated individual or organization (e.g., name, passport number, country of birth).

Smurfing/Structuring: A money laundering technique that involves splitting a large bank deposit into smaller deposits to evade the U.S. government's CTR and SAR requirements for financial institutions.

Special Recommendation: *See "40 + 9."*

TBML—Trade-Based Money Laundering: The process of disguising the proceeds of crime via fraudulent trade transactions and smuggling in order to legitimize their origin. One of the most common techniques is invoice fraud—that is, the misrepresentation of the price, quantity, or quality of imports or exports via over-invoicing, under-invoicing, double-invoicing, and so forth. The smuggling of precious metals and stones (particularly gold and diamonds) is also a part of many TBML schemes.

UNSCR—United Nations Security Council Resolution: *See "1267" and "1373."*

Notes

Separate sequences of endnotes have been used for separate sections within each chapter. For example, a chapter may have one set of notes for the main text, followed by additional sets for its various case studies and other boxes. These divisions are indicated by the various subheadings below; the notes pertaining to boxes are indicated by the original box titles.

Executive Summary

1. "Bush: 'We Will Starve the Terrorists,'" CNN, September 24, 2001. Available online (http://archives.cnn.com/2001/US/09/24/ret.bush.transcript).

Chapter 1

1. See U.S. State Department, "2008 International Narcotics Control Strategy Report," March 2008. Available online (www.state.gov/p/inl/rls/nrcrpt/2008/vol2/html/101353.htm).
2. Mark Sullivan, *Cuba and the State Sponsors of Terrorism List* (Washington, DC: Congressional Research Service, 2005), p. CRS-1. Available online (www.terrorisminfo.mipt.org/pdf/CRS_RL32251.pdf).
3. See U.S. State Department, "State Sponsors of Terrorism," (n.d.). Available online (www.state.gov/s/ct/c14151.htm).
4. See Asia/Pacific Group on Money Laundering, "History and Background," (n.d.). Available online (www.apgml.org/about/history.aspx).

The "Mother of All Snakeheads"

1. Emma Batha, "Chinese Gangs' Cruel Trade," BBC, April 2, 2001. Available online (http://news.bbc.co.uk/1/hi/world/asia-pacific/797489.stm).
2. See PBS, "Business of Human Trafficking: Criminal Groups," online article related to television program "Dying to Leave," an episode of the series *Wide Angle*, September 25, 2003 (available at www.pbs.org/wnet/wideangle/episodes/dying-to-leave/business-of-human-trafficking/criminal-groups/1423).
3. Ko-Lin Chin, *Smuggled Chinese: Clandestine Immigration into the United States* (Philadelphia: Temple University Press, 1999).
4. See European Parliament Intergroup on Organized Crime, "Snakeheads," (n.d.). Available online (www.organisedcrime.info/uploads/documents/4-38-snakeheads.doc).
5. See U.S. Justice Department, "Queen 'Snakehead' Sister Ping is Extradited from Hong Kong to New York to Face Alien Smuggling and Hostage Taking Charges," June 1, 2003. Available online (www.usdoj.gov/usao/nys/pressreleases/July03/ping222extradite.pdf).
6. Edward Barnes, "Two-Faced Woman," *Time*, July 23, 2000. Available online (www.time.com/time/magazine/article/0,9171,50610-1,00.html).
7. "'Mother of All Snakeheads' Faces Accusers," *Sydney Morning Herald*, May 17, 2005. Available online (www.smh.com.au/news/World/Mother-of-all-snakeheads-faces-accusers/2005/05/17/1116095938879.html).

8. Robert McFadden, "22 Illegal Immigrants Seized after a Jersey Shore Landing," *New York Times*, June 1, 1998. Available online (http://query.nytimes.com/gst/fullpage.html?res=9D01E5DC173BF932A35755C0A96E958260&sec=&spon=&pagewanted=all).
9. Christine Howlett, *Investigation & Control of Money Laundering via Alternative Remittance & Underground Banking Systems* (Australia: Churchill Trust, 2000). Available online (www.ncjrs.gov/pdffiles1/190720.pdf).
10. Ibid.
11. Barnes, "Two-Faced Woman."
12. Ibid.

Chiquita Pays Colombian Terrorist Group

1. For a description of the SDGT list, see chapter 10.
2. "Chiquita Admits to Paying Colombia Terrorists," Associated Press, March 15, 2007. Available online (www.msnbc.msn.com/id/17615143).
3. Eoin O'Carroll, "Colombia Seeks Eight in Chiquita Terrorist Scandal," *Christian Science Monitor,* March 22, 2007. Available online (www.csmonitor.com/2007/0322/p99s01-duts.html).
4. See U.S. Justice Department, "Chiquita Brands International Pleads Guilty to Making Payments to a Designated Terrorist Organization and Agrees to Pay $25 Million Fine," March 19, 2007. Available online (www.usdoj.gov/opa/pr/2007/March/07_nsd_161.html).
5. See U.S. State Department, "2008 International Narcotics Control Strategy Report," March 2008. Available online (www.state.gov/p/inl/rls/nrcrpt/2008/vol2/html/101353.htm).
6. See U.S. Justice Department, "Chiquita Brands International Pleads Guilty."
7. Matt Apuzzo, "Chiquita to Pay $25M Fine in Terror Case," Associated Press, March 15, 2007. Available online (www.washingtonpost.com/wp-dyn/content/article/2007/03/15/AR2007031500354.html).
8. See U.S. Justice Department, "Chiquita Brands International Pleads Guilty."
9. O'Carroll, "Colombia Seeks Eight."
10. "Victims of Colombian Conflict Sue Chiquita Brands," Associated Press, November 15, 2007. Available online (www.nytimes.com/2007/11/15/business/worldbusiness/15chiquita.html).
11. "Colombian Families' Suit Says Chiquita Liable for Torture, Murder," CNN, November 14, 2007. Available online (www.cnn.com/2007/US/law/11/14/chiquita.lawsuit).

Chapter 2

1. John Madinger and Sydney Zalopany, *Money Laundering* (Boca Raton, FL: CRC Press, 1999), p. 319.
2. Smurfs typically receive 0.5 to 1.5% of the cash they convert. Often their expenses are covered as well, including airline tickets, rental cars, food, and clothes. Ibid., p. 342.
3. See FinCEN, "Bank Secrecy Act Requirements," (n.d.). Available online (www.msb.gov/pdf/bsa_quickrefguide.pdf). It is also worth noting that according to a review of Suspicious Activity Reports filed by MSBs from 2002 to 2004, structuring is the most frequently reported activity. In addition, the Organized Crime Drug Enforcement Task Force (OCDETF) identified MSBs as an increasingly prevalent conduit for money laundering. See U.S. Treasury Department, *2005 U.S. Money Laundering Threat Assessment* (December 2005), p. 8; available online (www.treas.gov/offices/enforcement/pdf/mlta.pdf).
4. Patrick Jost, testimony before the Senate Banking, Housing, and Urban Affairs Committee hearing on "Hawala and Underground Terrorist Financing Mechanisms," November 14, 2001. Available online (www.banking.senate.gov/01_11hrg/111401/jost.htm).
5. Nikos Passas, "Hawala and Other Informal Value Transfer Systems: How to Regulate Them?" (U.S. State Department, 2003). Available online (www.usinfo.state.gov/eap/Archive_Index/Hawala_and_Other_Informal_Value_Transfer_Systems_How_to_Regulate_Them.html).
6. Ibid.

7. See FATF, "Trade-Based Money Laundering Typology Paper," June 23, 2006, p. 5. Available online (www.fatf-gafi.org/dataoecd/60/25/37038272.pdf).
8. Madinger and Zalopany, *Money Laundering*, p. 341.
9. See U.S. Treasury, *2005 U.S. Money Laundering Threat Assessment*, pp. 41–42.

White/Black Hawala

1. For more on the black/white hawala distinction, see Patrick Jost and Harjit Singh Sandhu, *The Hawala Alternative Remittance System and Its Role in Money Laundering* (Lyon, France: Interpol General Secretariat, January 2000). Available online (www.interpol.int/Public/FinancialCrime/MoneyLaundering/Hawala/default.asp).

Chapter 3

1. See U.S. State Department, "The Financial Action Task Force on Money Laundering," (n.d.). Available online (www.usinfo.state.gov/journals/ites/0501/ijee/fatffacts.htm).
2. FATF's members include Argentina, Australia, Austria, Belgium, Brazil, Canada, Denmark, Finland, France, Germany, Greece, Hong Kong–China, Iceland, Ireland, Italy, Japan, Luxembourg, Mexico, the Netherlands, New Zealand, Norway, Portugal, Russia, Singapore, South Africa, Spain, Sweden, Switzerland, Turkey, the United Kingdom, and the United States. The two regional organizations are the European Commission and the Gulf Cooperation Council. A number of affiliated international organizations hold observer status and can fully participate in all FATF activities; they are not, however, entitled to vote in any decisionmaking capacity. These organizations include the African Development Bank, Asian Development Bank, Commonwealth Secretariat, Egmont Group of Financial Intelligence Units, European Bank for Reconstruction and Development, European Central Bank (ECB), Europol, Inter-American Development Bank (IDB), International Association of Insurance Supervisors (IAIS), International Monetary Fund (IMF), Interpol, International Organization of Securities Commissions (IOSCO), Organization of American States/Inter-American Committee Against Terrorism (OAS/CICTE), Organization of American States/Inter-American Drug Abuse Control Commission (OAS/CICAD), Organization for Economic Co-operation and Development (OECD), Offshore Group of Banking Supervisors (OGBS), United Nations Office on Drugs and Crime (UNODC), United Nations Counter Terrorism Committee of the Security Council, World Bank, and World Customs Organization (WCO). See FATF, "FATF Members and Observers," (n.d.). Available online (www.fatf-gafi.org/document/52/0,2340,en_32250379_32237295_34027188_1_1_1_1,00.html#FATF_Members)
3. Initially, eight Special Recommendations were drafted, with a ninth added in October 2004.
4. The 40 + 9 are available on the FATF website (www.fatf-gafi.org).
5. Each of these organizations has officially endorsed FATF as the international standard-setter for AML/CFT. See United Nations, "The UN Political Declaration and Action Plan against Money Laundering," June 10, 1998; available online (www.imolin.org/imolin/en/ungadec.html). See also United Nations, "Security Council Resolution 1617," July 29, 2005; available online (www.un.org/Docs/sc/unsc_resolutions05.htm). See also IMF/WB, "IMF Advances Efforts to Combat Money Laundering and Terrorist Finance," August 8, 2002; available online (www.imf.org/external/np/sec/pn/2002/pn0287.htm). Other standard-setters that have recognized FATF include the Offshore Group of Banking Supervisors, the Basle Committee on Banking Supervision, and the Wolfsberg Group
6. Kathryn Gardner, "Fighting the FATF Way," *Global Governance* 13, no. 3 (July–September 2007). Available online (http://findarticles.com/p/articles/mi_7055/is_/ai_n28455371).
7. APG has 38 members: Afghanistan, Australia, Bangladesh, Brunei Darussalam, Cambodia, Canada, Chinese Taipei, Cook Islands, Fiji, Hong Kong–China, India, Indonesia, Japan, Lao People's Democratic Republic, Macau-China, Malaysia, Maldives, Marshall Islands, Mongolia, Myanmar, Nauru, Nepal, New Zealand, Niue, Pakistan, Palau, the Philippines, Republic of Korea (South Korea), Samoa, Singapore, Solomon Islands, Sri

Lanka, Thailand, Timor Leste, Tonga, the United States, Vanuatu, and Vietnam. See Asia/Pacific Group on Money Laundering, "Overlapping Membership," (n.d.). Available online (www.apgml.org/jurisdictions).

8. CFATF has 30 members: Anguilla, Antigua and Barbuda, Aruba, Bahamas, Barbados, Belize, Bermuda, British Virgin Islands, Cayman Islands, Costa Rica, Dominica, Dominican Republic, El Salvador, Grenada, Guatemala, Guyana, Haiti, Honduras, Jamaica, Montserrat, Netherlands Antilles, Nicaragua, Panama, Saint Kitts and Nevis, Saint Lucia, Saint Vincent and the Grenadines, Suriname, Trinidad and Tobago, Turks and Cacaos Islands, and Venezuela. See Caribbean Financial Task Force, "CFATF Overview," (n.d.). Available online (www.cfatf.org).
9. Moneyval has 27 permanent members: Albania, Andorra, Armenia, Azerbaijan, Bosnia and Herzegovina, Bulgaria, Croatia, Cyprus, Czech Republic, Estonia, Georgia, Hungary, Latvia, Liechtenstein, Lithuania, Malta, Moldova, Monaco, Poland, Romania, Russian Federation, San Marino, Serbia and Montenegro, Slovakia, Slovenia, "Former Yugoslav Republic of Macedonia," and Ukraine. There are two temporary members on a two-year basis, designated by the FATF Presidency. For the period 2005–2006, these two countries were France and the Netherlands. Israel was granted active observer status with MONEYVAL in January 2006 by the Committee of Ministers, which enables it to take part in the evaluation process. See Council of Europe, "About Moneyval," (n.d.). Available online (www.coe.int/t/e/legal_affairs/legal_co-operation/combating_economic_crime/5_money_laundering/General_information/About_MONEYVAL.asp#TopOfPage)
10. ESAAMLG has 14 members: Botswana, Kenya, Lesotho, Malawi, Mauritius, Mozambique, Namibia, Seychelles, South Africa, Swaziland, Tanzania, Uganda, Zambia, and Zimbabwe. See ESAAMLG, "Members and Cooperating Partners," (n.d.). Available online (www.esaamlg.org/MoU/index.php).
11. GIABA has 15 members: Benin, Burkina Faso, Cape Verde, Côte d'Ivoire, Gambia, Ghana, Guinea Bissau, Guinea Conakry, Liberia, Mali, Niger, Nigeria, Senegal, Sierra Leone, and Togo. See FATF, "Groupe Inter-gouvernemental d'Action contre le Blanchiment en Afrique (GIABA)," (n.d.). Available online (www.fatf-gafi.org/document/60/0,2340,en_32250379_32236869_34393596_1_1_1_1,00.html)
12. GAFISUD has 9 permanent members: Argentina, Bolivia, Brazil, Chile, Colombia, Ecuador, Paraguay, Peru, and Uruguay. See GAFISUD, "Contactenos," (n.d.). Available online (www.gafisud.org/miembros.htm).
13. MENAFATF has 17 members: Algeria, Bahrain, Egypt, Iraq, Jordan, Kuwait, Lebanon, Mauritania, Morocco, Oman, Qatar, Saudi Arabia, Sudan, Syria, Tunisia, United Arab Emirates, and Yemen. See MENAFATF, "Members and Observers," (n.d.). Available online (www.menafatf.org/topiclist.asp?ctype=about&id=430).
14. EAG has seven members: Belarus, China, Kazakhstan, Kyrgyzstan, Russia, Tajikistan, and Uzbekistan. See EAG, "List of Members and Observers of EAG," (n.d.). Available online (www.eurasiangroup.org/index-4.htm).
15. OGBS has 19 members and is the only nonregional FSRB. As its name indicates, its membership comprises offshore banking hubs around the globe: Aruba, Bahamas, Bahrain, Barbados, Bermuda, Cayman Islands, Cyprus, Gibraltar, Guernsey, Hong Kong (China), Isle of Man, Jersey, Labuan, Macau (China), Mauritius, Netherlands Antilles, Panama, Singapore, and Vanuatu. See OGBS, "Members and Observers," (n.d.). Available online (www.ogbs.net/members.htm).
16. Each of the FSRBs began as observers to FATF, which granted them access to FATF plenary sessions, working group meetings, and confidential documentation. In June 2005, FATF extended the option of becoming "Associate Members" to those FSRBs that meet certain criteria. Associate members are given a greater stake in the FATF decisionmaking process and are allowed to participate in FATF Mutual Evaluations, joint exercises, and typologies working groups. See FATF, "Financial Action Task Force: Annual Report 2005–2006," June 23, 2006, p. 5. Available online (www.fatf-gafi.org/dataoecd/38/56/37041969.pdf).
17. See FATF, "Recommendation 21—Applies to All NCCTs," (n.d.). Available online (www.fatf-gafi.org/document/39/0,2340,en_32250379_32236992_33916519_1_1_1_1,00.html)
18. See FATF, "About the Non-Cooperative Countries and Territories (NCCT) Initiative," (n.d.); available online (www.fatf-gafi.org/document/51/0,3343,en_32250379_32236992_33916403_1_1_1_1,00.html). See also U.S. State Department, "2006 Country Reports on Terrorism," April 30, 2007; available

online (www.state.gov/s/ct/rls/crt/2006/82728.htm).

19. See FATF, "Annual Review of Non-Cooperative Countries and Territories: 2005–2006," June 23, 2006, p. 2. Available online (www.fatf-gafi.org/dataoecd/0/0/37029619.pdf).
20. Ibid.
21. Jean-François Thony, "Money Laundering and Terrorist Financing: An Overview," May 10, 2000, p. 15. Available online (www.imf.org/external/np/leg/sem/2002/cdmfl/eng/thony.pdf).
22. See FATF, "Annual Review 2005–2006."
23. It is worth noting that the last country to come off the list was Myanmar, in October 2006.
24. See Hong Kong Office of the Commissioner of Insurance, memorandum to "Chief Executives of all authorized insurers carrying on long term business," titled "Non-Cooperative Countries and Territories, United Nations (Anti-Terrorism Measures) Ordinance, United States Executive Order 13224 & Combating Financing of Weapons of Mass Destruction Activities," October 31, 2006; available online (www.oci.gov.hk/download/cir_aml_20061031.pdf). See also British Virgin Islands Financial Services Commission, "Advisory Warning No. 1 of 2008," June 9, 2008; available online (www.bvifsc.vg/News/tabid/160/articleType/ArticleView/articleId/56/Advisory-Warning-No-1-of-2008-9-June-2008.aspx).
25. Craig Whitlock, "Terrorism Financing Blacklists at Risk," *Washington Post*, November 2, 2008. Available online (www.washingtonpost.com/wp-dyn/content/article/2008/11/01/AR2008110102214.html).
26. Named for the city in which it was signed, the convention came into force on November 11, 1990. See United Nations, "Convention against Illicit Traffic in Narcotic Drugs and Psychotropic Substances," 1988. Available online (www.unodc.org/pdf/convention_1988_en.pdf).
27. See UN Office on Drugs and Crime, "Monthly Status of Treaty Adherence," January 1, 2005; available online (www.unodc.org/unodc/treaty_adherence.html). See also UN Office on Drugs and Crime, "UN International Drug Control Conventions," (n.d.); available online (www.unodc.un.or.th/convention).
28. Specifically article 3, sections (b) and (c)(i).
29. Resolution 1267 has been followed by a number of related measures—including most recently Security Council Resolution 1617, adopted July 29, 2005. The text of both resolutions is available online (see www.un.org/Docs/scres/1999/sc99.htm and www.un.org/Docs/sc/unsc_resolutions05.htm).
30. Whitlock, "Terrorism Financing Blacklists at Risk."
31. Ibid.
32. Specifically, Resolution 1373 requires member states to impose sanctions against (1) "persons who commit, or attempt to commit, terrorist acts or participate in or facilitate the commission of terrorist acts," (2) "entities owned or controlled directly or indirectly by such persons," and (3) "persons and entities acting on behalf of, or at the direction of such persons and entities." Regarding the sanctions themselves, states must (1) freeze funds and other financial assets or economic resources of designated entities, (2) prohibit nationals or any entities within their territories from making funds available for the benefit of terrorist acts, (3) refrain from providing any form of support to designated entities or persons involved in terrorist acts, (4) prevent the movement of terrorists, and (5) deny safe haven to those who finance, plan, support, or commit terrorist acts. See United Nations, "Security Council Resolution 1373," September 28, 2001. Available online (www.un.org/Docs/scres/2001/sc2001.htm).
33. In March 2009, Britain announced "that it would engage in direct contacts with the political wing of the Hizbollah movement in Lebanon, recognising that the organisation has become part of the country's national unity government." At the same time, the Foreign Office "made clear that the UK would not be having contacts with Hizbollah's military wing." The United States has publicly rejected Britain's approach, though some British officials have claimed that the Obama administration is less opposed in private. See the opening paragraphs of chapter 8 for more on the "wings" issue. For Britain's announcement, see James Blitz, "UK to Engage with Hizbollah," *Financial Times*, March 4, 2009; available online (www.ft.com/cms/s/0/67fe86d0-08e6-11de-b8b0-0000779fd2ac.html?nclick_check=1). See also "US OK with UK's Overture to Hizbullah," Associated Press, April 5, 2009; available online (www.jpost.com/servlet/Satellite?cid=1238562907554&pagename=JPost%2FJPArticle%2FShowFull).

34. Victor Comras, "UN System for Designating Terrorists Is Faltering," CounterterrorismBlog.com, July 11, 2008. Available online (http://counterterrorismblog.org/2008/07/un_system_for_designating_terr.php).
35. "Blacklist Procedures 'Violate Human Rights,'" *Human Rights Tribune,* November 13, 2007. Available online (www.humanrights-geneva.info/Blacklist-procedures-violate-human,2447).
36. Whitlock, "Terrorism Financing Blacklists at Risk."
37. See Resolution 1822. Available online (http://daccessdds.un.org/doc/UNDOC/GEN/N08/404/90/PDF/N0840490.pdf?OpenElement).
38. Richard Barrett, "Al-Qaeda and Taliban Sanctions Threatened," *PolicyWatch* no. 1409 (Washington Institute for Near East Policy, October 6, 2008). Available online (www.washingtoninstitute.org/templateC05.php?CID=2935).
39. Whitlock, "Terrorism Financing Blacklists at Risk."
40. Ibid.
41. Ibid.
42. U.S. Treasury Department, "Treasury Targets Al Qaida Facilitators in South Africa," press release, January 26, 2007. Available online (www.treas.gov/press/releases/hp230.htm).
43. Jonathan Schanzer, "Where Is International Community in Fighting Terrorism's Financiers?" *Investor's Business Daily,* March 9, 2007. Available online (www.jewishpolicycenter.org/article/10).
44. See Egmont Group, "Principles for Information Exchange," June 13, 2001, p. 1. Available online (www.egmontgroup.org/princ_info_exchange.pdf).
45. See Egmont Group, "List of Egmont FIUs," (n.d.). Available online (www.egmontgroup.org).
46. See MENAFATF, "Mutual Evaluation of the Syrian Arab Republic on Anti-Money Laundering and Combating the Financing of Terrorism," November 15, 2006. Available online (www.menafatf.org/images/UploadFiles/MutualEvaluationReportofSyria.pdf).
47. Matthew Levitt, "Global Anti-Terrorism Financing Group Challenged by Syria's Application," *PolicyWatch* no. 1238 (Washington Institute for Near East Policy, May 31, 2007). Available online (www.washingtoninstitute.org/templateC05.php?CID=2609).

In Simple Terms: Recommendations or Obligations?

1. U.S. Treasury Department, "Prepared Remarks of Daniel L. Glaser, Acting Assistant Secretary for Terrorist Financing and Financial Crimes, Before the Latvian Commercial Bankers Association's Conference: The Fight Against Money Laundering and Financial Crimes," September 14, 2005. Available online (www.treas.gov/press/releases/js2717.htm).

Collapse of the UN Sanctions System? The Case of Yasin al-Qadi

1. Richard Morais and Denet Tezel, "The Al Qadi Affair," *Forbes,* January 24, 2008. Available online (www.forbes.com/2008/01/24/turkey-yasin-al-qadi-biz-cz_rm_0124alqadi.html).
2. Richard Barrett, "Al-Qaeda and Taliban Sanctions Threatened," *PolicyWatch* no. 1409 (Washington Institute for Near East Policy, October 6, 2008). Available online (www.washingtoninstitute.org/templateC05.php?CID=2935).

Chapter 4

1. FATF has issued the same preventive measures—albeit on a more limited basis—to designated nonfinancial businesses and professions (DNFBPs), which include jewelers, real-estate agents, and lawyers, among other professionals.
2. Such programs will vary depending on the institution's size, scope, and operations.
3. The international standard regarding customer due diligence and identification—described in FATF's Recommendation 5—was established in conjunction with the Basel Committee on Banking Supervision.

See FATF, "The 40 Recommendations" (available online at www.fatf-gafi.org/document/28/0,2340, en_32250379_32236930_33658140_1_1_1_1,00.html#40recs) and the Basel Core Principles for Effective Banking Supervision and Customer Due Diligence for Banks, principle 15 (available at www.bis.org/publ/bcbs30.pdf).

4. See FATF Recommendation 5.
5. For a complete definition, see FATF, "Key Topics, 40 Recommendations Glossary," (n.d.). Available online (www.fatf-gafi.org/glossary/0,2586,en_32250379_32236889_35433764_1_1_1_1,00.html).
6. See FATF Recommendation 6.
7. Interestingly, the relevant FATF standard calls for enhanced due diligence only on foreign PEPs, not domestic PEPs. FATF does encourage enhanced due diligence for domestic PEPs, but only as a side note to the main recommendation regarding foreign customers. See FATF, "Interpretative Notes to the 40 Recommendations of the FATF," Interpretative Note 6, (n.d.). Available online (www.fatf-gafi.org/document/28/0,2340, en_32250379_32236920_33988956_1_1_1_1,00.html).
8. See FATF Recommendation 7.
9. See FATF Recommendation 18.
10. Basel Committee on Banking Supervision, "Shell Banks and Booking Offices," January 2003. Available online (www.bis.org/publ/bcbs95.pdf).
11. See FATF Recommendation 8.
12. This period can be extended in specific cases if requested by a competent authority. This rule applies whether an account is active or closed. See FATF Recommendation 10.
13. See FATF Recommendation 13.
14. See FATF Recommendation 11.
15. See FATF Recommendation 14.
16. These laws should protect the financial institution and its directors, officers, and employees if they report their suspicions in good faith to the competent authorities. See FATF Recommendation 14.
17. See FATF Recommendation 19.
18. Financial Institutions may also substitute any of these requirements with national identity number, customer identification number and/or place and date of birth. See FATF, "9 Special Recommendations (SR) on Terrorist Financing (TF)," Special Recommendation VII (n.d.). Available online (www.fatf-gafi.org/document /9/0,2340,en_32250379_32236920_34032073_1_1_1_1,00.html).
19. It is worth noting that for the purposes of the Bank Secrecy Act (discussed later in this section), the financial sector includes banks, securities, insurance providers, money services businesses (e.g., money remitters and foreign exchange offices), accountants, casinos, dealers in precious metals and stones, lawyers, real-estate agents, trust and company service providers, and the nonprofit sector. For an exact breakdown of how large the U.S. formal and informal sectors are, see FATF, *Third Mutual Evaluation Report on Anti–Money Laundering and Combating the Financing of Terrorism: United States of America* (Paris: FATF, June 23, 2006), pp. 8–13, 199–201. Available online (www.fatf-gafi.org/dataoecd/44/9/37101772.pdf).
20. Ibid.
21. See section 358 of the BSA
22. See FATF, *Third Mutual Evaluation Report.*
23. Governor Susan Schmidt Bies, "Bank Secrecy Act Enforcement," testimony before the Senate Committee on Banking, Housing, and Urban Affairs, June 3, 2004; available online (www.federalreserve.gov/boarddocs/Testimony/2004/20040603/default.htm). It is also worth noting that all regulators must follow similar procedures as a result of their membership in the Federal Financial Institutions Examination Council (FFIEC). The FFIEC, established by statute in 1979, is a formal interagency body that "prescribes uniform principles, standards, and reporting forms for all banking and other depository institution examinations." See Congressional Research Service, "Terrorist Financing: U.S. Agency Efforts and Inter-Agency Coordination," August 3, 2005; available online (www.fas.org/sgp/crs/terror/RL33020.pdf).
24. Actions (including criminal charges) may also be taken against the bank's officers, directors, and/or other

individuals if they are knowingly involved in a money laundering or terrorism financing scheme. See Congressional Research Service, "Terrorist Financing."

25. See U.S. General Accounting Office, "Money Laundering: FinCEN's Law Enforcement Support, Regulatory, and International Roles," April 1, 1998. Available online (www.fas.org/irp/gao/ggd-98-083.htm).
26. See FinCEN, "History of Anti-Money Laundering Laws," (n.d.). Available online (www.fincen.gov/news_room/aml_history.html).
27. Matt Squire, "FinCEN Rated among Worst Government Agencies in Employee Satisfaction Poll," MoneyLaundering.com, April 27, 2007. Available online (www.moneylaundering.com/NewsBriefDisplay.aspx?id= 1277).
28. See John Cassara, "The Stalled War on Terrorist Finance," statement to the Senate Finance Committee, April 1, 2008. Available online (johncassara.com/articles/statement_senate.doc).
29. Ibid.
30. See FinCEN, "SAR Activity Review—By the Numbers," (n.d.). Available online (www.fincen.gov/news_room/rp/sar_by_number.html).
31. From its inception after the September 11 attacks through April 2004, the hotline resulted in 853 tips that were passed on to law enforcement. See Congressional Research Service, "Terrorist Financing."
32. See Code of Federal Regulations, 31 CFR 103.18(a)(2)(iii).
33. See also 31 CFR 103.121.
34. In FATF's last Mutual Evaluation of the U.S. financial sector in 2006, the American interpretation of the relevant international standard differed from that of the assessors. The standard mandates that banks conduct ongoing—not just initial—customer due diligence. The United States maintains that its SAR system fulfills this obligation, since such reports must be filed on any transaction that "is not the sort in which the particular customer would normally be expected to engage, and the bank knows of no reasonable explanation for the transaction after examining the available facts." In addition to initial identification procedures, the U.S. government also requires banks to conduct ongoing due diligence for certain activities—namely, correspondent banking, "private banking" (explained later in this chapter), and transactions involving PEPs (see 31 CFR 103.178(b)(4)). Finally, although federal regulations do not explicitly prohibit the use of anonymous accounts, identification rules mandate that institutions know the true identity of their customers. Despite all of these measures, FATF found the U.S. due diligence system to be deficient and strongly encouraged regulators to rectify it.
35. The guidelines were published by the Office of the Comptroller of the Currency in January 2001. Available online (www.occ.treas.gov/ftp/bulletin/2001-9a.pdf).
36. See section 313 of the PATRIOT Act
37. Specifically, Treasury's Office of Foreign Assets Control (OFAC) is responsible for the list. See the OFAC section of the Treasury website (www.treas.gov/offices/enforcement/ofac).
38. See U.S. State Department, "Country Reports on Terrorism," (n.d.). Available online (www.state.gov/s/ct/rls/crt).
39. See FinCEN, "Section 311—Special Measures," (n.d.). Available online (www.fincen.gov/statutes_regs/patriot/section311.html).
40. As discussed in chapter 3, the NCCT list was replaced by the International Cooperation Review Group (ICRG) list beginning in 2007. Sadly, however, the State Department website still has not yet caught up with this change, and FATF does not publicly release the ICRG list via the web or other means (though many countries have leaked information regarding designees). For information regarding the defunct NCCT list, see FATF, "Non Cooperative Countries and Territories," (n.d.). Available online (www.fatf-gafi.org/document/4/0,2340,en_32250379_32236992_33916420_1_1_1_1,00.html).
41. See U.S. State Department, "Narcotics Control Reports," (n.d.). Available online (www.state.gov/p/inl/rls/nrcrpt/index.htm). For more on the INCSR, see the concluding chapter of this book.
42. Also known as FinCEN form 104. CTRs must be filed within 15 days of the transaction (this deadline applies to paper filing; it is extended to 25 days for institutions filing electronically or via magnetic tape). It should be noted that institutions "are permitted to exempt certain customers from the reporting process. These

exemptions include banks, U.S. governmental departments and agencies, companies quoted on the major U.S stock exchanges (and their subsidiaries), and any U.S.-incorporated commercial enterprise (with respect only to its domestic business) that has maintained an account with the institution for at least 12 months and regularly engages in currency transactions in excess of $10,000. The exemption for commercial enterprises does not extend to a range of specified business activities." See 31 CFR 103.22(d) and 31 CFR 103.27(a)(3).

43. 31 CFR 103.38(d)
44. Businesses and trades—including insurance companies, jewelry stores, precious metals dealers, real estate firms, attorneys, accountants, automobile dealerships, boat dealerships, and so forth—that conduct transactions over $10,000 must go through a similar procedure by filing form 8300 with the Internal Revenue Service. See Internal Revenue Code 26 USC 60501 and the relevant BSA statute (31 USC 5331).
45. As mandated by the international standard, SAR records must be kept for at least five years. Reports can be filed via paper, magnetic tape, or BSA e-filing and should be completed within 30 calendar days of the suspicious transaction. Banks are also "encouraged" under Title 12 to file copies of their SARs with state and local law enforcement authorities. And in the case of terrorism-related transactions, FinCEN has encouraged institutions to contact a local FBI field office.
46. See FDIC, "Connecting the Dots...The Importance of Timely and Effective Suspicious Activity Reports," (n.d.); available online (www.fdic.gov/regulations/examinations/supervisory/insights/siwin07/article03_connecting.html). See also FinCEN "Annual Report: Fiscal Year 2006," (n.d.); available online (www.fincen.gov/news_room/rp/files/YEreport/AnnualReportFY2006.html).
47. See 31 CFR 103.18(a)(1) for banks.
48. See FATF, *Third Mutual Evaluation Report.* It is worth noting that from September 2001 to April 2004, financial institutions filed 4,294 SARs involving possible terrorism financing. See Congressional Research Service, "Terrorist Financing."
49. See FATF, *Third Mutual Evaluation Report.* It is worth noting that from April 1996 to June 2005, more than 2.6 million SARs were filed by the formal financial sector (ibid., p. 144).
50. 31 USC 5318(g)(3).
51. See 31 CFR 103.11 and 31 CFR 103.33(e)(1)(i).
52. See FATF, *Third Mutual Evaluation Report,* p. 135. See also 31 CFR 103.33.
53. See U.S. Treasury Department, "Written Testimony of David D. Aufhauser, General Counsel, before the Committee on Banking, Housing and Urban Affairs, September 25, 2003." Available online (www.treas.gov/press/releases/js760.htm).

Tightening the Noose around Banco Delta Asia and North Korea

1. See U.S. Treasury Department, "Treasury Designates Banco Delta Asia as Primary Money Laundering Concern under USA PATRIOT Act," September 15, 2005; available online (www.ustreas.gov/press/releases/js2720.htm). See also Todd Crowell, "North Korea, The 'Sopranos' State," *Asia Times,* January 18, 2006; available online (www.atimes.com/atimes/Korea/HA18Dg01.html).
2. Donald Greenlees and David Lague, "The Money Trail That Linked North Korea to Macao," *New York Times,* April 11, 2007. Available online (www.nytimes.com/2007/04/11/world/asia/11cnd-macao.html?scp=3&sq=greenlees%20and%20Lague%20north%20korea&st=cse).
3. See U.S. Treasury, "Treasury Designates Banco Delta Asia."
4. Mike Chinoy, "Macau Focus of Push on NK Activity," CNN, July 23, 2006; available online (www.cnn.com/2006/WORLD/asiapcf/05/18/nkorea.macau/index.html). See also Greenlees and Lague, "The Money Trail."
5. David Lague and Donald Greenlees, "Squeeze on Banco Delta Asia Hit North Korea Where It Hurt," *International Herald Tribune,* January 18, 2007. See also Greenlees and Lague, "The Money Trail."
6. Donald Greenlees and David Lague, "How a U.S. Inquiry Held Up the North Korea Peace Talks," *International Herald Tribune,* April 11, 2007; available online (www.iht.com/articles/2007/04/11/asia/bank.php?page=2). See also Raphael Perl and Dick Nanto, *North Korean Counterfeiting of U.S. Currency* (Congressional Research

Service, March 22, 2006); available online (www.fas.org/sgp/crs/row/RL33324.pdf).

7. See U.S. Treasury Department, "Prepared Remarks by Stuart Levey, Under Secretary for Terrorism and Financial Intelligence, before the American Enterprise Institute for Public Policy Research," September 8, 2006. Available online (www.ustreas.gov/press/releases/hp86.htm).
8. See Chinoy, "Macau Focus."

Yassir Arafat: PEP Par Excellence

1. Gideon Alon and Amira Hass, "MI Chief: Terror Groups Trying Hard to Pull Off Mega-Attack," *Haaretz,* August 14, 2002.
2. Lesley Stahl, "Arafat's Billions: One Man's Quest to Track Down Unaccounted-For Public Funds," CBS News, November 9, 2003. Available online (www.cbsnews.com/stories/2003/11/07/60minutes/main582487.shtml).
3. Adam Bennett et al., *Economic Performance and Reform under Conflict Conditions* (Washington, DC: International Monetary Fund, 2003), p. 91. Available online (www.imf.org/external/pubs/ft/med/2003/eng/wbg/wbg.pdf).
4. "Arafat's Investments Included Dotcoms, New York Bowling Alley," Bloomberg News, December 22, 2004. Available online (www.bloomberg.com/apps/news?pid=nifea&&sid=ag2fQ5pMZXc8).
5. Stahl, "Arafat's Billions."
6. Yaakov Katz, "Arafat Used Aid to Buy Weapons," *Jerusalem Report,* May 17, 2006. Available online (www.jpost.com/servlet/Satellite?cid=1145961361493&pagename=JPost/JPArticle/ShowFull).
7. Asaf Romirowsky, "One Man Bank," FrontPageMagazine.com, November 28, 2003; available online (www.frontpagemag.com/Printable.aspx?ArtId=15441). See also Youssef Ibrahim, "Arafat Found Safe in Libyan Desert after Crash," *New York Times,* April 9, 1992; available online (http://query.nytimes.com/gst/fullpage.html?res=9E0CE5D8143DF93AA35757C0A964958260&sec=&spon=&pagewanted=2).
8. This according to Ambassador Martin Indyk of the Saban Center at the Brookings Institution. See Lesley Stahl, "Arafat's Billions."
9. Ibid.
10. "Mrs Arafat's Bank Accounts Probed," BBC News, February 11, 2004; available online (http://news.bbc.co.uk/2/hi/middle_east/3479937.stm). See also "Arafat's Wife at Centre of Money-Laundering Inquiry," *Guardian Telegraph,* February 13, 2004; available online (www.smh.com.au/articles/2004/02/12/1076548163989.html).

Broadcasting Bank Accounts: Hizbollah's TV Station

1. These words appeared on al-Manar's former website (www.manartv.com).
2. See Christopher Dickey, "The Iran Connection," *Newsweek,* February 18, 2002; and Neil MacFarquhar, "Hezbollah Becomes Potent Anti-U.S. Force," *New York Times,* December 24, 2002. Information also confirmed by author interview with Nayef Krayem (al-Manar's general manager and chairman of the board), al-Manar Television station, Beirut, June 27, 2002.
3. Hizbollah's own Secretary-General Sheikh Hassan Nasrallah characterized the station in this manner, praising it "for its part in both supporting the Palestinian intifada and forcing the Israel Defense Forces (IDF) to withdraw from Lebanon." Avi Jorisch, *Beacon of Hatred: Inside Hizballah's al-Manar Television* (Washington, DC: Washington Institute for Near East Policy, 2004), p. 20.
4. See U.S. Treasury Department, "U.S. Designates Al-Manar as a Specially Designated Global Terrorist Entity: Television Station Is Arm of Hizballah Terrorist Network," March 23, 2006. Available online (www.ustreas.gov/press/releases/js4134.htm).
5. For samples of al-Manar footage promoting these and other messages, see Jorisch, *Beacon of Hatred,* which includes a multimedia CD-ROM containing video clips.
6. Avi Jorisch, "Hizballah's Unwitting U.S. Bankers," *PolicyWatch* no. 774 (Washington Institute for Near East Policy, July 22, 2003). Available online (www.washingtoninstitute.org/templateC05.php?CID=1652).

7. Avi Jorisch, "Hizbollah Hate with a U.S. Link," *Los Angeles Times*, October 13, 2002. Information also confirmed by author interview with Krayem.
8. See U.S. Treasury, "U.S. Designates Al-Manar." See also Minutes of the European Parliament Sitting, Strasbourg, France, July 6, 2005; available online (www.europarl.europa.eu/sides/getDoc.do?pubRef=-//EP//TEXT+CRE+20050706+ITEM-029+DOC+XML+V0//EN).
9. Channel lists available on the networks' websites: Arabsat (www.arabsat.com/ArabSat/English/Channels), Nilesat (www.nilesat.com.eg/channels.htm), and Palapa (www.lyngsat.com/palapac2.html). For more in-depth information about al-Manar, see Jorisch, *Beacon of Hatred.*

Banking AML Guidance

1. FFIEC, *Bank Secrecy Act Anti–Money Laundering Examination Manual* (available on FinCEN's website at www.ffiec.gov/bsa_aml_infobase/pages_manual/OLM_002.htm).

Citibank: Laundering through "Private Banking"

1. See Citibank, "Welcome to Citi Private Bank," (n.d.) Available online (www.citi.com/privatebank/worldwide.htm).
2. Eljay Bowron, *Private Banking: Raul Salinas, Citibank, and Alleged Money Laundering* (Washington DC: U.S. General Accounting Office, October 1998); available online (www.gao.gov/archive/1999/os99001.pdf). See also, "Citibank Secretly Helped Raul Salinas, Report Says," *Los Angeles Times*, December 5, 1998; available online (http://8.12.42.31/1998/dec/05/news/nc-50720).
3. Bowron, *Private Banking.* See also Tim Golden, "U.S. Report Says Salinas's Banker Ignored Safeguards," *New York Times*, December 4, 1998; available online (http://query.nytimes.com/gst/fullpage.html?res=9F07EFDE103BF937A35751C1A96E9582608&sec=&spon=&pagewanted=all).
4. Amy Elliott, remarks before the Senate Committee on Governmental Affairs, Subcommittee on Investigations, hearing on "Private Banking and Money Laundering: A Case Study of Opportunities and Vulnerabilities," November 9–10, 1999. Transcript available online (http://fdsys.gpo.gov/fdsys/pkg/CHRG-106shrg428/html/CHRG-106shrg428.htm).
5. Tim Golden, "U.S. Report Says Salinas's Banker Ignored Safeguards," *New York Times*, December 4, 1998. Available online (http://query.nytimes.com/gst/fullpage.html?res=9F07EFDE103BF937A35751C1A96E958260&sec=&spon=&pagewanted=all).

SWIFT and the Terrorist Finance Tracking Program

1. U.S. Treasury Department, "Terrorist Finance Tracking Program Fact Sheet," June 23, 2006. Available online (http://www.ustreas.gov/press/releases/js4340.htm).
2. Craig Whitlock, "Terrorism Financing Blacklists at Risk," *Washington Post*, November 2, 2008. Available online (www.washingtonpost.com/wp-dyn/content/article/2008/11/01/AR2008110102214_pf.html).
3. European Union, "USA to Take Account of EU Data Protection Principles to Process Data Received from Swift," June 28, 2007; available online (http://europa.eu/rapid/pressReleasesAction.do?reference=IP/07/968). See also European Union, "EU Review of the United States' 'Terrorist Finance Tracking Programme,'" March 7, 2008; available online (http://europa.eu/rapid/pressReleasesAction.do?reference=IP/08/400&format=HTML&aged=0&language=en&guiLanguage=en).

Chapter 5

1. Nikos Passas, "Informal Value Transfer Systems, Terrorism and Money Laundering" (study funded by the National Institute of Justice, November 2003), p. 7.
2. Steve Schifferes, "Migrants, Money Flows and Terrorism," BBC, December 16, 2008. Available online (http://news.bbc.co.uk/2/hi/business/7764823.stm).

3. Ibid. See also FATF, "Terrorist Financing," February 29, 2008; available online (www.fatf-gafi.org/dataoecd/28/43/40285899.pdf).
4. Harjit Sandhu, "Terrorism-Criminal Nexus: Non-banking Conduits," Organization for Security and Co-operation in Europe, March 11, 2004. Available online (www.osce.org/item/2723.html).
5. FATF has developed a helpful definition of these systems: "Any financial service that accepts cash, cheques, other monetary instruments or other stores of value in one location and pays a corresponding sum in cash or other form to a beneficiary in another location by means of a communication, message, transfer or through a clearing network to which the money/value transfer system belongs." See FATF, "Interpretative Notes to the 9 Special Recommendations on Terrorist Financing," Interpretative Note to Special Recommendation VI, (n.d.). Available online (www.fatf-gafi.org/document/53/0,2340,en_32250379_32236947_34261877_1_1_1_1,00.html#insrII).
6. See FATF, "Money Laundering and Terrorist Financing Typologies: 2004–2005," June 10, 2005. Available online (www.fatf-gafi.org/pages/0,2966,en_32250379_32237202_1_1_1_1_1,00.html). This typology report also includes a good overview of the regulatory frameworks in a sample of 12 countries.
7. See FATF, "Combating the Abuse of Alternative Remittance Systems: International Best Practices," June 20, 2003. Available online (www.fatf-gafi.org/dataoecd/39/17/34033713.pdf).
8. For an excellent overview of Hawala, see FinCEN, "Advisory Issue 33," March 2003. Available online (www.fincen.gov/advis33.pdf).
9. Patrick Jost and Harjit Singh Sandhu, *The Hawala Alternative Remittance System and Its Role in Money Laundering* (Lyon, France: Interpol General Secretariat, January 2000). Available online (www.interpol.int/Public/FinancialCrime/MoneyLaundering/Hawala/default.asp).
10. See FATF, "Combating the Abuse," p. 3.
11. See FATF, Interpretative Note to Special Recommendation VI. Ideally, this recommendation should apply to all of a given network's agents. At minimum, the principal operator to be licensed should maintain a list of current agents and make it available to the relevant authorities.
12. See FATF, "9 Special Recommendations (SR) on Terrorist Financing (TF)," Special Recommendation VI, (n.d.). Available online (www.fatf-gafi.org/document/9/0,2340,en_32250379_32236920_34032073_1_1_1_1,00.html).
13. See FATF Special Recommendation VII.
14. See FATF, "The 40 Recommendations." Available online (www.fatf-gafi.org/document/28/0,2340,en_32250379_32236930_33658140_1_1_1_1,00.html#40recs).
15. Other kinds of MSBs include currency dealers, check cashers, and issuers and sellers of travelers checks, money orders, or stored value. U.S. government agencies and outside analysts use many different terms to refer to MSBs, including alternative remittance system/house, value transfer business/system/operator, money remitter/remittance business, money transmittal business, informal financial network, hawaladar, hawala operator, hawala network, informal broker, informal banking business, and so forth. FATF defines an MSB as follows: "Any person, whether or not licensed or required to be licensed, who engages as a business in accepting currency, or funds denominated in currency, and transmits the currency or funds, or the value of the currency or funds, by any means through a financial agency or institution, a Federal Reserve Bank or other facility of one or more Federal Reserve Banks, the Board of Governors of the Federal Reserve System, or both, or an electronic funds transfer network." See FATF, *Third Mutual Evaluation Report on Anti–Money Laundering and Combating the Financing of Terrorism: United States of America* (Paris: FATF, June 23, 2006), p. 190. Available online (www.fatf-gafi.org/dataoecd/44/9/37101772.pdf).
16. See U.S. Treasury Department, *2005 U.S. Money Laundering Threat Assessment* (December 2005), p. 7. Available online (www.treas.gov/offices/enforcement/pdf/mlta.pdf).
17. See U.S. Treasury Department, "Remarks by Deputy Assistant Secretary for International Monetary and Financial Policy Mark Sobel on the Committee on Payment and Settlement Systems of the Bank for International Settlements–World Bank," May 11, 2006. Available online (www.treas.gov/press/releases/js4252.htm).
18. This requirement became effective in December 2001. Each MSB must provide contact information,

identify its owner, provide a governmentally issued identification number for the owner, identify its primary transaction banking account, and indicate whether it uses informal means of transferring money.

19. See 18 USC 1960 and 31 USC 5322.
20. See FinCEN, "MSB Registration List," (n.d.). Available online (http://msb.gov/pdf/msb_registration_list.pdf).
21. Congress recommended that states do away with these licensing disparities as long ago as 1994, in the Money Laundering Suppression Act, but the problem persists.
22. See Code of Federal Regulations, 31 CFR 103.125. See also U.S. Treasury, *2005 U.S. Money Laundering Threat Assessment,* p. 10.
23. FinCEN is responsible for civil enforcement actions and assessing civil money penalties with respect to violations of BSA regulations. The Justice Department is responsible for enforcing criminal penalties.
24. 18 USC 1960. Any person who knowingly conducts, controls, manages, supervises, directs, or owns all or part of an MSB and fails to register as required with FinCEN, or in certain circumstances operates without a required state license, is in breach of 18 USC 1960.
25. For recordkeeping violations, the government may assess a civil penalty of up to $100,000. See 31 CFR 103.57.
26. Carol Van Cleef and Maureen Sanders, "Insights: New MSB Examination Manual Challenges Regulators, Industry and Banks" (Fortent, April 1, 2009). Available online (www.pattonboggs.com/files/News/187d3d87-564d-4124-b721-0ce69bd0991e/Presentation/NewsAttachment/bc998c3b-ae3f-40a4-b3ee-0de77c82cc79/Fortent%20Insights%20VanCleef%20040109.pdf).
27. See U.S. Treasury, *2005 U.S. Money Laundering Threat Assessment,* p. 31.
28. Ibid., p. 30.
29. Ibid., p. 9.
30. See FATF, *Third Mutual Evaluation Report,* p. 198.
31. Robert Looney, "Following the Terrorist Informal Money Trail: The Hawala Financial Mechanism," *Strategic Insights* 1, no. 9 (November 2002). Available online (www.ccc.nps.navy.mil/si/nov02/southAsia.asp).

United Arab Emirates—The Mecca of Illicit Finance

1. See U.S. State Department, "2008 International Narcotics Control Strategy Report," March 2008. Available online (www.state.gov/p/inl/rls/nrcrpt/2008/vol2/html/101353.htm).
2. "An Unlikely Criminal Crossroads," *U.S. News & World Report,* November 27, 2005. Available online (www.usnews.com/usnews/news/articles/051205/5terror.b1.htm).
3. John Willman, "Trail of Terrorist Dollars That Spans the World," *Financial Times,* November 29, 2001. Available online (http://specials.ft.com/attackonterrorism/FT3RNR3XMUC.html).
4. See 9/11 Commission, *The 9/11 Commission Report* (Washington, DC: U.S. Government Printing Office, 2004), p. 162; available online (www.9-11commission.gov/report/911Report.pdf). See also "UAE Says Suspect Received $100,000," *Chicago Tribune,* October 25, 2001; available online (www.chicagotribune.com/news/local/chi-0110250282oct25,0,5256351.story).
5. Mark Pieth, *Financing Terrorism* (Norwell, MA.: Kluwer Academic Publishers, 2002), pp. 24–26.
6. "Officials: Alleged al Qaeda Paymaster in Custody," CNN, March 4, 2003; available online (www.cnn.com/2003/WORLD/asiapcf/south/03/03/pakistan.arrests). See also Paul Thompson, *The Terror Timeline* (New York: Harper Collins, 2004), p. 253.
7. Paul Helminger, "The Economic Consequences of September 11, 2001 and the Economic Dimension of Anti-Terrorism," NATO Parliamentary Assembly, 2002 Annual Session [AV 187 EC(02)7]. Available online (www.nato-pa.int/default.asp?SHORTCUT=248).
8. It should also be mentioned that infamous Pakistani nuclear scientist Abdul Qadir Khan used the UAE as his black market of choice to peddle his nuclear proliferation know-how. In addition, according to one U.S. official, "Iran is building a [nuclear] bomb through Dubai." See "Bin Laden's Operatives Still Using Freewheeling Dubai," *USA Today,* September 2, 2004; available online (www.usatoday.com/news/world/2004-09-02-terror-dubai_x.htm). See also "An Unlikely Criminal Crossroads."

9. See MENAFATF, "Mutual Evaluation of the United Arab Emirates on Anti-Money Laundering and Combating the Financing of Terrorism," April 9, 2008. Available online (www.menafatf.org/images/UploadFiles/UAEoptimized.pdf).
10. Kevin Whitelaw, "Trying to Cut Off Terrorists' Money Supplies," *U.S. News & World Report*, April 11, 2008. Available online (www.usnews.com/articles/news/world/2008/04/11/trying-to-cut-off-terrorists-money-supplies.html).
11. Ibid.
12. See "An Unlikely Criminal Crossroads."

Al-Barakat: Informal Terrorism Financing Network

1. "Remittance Firms Continue Services Despite Constraints," SomaliUK.com, September 2002. Available online (www1.somaliuk.com/News/archive.php?month=9&year=2002).
2. Edward Alden and Mark Huband, "Case Not Proved against Terror's Quartermasters," FT.com, February 19 2002; available online (http://specials.ft.com/attackonterrorism/FT3Y1UAAXXC.html). See also "Somali Men Sentenced for Sending Money to al-Qaida," *Mail and Guardian*, January 1, 2002; available online (www.mg.co.za/article/2002-01-01-somali-men-sentenced-for-sending-money-to-alqaida). See also "Somali Nationals Get Harsher Sentence," SomaliUK.com, December 2003; available online (www1.somaliuk.com/News/archive.php?month=12&year=2003).
3. See *United States v. Abdirahman Sheik-Ali Isse and United States v. Abdillah S. Abdi*. Available online (http://bulk.resource.org/courts.gov/c/F3/342/342.F3d.313.02-4815.02-4814.02-4774.02-4759.html).
4. Ibid.
5. Ibid.
6. See "Somali Men Sentenced." See also *United States v. Abdirahman Sheik-Ali Isse and United States v. Abdillah S. Abdi*.
7. John Kane and April Wall, *Identifying the Links between White-Collar Crime and Terrorism* (Glen Allen, VA: National White Collar Crime Center, 2004), p. 14. Available online (www.ncjrs.gov/pdffiles1/nij/grants/209520.pdf).
8. "2 Somalis with Terrorist Ties to Be Resentenced," *Los Angeles Times*, September 4, 2003; available online (http://articles.latimes.com/2003/sep/04/nation/na-somalis4). See also *United States v. Abdirahman Sheik-Ali Isse and United States v. Abdillah S. Abdi*.

Licensing or Registering?

1. FATF Task Force on Money Laundering, "Combating the Abuse of Alternative Remittance Systems: International Best Practices," June 20, 2003, p. 3. Available online (www.fatf-gafi.org/dataoecd/39/17/34033713.pdf).

Hawala and AML/CFT

1. Code of Federal Regulations, 31 CFR 103.125.
2. Section 359(a) of the PATRIOT Act. See also U.S. Department of the Treasury, "A Report to the Congress in Accordance with Section 359 of the USA PATRIOT Act," (November 2002). See also Code of Federal Regulations, 31 CFR 103.38.
3. See Code of Federal Regulations, 31 CFR 103.29 and 31 CFR 103.33(f).
4. See Code of Federal Regulations, 31 CFR 103.22.

Beacon on the Hill

1. National Drug Intelligence Center, "Unlicensed Money Transmittal Business Prosecuted in New York," in *National Drug Threat Assessment 2005*, February 2005; available online (www.usdoj.gov/ndic/

pubs11/12620/money.htm). See also "Wells Fargo Skirts Money-Laundering Charges as Clients Probed," *Bloomberg News*, December 23, 2003; available online (www.bloomberg.com/apps/news?pid=10000039&sid=axnIyNZ5tqmM&refer=columnist_evans#).

2. Susan Saulny, "Laundering of Billions Is Alleged," *New York Times*, June 27, 2003. Available online (http://query.nytimes.com/gst/fullpage.html?res=9C04E3DC1E3BF934A15755C0A9659C8B63).
3. New York County District Attorney's Office, news release, February 23, 2004. Available online (http://manhattanda.org/whatsnew/press/2004-02-23.shtml).
4. "Bank of America Settles Money Laundering Probe," *North Country Gazette*, September 27, 2006; available online (www.northcountrygazette.org/articles/092706MoneyLaundering.html). See also Robert Morgenthau, "Tax Evasion Nation," *The American Interest* 4, no. 1 (September–October 2008); available online (www.the-american-interest.com/ai2/article-bd.cfm?Id=465&MId=21).
5. Saulny, "Laundering of Billions."
6. See "Bank of America Settles."
7. Ibid.
8. See State of New York Banking Department, "Banking Department Joins Manhattan District Attorney in Announcing Joint Settlement with Israel Discount Bank," press release, December 16, 2005. Available online (www.banking.state.ny.us/pr051216.htm).
9. See "Wells Fargo Skirts."

Manhattan Foreign Exchange

1. Benjamin Weiser, "Federal Prosecutors Charge Man in Money-Laundering Scheme," *New York Times*, March 22, 2003. Available online (http://query.nytimes.com/gst/fullpage.html?res=9C04E1DA1F31F931A15750C0A9659C8B63).
2. "Terror Finance Schemes Busted," Fox News, March 24, 2003. Available online (www.foxnews.com/story/0,2933,81821,00.html).
3. See U.S. Department of Homeland Security, "Investigative Programs: Protecting America's Financial Systems," (n.d.); available online (www.dhs.gov/xlibrary/assets/Financial_Crimes_Press_Kit.doc). See also John Solomon, "Feds Launch New Raids against Financing Schemes," Associated Press, March 22, 2003; available online (www.smdp.com/site/archives/032203.pdf).
4. Khalid Hasan, "Kashmiri Held for Money Laundering out on Bail," *Daily Times*, March 23, 2003. Available online (www.dailytimes.com.pk/default.asp?page=story_23-3-2003_pg7_2).
5. Greg Smith, "Cash for Terror Busts Say Times Sq. Biz Laundered $33 M for Pakistanis," *New York Daily News*, March 22, 2003. Available online (www.nydailynews.com/archives/news/2003/03/22/2003-03-22_cash_for_terror_busts____say_.html).
6. See "Terror Finance Schemes Busted."

Chapter 6

1. John Diamond, "Terror Funding Shifts to Cash," *USA Today*, June 18, 2006. Available online (www.usatoday.com/news/washington/2006-06-18-terror-cash_x.htm).
2. See Asia/Pacific Group on Money Laundering, "Annual Typologies Report: 2003–2004," (n.d.). Available online (apgml.org/frameworks/docs/4/APG%20Typologies%20Yearly%20Report%202003-04%20_public_.pdf).
3. In many countries, customs authorities are not part of the regular law enforcement community and are therefore even less likely to have the resources, training, or authority needed to conduct effective enforcement operations. See FATF, "Detecting and Preventing the Cross-Border Transportation of Cash by Terrorists and Other Criminals: International Best Practices," February 12, 2005. Available online (www.fatf-gafi.org/dataoecd/50/63/34424128.pdf).
4. In this context, "currency" refers to banknotes and coins, and "bearer negotiable instruments" refers to

checks, promissory notes, money orders, and travelers checks,. It should be noted that for the purposes of Special Recommendation IX, gold, precious metals, and precious stones are not included despite their high liquidity and use in certain situations as a means of exchange or transmitting value. See FATF, "Interpretative Notes to the 9 Special Recommendations on Terrorist Financing," (n.d.). Available online (www.fatf-gafi.org/document/53/0,2340,en_32250379_32236947_34261877_1_1_1_1,00.html#insrII).

5. All of these measures apply to bearer negotiable instruments as well (see definition in previous note).
6. See FATF, Interpretative Note to Special Recommendation IX.
7. FATF, "Detecting and Preventing."
8. See FATF, Interpretative Note to Special Recommendation IX.
9. See FATF, "Detecting and Preventing," p. 3.
10. U.S. Treasury Department, *2005 U.S. Money Laundering Threat Assessment* (December 2005), p. 35; available online (www.treas.gov/offices/enforcement/pdf/mlta.pdf). See also Janice Cheryl Beaver, "U.S. International Borders: Brief Facts" (Congressional Research Service, 2006), pp. CRS 1–2; available online (www.fas.org/sgp/crs/misc/RS21729.pdf).
11. See U.S. Treasury, *2005 U.S. Money Laundering Threat Assessment,* p. 33.
12. Ibid.
13. In technical terms, a CMIR must be filed whenever a person "physically transports, mails, ships, or causes to be physically transported, mailed or shipped, currency (U.S. or foreign) or other monetary instruments in an aggregate amount exceeding USD 10,000 at any one time" to or from the United States (the latest version of the CMIR form and definitions are available online at www.fincen.gov/fin105_cmir.pdf). The CMIR requirement does not apply to certain types of financial institutions, including the Federal Reserve, banks, or SEC-registered securities brokers, per 31 CFR 103.23(c). It should also be noted that these same obligations apply equally to both containers and mail. Individuals or entities that use shipping containers are informed of their obligations in a Shippers Export Declaration form (SED).
14. Section 371 of Patriot Act (31 USC 5332)
15. CBP Form 6059B.
16. CBP/ICE have the following powers during investigations: authority to search persons and conveyances (19 USC 482), authority to administer oaths (19 USC 1486), authority to search and seize (19 USC 1581), authority to detain persons (19 USC 1582), and authority to carry weapons, make arrests, and execute warrants (19 USC 1589).
17. This database is known as the Treasury Enforcement Communications System (TECS). It is worth noting that in July 2003, the CMIR became a FinCEN form like other Bank Secrecy Act reporting forms. See FATF, *Third Mutual Evaluation Report on Anti–Money Laundering and Combating the Financing of Terrorism: United States of America* (Paris: FATF, June 23, 2006), p. 76. Available online (www.fatf-gafi.org/dataoecd/44/9/37101772.pdf).
18. See the international money laundering offense section of 18 USC 1956(a)(2). See also 18 USC 2339C (Prohibitions against Terrorist Financing).
19. 31 USC 5317(c).
20. See FATF, *Third Mutual Evaluation Report,* p. 81.
21. All of these seizures were made pursuant to 31 USC 5316, 31 USC 5317, and 31 USC 5332. See ibid., p. 82.
22. See Drug Enforcement Administration, "National Drug Threat Assessment," October 2006. Available online (www.dea.gov/concern/18862/index.htm).

Southeast Asia

1. See Asia/Pacific Group on Money Laundering, "Annual Typologies Report: 2003–2004," (n.d.), p. 34. Available online (apgml.org/frameworks/docs/4/APG%20Typologies%20Yearly%20Report%202003-04%20_public_.pdf).
2. *Transnational Terrorism: The Threat to Australia* (Canberra: Commonwealth of Australia, 2004), p. 68. Available online (www.dfat.gov.au/publications/terrorism/transnational_terrorism.pdf).

3. See Asia/Pacific Group, "Annual Typologies Report," p. 34.
4. For a sampling of this evidence, see the following articles: "Jakarta Forensic Team Finds Possible Bali Link," CNN, August 5, 2003 (available online at www.cnn.com/2003/WORLD/asiapcf/southeast/08/05/indonesia.blast/index.html); "Al-Qaeda Singles Out Australia: Report," *Sydney Morning Herald*, August 12, 2003 (available online at www.smh.com.au/articles/2003/08/12/1060588349256.html); "Marriott Blast Suspects Named," CNN, August 19, 2003 (available online at www.cnn.com/2003/WORLD/asiapcf/southeast/08/19/indonesia.arrests.names); "Severed Head Clue to Jakarta Bomb," BBC, August 9, 2003 (available online at http://news.bbc.co.uk/2/hi/asia-pacific/3134179.stm).

Al-Qaeda Funds Attacks in Turkey

1. "Bin Laden Allegedly Planned Attack in Turkey," Associated Press, December 17, 2003. Available online (www.msnbc.msn.com/id/3735645).
2. It is worth noting that only six Jews were among the dead. See "Film Clue to Turkey Jewish Attack," BBC, November 17, 2003; available online (http://news.bbc.co.uk/2/hi/middle_east/3276549.stm). See also Yigal Schleifer, "Bombed Istanbul Synagogue Reopens, Heartening Turkey's Vulnerable Jews," Jewish Telegraphic Agency, October 12, 2004; available online (www.ujc.org/page.aspx?id=75158).
3. "Film Clue to Turkey Jewish Attack."
4. "Turkey Bomb Suspect Says al Qaeda Was Financier," Associated Press, December 21, 2003; available online (www.ctv.ca/servlet/ArticleNews/story/CTVNews/20031221/turkey_suspect031220?s_name=&no_ads=). See also Peter Brookes, "Al Qaeda's Cash," *New York Post*, December 29, 2003; available online (www.heritage.org/Press/Commentary/ed122903a.cfm).
5. Karl Vick, "Al-Qaeda's Hand in Istanbul Plot," *Washington Post*, February 13, 2007. Available online (www.washingtonpost.com/wp-dyn/content/article/2007/02/12/AR2007021201715_pf.html).
6. "Al Qaeda Associates Jailed for Istanbul Bombings," Agence France-Presse, February 17, 2007. Available online (www.abc.net.au/news/newsitems/200702/s1850227.htm).

Operation Dragon: Largest Single Drug-Money Seizure in History

1. The amount included 205.6 million in U.S. dollars, 200,000 in euros, and 17.3 million in pesos. See "Mexico: World's Largest Drug Cash Seizure Is Larger Than Originally Announced," Associated Press, March 22, 2007. Available online (www.iht.com/articles/ap/2007/03/22/america/LA-GEN-Mexico-Drug-Money.php).
2. U.S. Justice Department, "Statement by Administrator Karen P. Tandy on Two Hundred and Seven Million in Drug Money Seized in Mexico City," March 20, 2007. Available online (www.usdoj.gov/dea/pubs/pressrel/pr032007.html).
3. See Laurence Iliff, "Meth Production Flourishes South of the Border," *Dallas Morning News*, April 28, 2007. Available online (www.fox11az.com/sharedcontent/dws/news/dmn/stories/042807dnintmexmeth.3794852.html). Mexican trafficking organizations operating on both sides of the border are the source of at least 80 percent of the meth consumed in the United States.
4. Ibid. It is also worth noting that Gon became a naturalized Mexican citizen in 2002. See Mark Stevenson and Michael Rubinkam, "Biggest Cash Seizure In History — $205M — in Mexico City," Associated Press, July 2, 2007. Available online (http://seattletimes.nwsource.com/html/nationworld/2003771087_webmillions02.html).
5. See "Mexico: World's Largest Drug Cash Seizure." See also Paul Duggan and Ernesto Londoño, "Not Your Average Drug Bust," *Washington Post*, July 25, 2007; available online (www.washingtonpost.com/wp-dyn/content/article/2007/07/24/AR2007072400150.html). See also Iliff, "Meth Production Flourishes."
6. Duggan and Londoño, "Not Your Average Drug Bust."
7. U.S. Justice Department, "Affidavit in Support of Complaint and Arrest Warrant For Zhenli Ye Gon," (n.d.).

Available online (www.washingtonpost.com/wp-srv/metro/gon-affidavit.pdf).

8. "U.S. Nabs Alleged Mexican Meth Lord," CBS News, July 24, 2007. Available online (www.cbsnews.com/stories/2007/07/24/national/main3092132.shtml?source=related_story).
9. "Authorities Nab Alleged Mexico Drug Kingpin Zhenli Ye Gon in Maryland," Associated Press, July 24, 2007. Available online (www.foxnews.com/story/0,2933,290520,00.html#).
10. Stevenson and Rubinkam, "Biggest Cash Seizure in History."

Who Is Responsible for Stopping Smugglers?

1. See 19 USC 1595, 31 USC 5316, and 31 USC 5317. CBP and ICE also have the authority to stop or restrain unreported or falsely reported currency for a reasonable time (31 USC 5316, 31 USC 5317, and 31 USC 5332).

American Contractor in Iraq Busted for Cash Smuggling

1. "Air Force Contract Augmentation Program (AFCAP)," GlobalSecurity.org, (n.d.); available online (www.globalsecurity.org/military/agency/usaf/afcap.htm). See also "Documents Say Contractor Shipped Home Cash in Box," *San Antonio Express News*, March 5, 2008; available online (www.mysanantonio.com/news/MYSA030608_01A_fraud_38e1e38_html91.html).
2. See "Documents Say Contractor."
3. "Man Pleads Guilty to Cash Smuggling," *San Antonio Express News*, October 10, 2008. Available online (www.mysanantonio.com/news/local_news/Man_pleads_guilty_to_cash_smuggling.html).
4. Jeremy Landers, "Iraq Contractor Indicted in Cash Smuggling Case," Associated Press, March 6, 2008.
5. "Man Pleads Guilty to Cash Smuggling."
6. Ibid.
7. Ibid.

Chapter 7

1. Although quantifying the exact amount of money laundered through trade is impossible, U.S. officials estimate losses of tens of billions of dollars in tax revenue annually due to "over- and under-invoicing" products entering and leaving the country. See U.S. State Department, "2003 International Narcotics Control Strategy Report," March 2004. Available online (www.state.gov/p/inl/rls/nrcrpt/2003/vol2/html/29910.htm).
2. See Rand Beers (assistant secretary for international narcotics and law enforcement affairs) and Francis Taylor (ambassador-at-large for counterterrorism), joint testimony before the Senate Judiciary Subcommittee on Technology, Terrorism, and Government Information, hearing on "Narco-Terror: The Worldwide Connection between Drugs and Terror," March 13, 2002. Available online (http://judiciary.senate.gov/hearings/testimony.cfm?id=196&wit_id=331).
3. See FATF, *Trade Based Money Laundering* (Paris: FATF, June 23, 2006), p. 1. Available online (www.fatf-gafi.org/dataoecd/60/25/37038272.pdf).
4. Ibid. According to the World Trade Organization, global merchandise trade now exceeds $9 trillion per year, and global trade in services accounts for a further $2 trillion. See World Trade Organization, *International Trade Statistics 2005*; available online (www.wto.org/English/res_e/statis_e/its2005_e/its05_toc_e.htm).
5. See U.S. State Department, "2003 International Narcotics Control Strategy Report."
6. Loren Yager (director, international affairs and trade, U.S. General Accountability Office), testimony before the Senate Governmental Affairs Subcommittee on Oversight of Government Management, Restructuring, and the District of Colombia, February 13, 2002. See also U.S. Treasury Department, *2005 U.S. Money Laundering Threat Assessment* (December 2005), p. 43; available online (www.treas.gov/offices/enforcement/pdf/mlta.pdf).
7. David Kaplan, "The Golden Age of Crime: Why International Drug Traffickers Are Invading the Global Gold Trade," *U.S. News & World Report*, November 29, 1999.

8. Ibid.
9. John Cassara, interview by author, May 2009.
10. See U.S. Treasury, *2005 U.S. Money Laundering Threat Assessment,* p. 43.
11. See the initiative's main website (www.kimberleyprocess.com).
12. Cassara, interview by author.
13. Robert Block, "Policing Trade to Nab Terrorists: New Effort Spots Illegal Exports Masking Money Laundering," *Wall Street Journal,* March 11, 2006.
14. See the ICE website (www.ice.gov). It is worth noting that TBML is always customs fraud, but customs fraud is not always TBML. For example, if money is being moved for tax evasion purposes or asset flight but does not stem from illicit sources, then it is simply customs fraud.
15. See the DEA website (www.dea.gov).
16. See FinCEN's website (www.fincen.gov).
17. See both agencies' websites (www.cbp.gov and www.commerce.gov).
18. Also known as Form 8300; see the IRS website (www.irs.gov).
19. The "interim" tag was applied so that FinCEN could solicit additional public comment; the rule is nevertheless considered final and binding.
20. See Code of Federal Regulations, 31 CFR 103.140 (70 FR 33702 [2005]). Available online (www.fincen.gov/statutes_regs/frn/pdf/antimoneylaundering060905.pdf).
21. The rule only recommends that dealers file SARs. Separately, before this rule was passed, dealers were obligated to report any transaction they conducted over $10,000 by filing IRS Form 8300. See 26 USC 6050I and 31 CFR 103.30.
22. See U.S. State Department, "2005 International Narcotics Control Strategy Report," March 2005. Available online (www.state.gov/p/inl/rls/nrcrpt/2005/vol2/html/42381.htm).
23. U.S. Immigration and Customs Enforcement, "ICE Launches Trade Transparency Unit in Mexico City as Part of Bi-lateral Cooperation with Mexico Customs," press release, June 12, 2008. Available online (www.ice.gov/pi/news/newsreleases/articles/080612mexicocity.htm). See also U.S. State Department, "2005 International Narcotics Control Strategy Report."
24. See FATF, *Trade Based Money Laundering,* p. 21.
25. See ICE, "ICE Partners with Argentina, Brazil and Paraguay in Creating Trade Transparency Units to Combat Money Laundering & Crimes," press release, March 13, 2006; available online (http://useu.usmission.gov/Article.asp?ID=242FAE42-FE2D-48D5-A4AB-FD07DE301770). See also Jerry Seper, "Teams to Target Financial Crimes," *Washington Times,* March 24, 2006.
26. Block, "Policing Trade to Nab Terrorists."
27. The software was developed by Data Mining International Inc. (see www.dataminininternational.com). See also U.S. State Department, "2005 International Narcotics Control Strategy Report."
28. Block, "Policing Trade to Nab Terrorists."
29. See U.S. State Department, "2005 International Narcotics Control Strategy Report."
30. Ibid.
31. See U.S. Immigration and Customs Enforcement, "Trade-Based Money Laundering," (n.d.). Available online (www.ice.gov/partners/financial/topics.htm).

Terrorist Groups and Latin America's Black Market Peso Exchange

1. Karen Tandy (administrator, Drug Enforcement Administration), testimony before the U.S. Senate Caucus on International Narcotics Control, March 4, 2004; available online (www.dea.gov/pubs/cngrtest/ct030404.htm). The DEA believes that Mexican and Colombian drug traffickers are responsible for most wholesale-level drug money laundering in the United States. Together, these organizations generate, remove, and launder between $8.3 billion and $24.9 annually from marijuana, methamphetamine, heroin, and

cocaine sales. See National Drug Intelligence Center, "National Drug Threat Assessment 2007," October 2006; available online (www.usdoj.gov/ndic/pubs21/21137/mlaund.htm).

2. Rand Beers (assistant secretary for international narcotics and law enforcement affairs) and Francis Taylor (ambassador-at-large for counterterrorism), joint testimony before the Senate Judiciary Subcommittee on Technology, Terrorism, and Government Information, hearing on "Narco-Terror: The Worldwide Connection between Drugs and Terror," March 13, 2002. Available online (http://judiciary.senate.gov/hearings/testimony.cfm?id=196&wit_id=331).
3. Ibid.
4. "Police Link 17 'Drug Traders' in Curacao with Hizbullah," Agence France-Presse, April 30, 2009; available online (www.dailystar.com.lb/article.asp?edition_id=1&categ_id=2&article_id=101522). See also "Gang Allied to Hezbollah Rounded Up in the Caribbean," *NIS News Bulletin,* April 30, 2009; available online (www.nisnews.nl/public/300409_2.htm).

Al-Qaeda Uses Gold to Move Value

1. For more on al-Qaeda's abuse of the gold sector, see the following: U.S. General Accounting Office, "Terrorist Financing: U.S. Agencies Should Systematically Assess Terrorists' Use of Alternative Financing Mechanisms," December 12, 2003 (available online at www.gao.gov/htext/d04163.html); Douglas Farah, "Al Qaeda's Road Paved with Gold," *Washington Post,* February 17, 2002 (available online at www.washingtonpost.com/ac2/wp-dyn/A22303-2002Feb16?language=printer); "Al-Qaeda Gold Moved to Sudan," BBC, September 4, 2002 (available online at http://news.bbc.co.uk/2/hi/middle_east/2233989.stm); Syed Saleem Shahzad, "From the al-Qaeda Puzzle, A Picture Emerges," *Asia Times,* September 11, 2002 (available online at www.atimes.com/atimes/South_Asia/DI11Df02.html). For a detailed study of al-Qaeda's use of both diamonds and gold, see *For a Few Dollars More: How al-Qaeda Moved into the Diamond Trade* (London: Global Witness, April 2003); available online (www.allafrica.com/peaceafrica/resources/view/00010304.pdf). More generally, FATF's Annual Typologies Report of 2002–2003 contains a section on the use of gold and diamonds in money laundering (see www.oecd.org/LongAbstract/0,3425,en_32250379_32237277_34037959_32247552_1_1_1,00.html)
2. See U.S. General Accounting Office, "Terrorist Financing." See also *For a Few Dollars More.*
3. Commonwealth Secretariat, "Money Laundering: Special Problems of Parallel Economies," paper presented at the Joint Meeting of Commonwealth Finance and Law Officials on Money Laundering, London, June 1–2, 1998.

Operation White Dollar

1. See U.S. Drug Enforcement Administration, "U.S., Colombia, Canada and United Kingdom Jointly Announce Dismantling of Massive International Money-Laundering Ring," press release, May 4 2004. Available online (www.usdoj.gov/dea/pubs/pressrel/pr050404.html).
2. Ibid.
3. See U.S. Drug Enforcement Administration, "U.S. Announces Extradition of Three Defendants from Canada on International Money Laundering Charges," press release, January 3, 2008. Available online (www.usdoj.gov/usao/nys/pressreleases/January08/whitedollarextraditionpr.pdf).
4. See U.S. Drug Enforcement Administration, "U.S. Announces Extradition." See also Paul Cherry, "Montreal-Area Men in N.Y. Court on Money-Laundering Charges," Canada.com, January 3, 2008; available online (www.canada.com/calgaryherald/story.html?id=27240614-284c-43f0-a3e8-5611da28d723&k=7407).
5. See Royal Canadian Mounted Police, "Five Montreal Residents Arrested by the RCMP in Operation White Dollar," press release, May 4, 2004. Available online (www.rcmp-grc.gc.ca/qc/comm/archives/2004/mai04/040503_e.htm).
6. See U.S. State Department, "International Narcotics Control Strategy Report," March 2005. Available online (www.state.gov/p/inl/rls/nrcrpt/2005/vol2/html/42382.htm).

Operation Deluge

1. In Brazil, this operation was referred to as "Operação Dilúvio." See Stephanie Ayres, "Investigation by New 'Trade Transparency Unit' Leads to Hundreds of Raids in Brazil," Financial Crime News, January 8, 2007. Available online (http://home.att.net/~fcwriter/news131.htm).
2. Kenneth Rijock, "Operation Deluge, Brazilian-American Joint Operation, Shuts Down $234m trade Fraud Scheme," World-Check, August 21, 2006. Available online (www.world-check.com/articles/2006/08/21/brazil-and-us-shut-down-234m-trade-fraud-scheme).
3. "79 Arrested in Brazil's Biggest Foreign Trade Fraud," *People's Daily Online,* August 17, 2006. Available online (http://english.people.com.cn/200608/17/eng20060817_294109.html).
4. See U.S. Immigration and Customs Enforcement, "ICE Assists Brazilian Officials in Dismantling $200 Million Trade Fraud Scheme," news release, August 18, 2006. Available online (www.dataminingintern ational.com/OperationDelugeBrazil_060818dc.pdf).
5. Ibid.
6. Francesco Neves, "Brazilian Police Have No Rest: They Bust International Importing Gang," *Brazzil Magazine,* August 16, 2006. Available online (www.brazzilmag.com/content/view/7077).
7. See U.S. Immigration and Customs Enforcement, "ICE Assists Brazilian Officials."

Chapter 8

1. Affidavit by Senior Special Agent David Kane (U.S. Immigration and Customs Enforcement), *United States of America v. Soliman S. Biheiri,* U.S. District Court for the Eastern District of Virginia, Alexandria Division, case #03-365-A, August 14, 2003.
2. By July 2005, Treasury had designated 41 charities worldwide, with 36 based abroad and five based in the United States. In addition, two of the 36 international organizations had offices on U.S. soil. In 2006, Treasury blocked the assets of a sixth U.S.-based charity: Kindhearts International, based in Toledo, Ohio. Once a charity is designated, its U.S. assets are frozen, and American nationals are prohibited from transacting with it. See U.S. Treasury Department, "Protecting Charitable Organizations," (n.d.). Available online (www.ustreas.gov/offices/enforcement/key-issues/protecting/charities_exec-orders.shtml).
3. Robert Looney, "The Mirage of Terrorist Financing: The Case of Islamic Charities," *Strategic Insights* 5, no. 3 (March 2006). Available online (www.ccc.nps.navy.mil/si/2006/Mar/looneyMar06.asp).
4. Ibid.
5. See FATF, "Combating the Abuse of Non-Profit Organizations: International Best Practices," October 11, 2002, p. 1. Available online (www.fatf-gafi.org/dataoecd/39/19/34033761.pdf).
6. According to FATF's "Best Practices" on the subject, government oversight should be flexible, effective, and proportional to the risk of abuse. See ibid.
7. FATF, "Interpretative Notes to the 9 Special Recommendations on Terrorist Financing," Interpretative Note to Special Recommendation VIII, (n.d.). Available online (www.fatf-gafi.org/document/53/0,2340,en_32250379_32236947_34261877_1_1_1_1,00.html#insrII).
8. Per FATF's Interpretative Note to Special Recommendation VIII, this review should include the participation of all relevant agencies—e.g., financial intelligence units, tax authorities, intelligence and law enforcement agencies, and so forth. Thereafter, governments should conduct periodic reassessments.
9. Ibid.
10. Ibid.
11. Ibid.
12. See U.S. Treasury, "Protecting Charitable Organizations."
13. See FATF, *Third Mutual Evaluation Report on Anti–Money Laundering and Combating the Financing of Terrorism: United States of America* (Paris: FATF, June 23, 2006), p. 240; available online (www.fatf-gafi.org/dataoecd/44/9/37101772.pdf). According to the National Center for Charitable Statistics, a private sector watchdog organization, there are nearly 1.5 million NPOs in the United States. See the "Frequently Asked

Questions" page on the Foundation Center website (www.foundationcenter.org/getstarted/faqs/html/howmany.html).

14. For purposes of this chapter, public charities and private foundations are collectively referred to as charities, charitable organizations, or the charitable sector.
15. In addition, approximately 350,000 religiously affiliated or smaller public charities are exempt from applying to the IRS. See FATF, *Third Mutual Evaluation Report,* p. 240.
16. Public charities use Form 990, private foundations use Form 990-PF. Organizations with less than $25,000 in gross receipts are exempted from this annual filing requirement, along with churches, church associations, and certain church-affiliated organizations. Regarding foreign organizations, only those with less than $25,000 of U.S.-based income are exempt from IRS recognition, along with any specific organizations exempted at the IRS commissioner's discretion. See FATF, *Third Mutual Evaluation Report.*
17. Ibid., p. 248.
18. Other important watchdogs include the Evangelical Council for Financial Accountability (ECFA), the International Committee for Fundraising Organizations, Guidestar, the Better Business Bureau (BBB) Wise Giving Alliance, the National Council on Charitable Statistics (NCCS), the National Center on Philanthropy and Law of the New York University Law School, and the Center on Philanthropy at Indiana University.
19. See U.S. Treasury, "Protecting Charitable Organizations."
20. OFAC may make exceptions at its discretion, authorizing certain individuals or entities to deal with a designated organization. For further elaboration on risk in the charitable sector, readers are advised to consult the OFAC Risk Matrix. See U.S. Treasury Department, "Risk Matrix for the Charitable Sector," (n.d.). Available online (http://treasury.gov/offices/enforcement/ofac/policy/charity_risk_matrix.pdf).

Saudi Arabia

1. "Saudis Said Failing to Crack Down on al Qaeda Donors," Reuters, September 12, 2007. Available online (http://in.reuters.com/article/worldNews/idINIndia-29474720070912).
2. Saudi-US Relations Information Service (SUSRIS), "Saudi Arabia and the Fight against Terror Financing" (digest of House testimony by J. Cofer Black, Juan Zarate, and Thomas Harrington, March 24, 2004), March 29, 2004. Available online (www.saudi-us-relations.org/articles/2004/ioi/040329a-testimony-black.html).
3. See U.S. Senate Select Committee on Intelligence, "Implementing Recommendations of the 9/11 Commission Act of 2007," August 3, 2007. Available online (http://intelligence.senate.gov/laws/pl11053.pdf).
4. See U.S. State Department, "2007 International Narcotics Control Strategy Report," March 2008. Available online (www.state.gov/p/inl/rls/nrcrpt/2008/vol2/html/101353.htm).
5. See 9/11 Commission, *The 9/11 Commission Report* (Washington, DC: U.S. Government Printing Office, 2004), Available online (www.9-11commission.gov/report/911Report.pdf).
6. See Christopher Blanchard and Alfred Prados, *Saudi Arabia: Terrorist Financing Issues* (Washington, DC: Congressional Research Service, September 14, 2007). Available online (www.fas.org/sgp/crs/terror/RL32499.pdf).
7. See Blanchard and Prados, *Saudi Arabia: Terrorist Financing Issues.*
8. See Jonathan Winer (former U.S. deputy assistant secretary of state), "Origins, Organization and Prevention of Terrorist Finance," testimony before the U.S. Senate Committee on Governmental Affairs, July 31, 2003; available online (www.iwar.org.uk/cyberterror/resources/terror-financing/073103winer.htm). Saudi officials estimate that the amount sent abroad annually is only $100 million. See remarks by Adel al-Jubeir (foreign affairs adviser to Crown Prince Abdullah) in "U.S. and Saudi Officials Hold a News Conference on a Major Development in the War on Terrorism," Political Transcript Wire, June 2, 2004. Available online (www.accessmylibrary.com/coms2/summary_0286-2886896_ITM).
9. "Saudi Arabia to Impose Stricter Controls on Charities," VOA News, December 4, 2002. Available online (www.voanews.com/english/archive/2002-12/a-2002-12-04-15-Saudi.cfm).
10. See "Written Testimony of Mallory Factor," U.S. Senate Committee on Banking, Housing, and Urban Affairs, September 29, 2004. Available online (http://banking.senate.gov/public/_files/factor.pdf).

11. See Embassy of Saudi Arabia, "Saudi Arabian Monetary Agency Implements New Regulations Regarding Charities," Washington, D.C., June 12, 2003. Available online (www.saudiembassy.net/2003News/Press/PressDetail.asp?cYear=2003&cIndex=99).
12. See Blanchard and Prados, *Saudi Arabia: Terrorist Financing Issues.*
13. See "U.S. and Saudi Officials Hold a News Conference."
14. See Daniel Glaser (deputy assistant secretary, Office of Terrorist Financing and Financial Crime, U.S. Treasury Department), testimony before the Senate Judiciary Committee, November 8, 2005. Available online (www.treasury.gov/press/releases/js3011.htm).
15. See U.S. Treasury Department, "Treasury Announces Joint Action with Saudi Arabia Against Four Branches of al-Haramain In The Fight Against Terrorist Financing," January 22, 2004. Available online (www.treasury.gov/press/releases/js1108.htm).
16. See U.S. Treasury, "Protecting Charitable Organizations: Additional Background Information on Charities Designated under Executive Order 13224," (n.d.). Available online (www.treas.gov/offices/enforcement/key-issues/protecting/charities_execorder_13224-a.shtml).
17. According to the Saudi embassy, "The total amount of the assistance that has been extended to the Palestinians by the government and people of the Kingdom of Saudi Arabia is close to ten billion riyals. Government aid has reached SR 7.44 billion [USD 1.99 billion], including SR 4.73 billion [USD 1.26 billion] in non-repayable grants issued prior to the 1993 Palestinian-Israeli agreement. Following this agreement the Kingdom committed SR 1.13 billion [USD 300 million] in support of the Palestinian Authority. This sum was paid through the Saudi Development Fund for the financing of development projects implemented by international organizations such as the Islamic Development Bank." See Embassy of Saudi Arabia, "Kingdom's Aid to Palestenians [sic] Nears Ten Billion Saudi Riyals," Washington, D.C., May 2, 2002. Available online (www.saudiembassy.net/2002News/News/ForDetail.asp?cIndex=1122).
18. See Embassy of Saudi Arabia, "Humanitarian Relief Handed Over to Palestinian Officials in Kingdom," Washington, D.C., December 31, 2003. Available online (www.saudiembassy.net/2003News/News/ForDetail.asp?cIndex=1189).
19. "Saudi Arabia to Fund Construction of 100 Housing Units in West Bank," Middle East and North Africa Business Report, September 2006. Available online (http://findarticles.com/p/articles/mi_hb5614/is_200609/ai_n23617832).
20. Ben Barber, "Saudi Millions Finance Terror against Israel," *Washington Times*, May 7, 2002. Available online http://nucnews.net/nucnews/2002nn/0205nn/020507nn.htm#550). Israel also released allegedly seized documents that featured "the letterhead of the 'Saudi Arabian Committee for Support of the Al Quds Intifada.'"
21. See Embassy of Saudi Arabia, "The Kingdom of Saudi Arabia Responds to False Israeli Charges," Washington, D.C., May 6, 2002; available online (www.saudiembassy.net/2002News/Press/PressDetail.asp?cYear=2002&cIndex=36). See also Embassy of Saudi Arabia, "Saudi Arabia Doesn't Reward Terrorism," Washington, D.C., May 11, 2002; available online (http://saudiembassy.net/2002News/News/TerDetail.asp?cIndex=45).
22. See Blanchard and Prados, *Saudi Arabia: Terrorist Financing Issues.*
23. See Embassy of Saudi Arabia, "Saudi Arabia Does Not Support Terrorism," Washington, D.C., May 10, 2002. Available online (www.saudiembassy.net/2002News/Statements/TransDetail.asp?cIndex=149).
24. Don Van Natta Jr. and Timothy O'Brien, "Flow of Saudis' Cash to Hamas Is Scrutinized," *New York Times*, September 17, 2003. Available online (http://query.nytimes.com/gst/fullpage.html?res=9D03E4DB143AF934A2575AC0A9659C8B63).
25. "Saudi Official Condemns Terrorism, But Not Hamas," Agence France-Presse, June 12, 2003.
26. See U.S. State Department, *Patterns of Global Terrorism 2001* (May 2002). Available online (www.state.gov/s/ct/rls/crt/2001).
27. See U.S. State Department, Office of the Coordinator for Counterterrorism, *Country Reports on Terrorism 2005* (April 2006). Available online (www.state.gov/documents/organization/65462.pdf).

28. See Blanchard and Prados, *Saudi Arabia: Terrorist Financing Issues.*
29. See U.S. Treasury Department, "Testimony of Stuart Levey, Under Secretary Office of Terrorism and Financial Intelligence U.S. Department of the Treasury Before the Senate Committee on Banking, Housing, and Urban Affairs," July 13, 2005. Available online (www.treasury.gov/press/releases/js2629.htm).
30. "Saudis Reportedly Funding Iraqi Sunni Insurgents," Associated Press, December 8, 2006. Available online (www.usatoday.com/news/world/iraq/2006-12-08-saudis-sunnis_x.htm).
31. Ghaith Abdul-Ahad, "Outside Iraq but Deep in the Fight," *Washington Post*, June 8, 2005. Available online (www.washingtonpost.com/wp-dyn/content/article/2005/06/07/AR2005060702026.html).
32. Tarek el-Tablawy, "Iraq Minister Urges Neighbors on Militants," Associated Press, May 11, 2005. Available online (www.kerkuk.net/haberler/haber.aspx?dil=2057&metin=200505111).

Foundation of Terror: Benevolence International

1. These mission statements appeared on BIF's website (www.benevolence.org). Although the original site is no longer in operation, its content is intermittently accessible via two other websites: the "Wayback Machine" tool (www.archive.org/web/web.php) and IslamicArchitecture.org (www.islamicarchitecture.org/islam/relief-organizations/Benevolence-International-Foundation.html).
2. See U.S. Justice Department, "Benevolence Director Indicted for Racketeering Conspiracy; Providing Material Support to Al Qaeda and Other Violent Group," press release, October 9, 2002; available online (www.usdoj.gov/usao/iln/pr/chicago/2002/pr1009_01.pdf). See also Rohan Gunaratna, *Inside al-Qaeda* (New York: Berkeley Publishing Group, 2002), pp. 112–113.
3. See U.S. Justice Department, "Benevolence Director Indicted."
4. Ibid.
5. "Feds Arrest Man Linked to 'Dirty Bomb' Suspect," CNN, June 15, 2002; available online (http://archives.cnn.com/2002/US/06/15/padilla.associate/index.html). See also Curt Anderson, "Defense Urges Acquittal in Padilla Trial," Associated Press, August 14, 2007; available online (www.usatoday.com/news/topstories/2007-08-13-2070374513_x.htm).
6. See United Nations, "1267 Consolidated List," October 17 2008; available online (www.un.org/sc/committees/1267/consoltablelist.shtml). See also "BIF Activities in the Current Crisis," Relief Web, (n.d); available online (www.reliefweb.int/rw/rwb.nsf/db900sid/OCHA-64CDKQ?OpenDocument).
7. See U.S. Treasury Department, "Treasury Designates Benevolence International Foundation and Related Entities as Financiers of Terrorism," press release, November 19, 2002. Available online (www.ustreas.gov/press/releases/po3632.htm).
8. Georg Mascolo and Erich Follath, "Osama's Road to Riches and Terror," Spiegel Online, June 6, 2005; available online (www.spiegel.de/international/spiegel/0,1518,359690,00.html). See also "UK Freezes Assets of 'Bin Laden Charity," BBC, November 19, 2002; available online (http://news.bbc.co.uk/2/hi/uk_news/politics/2491681.stm).
9. See U.S. Treasury, "Treasury Designates Benevolence."
10. Ibid. See also Kevin Johnson and Richard Willing, "Bosnian Evidence Makes FBI Case," *USA Today*, May 1, 2002; available online (www.usatoday.com/news/sept11/2002/05/01/charity-terrorism.htm).
11. Dan Eggen and Julie Tate, "U.S. Campaign Produces Few Convictions on Terrorism Charges," *Washington Post*, June 12, 2005. Available online (www.washingtonpost.com/wp-dyn/content/article/2005/06/11/AR2005061100381.html).
12. Ibid.

International Pariah: Tamil Tigers and the Tamils Rehabilitation Organization

1. Preeti Bhattacharji, *Liberation Tigers of Tamil Eelam* (New York: Council on Foreign Relations, 2008). Available online (www.cfr.org/publication/9242).

2. "Tamil Tiger Credit Card Racketeers Busted in New York," *Asian Tribune*, October 17, 2007. Available online (www.asiantribune.com/index.php?q=node/7841).
3. Tom Whipple, "British Tamils Are Intimidated into Giving Money to Terrorists," *The Times*, February 5, 2007. Available online (www.timesonline.co.uk/tol/news/uk/article1329397.ece).
4. "Frozen TRO Funds in Local Banks Just a Trickle," *Sunday Times* (Sri Lanka), November 25, 2007. Available online (www.sundaytimes.lk/071125/News/RelatedLink-news3.html).
5. See U.S. Treasury Department, "Treasury Targets Charity Covertly Supporting Violence in Sri Lanka," press release, November 15, 2007. Available online (www.treasury.gov/press/releases/hp683.htm).

Holy Land Foundation: Humanitarian Relief and Terrorism Financing

1. Robert Barnes, "Case against Islamic Charity Opens," *Washington Post*, July 25, 2007. Available online (www.washingtonpost.com/wp-dyn/content/article/2007/07/24/AR2007072402273.html).
2. See U.S. Treasury, "Protecting Charitable Organizations: Additional Background Information on Charities Designated under Executive Order 13224," (n.d.). Available online (www.ustreas.gov/offices/enforcement/key-issues/protecting/charities_execorder_13224-e.shtml).
3. Ibid.
4. Jordan Hirsch, "Deception and Discord in Dallas: The Undoing of a Flagship Anti-Terrorism Case," *The Current* (Spring 2008). Available online (www.columbia.edu/cu/current/articles/spring2008a/deception-discord.html).
5. "Hamas Leader Refutes 'Untrue' U.S. Terror Charges," *Islamonline & News*, December 19, 2002. Available online (www.islamonline.net/English/News/2002-12/19/article12.shtml).
6. See U.S. Treasury Department, Office of Foreign Assets Control, "Specially Designated Nationals and Blocked Persons," October 2, 2008; available online (www.ustreas.gov/offices/enforcement/ofac/sdn/t11sdn.pdf). See also U.S. Treasury Department, "Statement of Secretary Paul O'Neill on the Blocking of Hamas Financiers' Assets," December 4, 2001; available online (www.ustreas.gov/press/releases/po837.htm). See also U.S. Treasury, "Protecting Charitable Organizations."
7. See European Union, "Council Common Position 2005/936/CFSP," December 21, 2005. Available online (http://eur-lex.europa.eu/LexUriServ/site/en/oj/2005/l_340/l_34020051223en00800084.pdf).
8. Barnes, "Case against Islamic Charity Opens."
9. Eric Lichtblau, "Islamic Charity Says F.B.I. Falsified Evidence against It," *New York Times*, July 27, 2004. Available online (www.nytimes.com/2004/07/27/politics/27muslim.html?pagewanted=all).
10 Jason Trahan and Michael Grabell, "Judge Declares Mistrial in Holy Land Foundation Case," *Dallas Morning News*, October 22, 2007. Available online (www.dallasnews.com/sharedcontent/dws/news/localnews/stories/102207dnmetholyland.1878fd716.html).
11. Jason Trahan and Tanya Eiserer, "Holy Land Foundation Defendants Guilty on All Counts," *Dallas Morning News*, November 25, 2008. Available online (www.dallasnews.com/sharedcontent/dws/news/localnews/stories/112508dnmetholylandverdicts.1e5022504.html).

Chapter 9

1. Paul Allan Schott, *Reference Guide to Anti–Money Laundering and Combating the Financing of Terrorism* (Washington, DC: World Bank, 2006), p. V-1. Available online (www1.worldbank.org/finance/html/amlcft/referenceguide.htm).
2. FATF, Recommendation 1, in "The 40 Recommendations." Available online at www.fatf-gafi.org/document/28/0,2340,en 32250379_32236930_33658140_1_1_1_1,00.html#40recs).
3. See United Nations, "Convention against Illicit Traffic in Narcotic Drugs and Psychotropic Substances," article 3, sections b, c, and i, 1988; available online (www.unodc.org/pdf/convention_1988_en.pdf). See also United Nations, "UN Convention against Transnational Organized Crime," articles 6 and 1, November

2, 2000; available online (www.unodc.org/adhoc/palermo/convmain.html).

4. Relevant provisions include article 3(1)(b)(i), 3(1)(b)(ii), and (3)(c)(i). See UN, "Convention against Illicit Traffic."
5. Relevant provisions include article 2(a). See UN, "UN Convention against Transnational Organized Crime."
6. The 20 predicate offenses include (1) participation in an organized criminal group and racketeering; (2) terrorism, including terrorism financing; (3) trafficking in human beings and migrant smuggling; (4) sexual exploitation, including sexual exploitation of children; (5) illicit trafficking in narcotic drugs and psychotropic substances; (6) illicit arms trafficking; (7) illicit trafficking in stolen and other goods; (8) corruption and bribery; (9) fraud; (10) counterfeiting currency; (11) counterfeiting and piracy of products; (12) environmental crime; (13) murder or grievous bodily injury; (14) kidnapping, illegal restraint, and hostage taking; (15) robbery or theft; (16) smuggling; (17) extortion; (18) forgery; (19) piracy; and (20) insider trading and market manipulation. It is worth nothing that the three Vienna categories described earlier are applicable to FATF's predicate offenses. See FATF, "Key Topics, 40 Recommendations Glossary," (n.d.). Available online (www.fatf-gafi.org/glossary/0,3414,en_32250379_32236889_35433764_1_1_1_1,00.html#34277114).
7. See Moses Naim, *Illicit: How Smugglers, Traffickers and Copycats Are Hijacking the Global Economy* (New York: Doubleday, 2005).
8. Schott, *Reference Guide,* chapter V, p. V-9.
9. Examples of categories of serious offenses include "indictable offenses" (as opposed to summary offenses), "felonies" (as opposed to misdemeanors), and "crimes" (as opposed to délits). In all likelihood, if a country were to use the threshold system, it would have many more than 20 predicate offenses. Ibid., pp. V-8, V-9.
10. See FATF Recommendation 37.
11. See FATF Recommendations 1 and 2.
12. It is important to underscore that administrative actions such as asset freezing should not delay or preclude the criminal process—courts should have be given the opportunity to put terrorists behind bars whenever possible. See FATF, "Interpretative Notes to the 9 Special Recommendations on Terrorist Financing," Interpretative Note to Special Recommendation II, (n.d.). Available online (www.fatf-gafi.org/document/53/0,2340,en_32250379_32236947_34261877_1_1_1_1,00.html#insrII).
13. To further assist countries in implementing the recommendations, FATF has gone to extraordinary lengths to provide standardized definitions for terms such as "funds," "terrorists," "terrorist acts," "terrorist financing," and "terrorist organizations." See FATF, Interpretative Note to Special Recommendation II.
14. Title 18 USC 1956 and 1957, Money Laundering Control Act of 1986.
15. FATF, *Third Mutual Evaluation Report on Anti–Money Laundering and Combating the Financing of Terrorism: United States of America* (Paris: FATF, June 23, 2006), pp. 85. Available online (www.fatf-gafi.org/dataoecd/44/9/37101772.pdf).
16. Relevant articles of the Vienna Convention include 3(1)(b)(i)-(ii); relevant articles of Palermo include 6(1)(a)(i)-(ii).
17. Predicate offenses are listed in section 1956(c)(7). All of the "Racketeer Influenced and Corrupt Organization" (RICO) predicates listed in 18 USC 1961(1) are included as well.
18. Namely, piracy and insider trading/market manipulation. See FATF, *Third Mutual Evaluation Report,* p. 32.
19. The following eight offenses are not included: (1) participation in an organized criminal group and racketeering; (2) illicit trafficking in stolen and other goods; (3) fraud which is not fraud against a foreign bank; (4) counterfeiting currency; (5) counterfeiting and piracy of products; (6) environmental crime; (7) forgery; and (8) piracy. See FATF, *Third Mutual Evaluation Report,* p. 33.
20. Ibid.
21. *Report on the Activities of the Committee on Finance of the United States Senate during the 110th Congress* (Report 111–13) (Washington, DC: U.S. Government Printing Office, March 31, 2009), p. 48; available online (http://frwebgate.access.gpo.gov/cgi-bin/getdoc.cgi?dbname=111_cong_reports&docid=f:sr013.111.pdf). See also "Combating Money Laundering and Terrorist Financing Act of 2006," (n.d.); available online (www.govtrack.us/congress/bill.xpd?bill=s109-2402).

22. 18 USC 2339A. Enacted in September 1994, this law came into effect in April 1996.
23. 18 USC 2339B. Enacted by Congress and signed by the president in April 1996, and implemented with State Department designations of FTOs on October 8, 1997.
24. 18 USC 2339C(a). Enacted June 25, 2002.
25. Ibid.
26. See 18 USC 1956(c)(7)(D).
27. See 18 USC 2. Available online (www4.law.cornell.edu/uscode/html/uscode18/usc_sec_18_00000002----000-.html).
28. 18 USC 3286.
29. Prosecutions under Executive Order 13224 operate as alternatives to prosecutions under 18 USC 2339A, 2339B, and 2339C.
30. See FATF, *Third Mutual Evaluation Report*, p. 43.

Latin America's Tri-Border Area

1. Lt. Col. Philip Abbott, "Terrorist Threat in the Tri-Border Area: Myth or Reality?," *Military Review* (September–October 2004). Available online (www.army.mil/professionalwriting/volumes/volume3/january_2005/1_05_4.html).
2. See U.S. State Department, "2008 International Narcotics Control Strategy Report," March 2008; available online (www.state.gov/p/inl/rls/nrcrpt/2008/vol2/html/101353.htm). See also John Price, "International Terrorism in Latin America, A Broad and Costly Security Risk," *InfoAmericas*, October 2001; available online (http://tendencias.infoamericas.com/ article_archive/ 2001/1001/1001_regional_trends.htm).
3. Pablo Gato and Robert Windrem, "Hezbollah Builds a Western Base," MSNBC, May 9, 2007. Available online (www.msnbc.msn.com/id/17874369)
4. Ibid.
5. Rex Hudson (Federal Research Division, Library of Congress), *Terrorist and Organized Crime Groups in the Tri-Border Area (TBA) of South America* (Washington, DC: U.S. Government Printing Office, July 2003); available online www.au.af.mil/au/awc/awcgate/loc/terr_org_crime_tba.pdf). See also Gato and Windrem, "Hezbollah Builds." Most of the area's Arab and Muslim immigrants work in Paraguay but actually live in Brazil—a jurisdictional problem that makes law enforcement efforts much more difficult.
6. Hudson, *Terrorist and Organized Crime Groups.*
7. Gato and Windrem, "Hezbollah Builds."
8. See "Joint Statement of the Fifth Plenary Session of the 3+1 Mechanism on Triple Border Security," U.S. Embassy in Buenos Aires, Argentina, December 4–5, 2006. Available online (argentina.usembassy.gov/comeng).
9. Gato and Windrem, "Hezbollah Builds."
10. Hudson, *Terrorist and Organized Crime Groups.*
11. See U.S. State Department, "Philip Wilcox on International Terrorism in Latin America," September 28, 1995. Available online (http://dosfan.lib.uic.edu/ERC/bureaus/lat/1995/950928WilcoxTerrorism.html).
12. Gato and Windrem, "Hezbollah Builds."
13. Ronen Bergman, *The Secret War against Iran* (New York: Free Press, 2008), pp. 169–184.
14. The group called itself "Islamic Jihad," not to be confused with the plethora of Middle Eastern groups bearing the same name. See U.S. State Department, "Philip Wilcox."
15. Mike Boettcher, "South America's Tri-Border Back on Terrorism Radar," CNN, November 8, 2002. Available online (www.cnn.com/2002/WORLD/americas/11/07/terror.triborder).
16. Gato and Windrem, "Hezbollah Builds."
17. Matthew Levitt and Jake Lipton, "Dangerous Partners: Targeting the Iran-Hizballah Alliance," *PolicyWatch* no. 1267 (Washington Institute for Near East Policy, July 31, 2007). Available online (www.washingtoninstitute.org/templateC05.php?CID=2643).
18. Ibid.

19. Matthew Levitt, prepared testimony submitted to "Iran: A Quarter-Century of State-Sponsored Terror," joint hearing of the House Committee on International Relations, February 16, 2005; available online (http://commdocs.house.gov/committees/intlrel/hfa98810.000/hfa98810_0f.htm). See also Mark Steinitz, "Middle East Terrorist Activity in Latin America," *Policy Papers on the Americas* 14, Study 7 (Center for Strategic and International Studies, July 2003).
20. Andrew Buncombe, "Menem Took Iran Bribe to Cover Up Attack on Jewish Centre," *The Independent*, July 23, 2002. Available online (www.independent.co.uk/news/world/americas/menem-took-iran-bribe-to-cover-up-attack-on-jewish-centre-649204.html). According to author interviews with Argentinean prosecutor Alberto Nisman, Menem purportedly attempted to shield a prime suspect—Alberto Kannore Edul—from further inquiries only days after the AMIA attack. Specifically, he asked the justice department not to investigate Edul and even granted the suspect secret service and police protection. Argentinean authorities are still seeking to prosecute Menem on these allegations.
21. "Argentine Bomb Probe Judge Sacked," BBC, August 3, 2005. It should be mentioned that many of the improprieties that led to the judge's dismissal (e.g., paying a witness for evidence) appeared to be rooted in a misguided effort to ensure that the inquiry was successful, rather than an attempt to impede the investigation.
22. "Breakthrough Made in '94 Argentina Bombing: Hezbollah Militant Named in Attack on Jewish Community Center," Associated Press, November 9, 2005. Available online (www.msnbc.msn.com/id/9983810).
23. Hudson, *Terrorist and Organized Crime Groups.*
24. See U.S. Treasury Department, "Treasury Targets Hizballah Fundraising Network in the Triple Frontier of Argentina, Brazil, and Paraguay," press release, December 6, 2006; available online (www.treas.gov/press/releases/hp190.htm). See also U.S. Treasury Department, "Treasury Designates Islamic Extremist, Two Companies Supporting Hizballah in Tri-Border Area," June 10, 2004; available online (www.treas.gov/press/releases/js1720.htm).

U.S. Efforts Recognized by FATF

1. See FATF, "Third Mutual Evaluation Report on Anti-Money Laundering and Combating the Financing of Terrorism of the United States of America," June 23, 2006, pp. 25–26. Available online (www.fatf-gafi.org/dataoecd/44/9/37101772.pdf).

Riggs Bank: Laundering for a Dictator

1. Terence O'Hara and Kathleen Day, "Riggs Bank Hid Assets of Pinochet, Report Says," *Washington Post*, July 15, 2004; available online (www.washingtonpost.com/wp-dyn/articles/A50222-2004Jul14.html). See also Senate Committee on Homeland Security and Governmental Affairs, Permanent Subcommittee on Investigations, "Money Laundering and Foreign Corruption: Enforcement and Effectiveness of the Patriot Act," March 16, 2005. Available online (http://hsgac.senate.gov/public/_files/PINOCHETREPORTFINALwcharts0.pdf).
2. Ibid.

Smuggling Ring Uses Commodities to Launder Money for Hizbollah

1. "U.S. Authorities Bust Cigarette-Smuggling Ring Linked to Hezbollah," CNN, July 21, 2000. Available online (http://archives.cnn.com/2000/LAW/07/21/charlotte.raids.02/index.html).
2. *Terrorist Financing: U.S. Agencies Should Systematically Assess Terrorists' Use of Alternative Financing Mechanisms* (Washington, DC: General Accounting Office, November 2003). Available online (www.gao.gov/new.items/d04163.pdf).
3. Jeffrey Goldberg, "In the Party of God, Part Two," *New Yorker*, October 28, 2002. Available online (www.newyorker.com/archive/2002/10/28/021028fa_fact2).

4. Jason Burke, "Suburban Cigarette Gang Raised Cash for Hizbollah," *Guardian*, July 23, 2000. Available online (www.guardian.co.uk/world/2000/jul/23/israel).
5. See FINCEN, "The SAR Activity Review: Trends, Tips and Issues," August 2004, p. 31. Available online (www.fincen.gov/news_room/rp/files/sar_tti_07.pdf).
6. Don Van Natta Jr., "Terrorists Blaze a New Money Trail," *New York Times*, September 28, 2003. Available online (http://query.nytimes.com/gst/fullpage.html?res=9C07E2D7133DF93BA1575AC0A9659C8B63).
7. "Two Men in United States Convicted of Aiding Hizballah," Associated Press, June 23, 2002.
8. See FBI, *Terrorism 2002–2005*, (n.d.). Available online (www.fbi.gov/publications/terror/terrorism2002_2005.htm).
9. United States v. Mohamad Youssef Hammoud et al., United States Court of Appeals for the Fourth District.

Chapter 10

1. Also commonly referred to as targeted financial sanctions.
2. See Watson Institute for International Studies, Brown University, "Targeted Sanctions Project," (n.d.). Available online (www.watsoninstitute.org/project_detail.cfm?id=4).
3. See FATF, "Freezing of Terrorist Assets: International Best Practices," October 3, 2003. Available online (www.fatf-gafi.org/dataoecd/39/15/34033495.pdf).
4. The freezing of terrorism-related funds should be done in accordance with FATF Special Recommendation 3; see FATF, "9 Special Recommendations (SR) on Terrorist Financing (TF)," (n.d.) (available online at www.fatf-gafi.org/document/9/0,2340,en_32250379_32236920_34032073_1_1_1_1,00.html). The phrase "without delay" stems from UNSCR 1267 (which defines it as "ideally, within a matter of hours of a designation by the Al-Qaeda and Taliban Sanctions Committee") and UNSCR 1373 (which defines it as "upon having reasonable grounds, or a reasonable basis, to suspect or believe that a person or entity is a terrorist, one who finances terrorism or a terrorist organization"). It is important to note that freezing action should be taken whether the funds were derived from legal or illegal sources. See FATF, "Interpretative Notes to the 9 Special Recommendations on Terrorist Financing," Interpretative Note to Special Recommendation III, (n.d.); available online (www.fatf-gafi.org/document/53/0,2340,en_32250379_32236947_34261877_1_1_1_1,00.html#insrII).
5. See FATF, Interpretative Note to Special Recommendation III.
6. Ibid.
7. Ibid.
8. See FATF, Recommendation 3, in "The 40 Recommendations." Available online (www.fatf-gafi.org/document/28/0,2340,en_32250379_32236930_33658140_1_1_1_1,00.html#40recs).
9. Interpretative Note to Special Recommendation III.
10. Ibid.
11. Ibid.
12. See UNSCR 1735 (December 22, 2006). Available online (www.un.org/sc/committees/1267/resolutions.shtml).
13. See UNSCR 1452 (December 20, 2002). Available online (www.un.org/Docs/scres/2002/sc2002.htm).
14. It is worth mentioning that the United States has other domestic targeting programs, all conducted in the same fashion as the EO 13224 program. For a full list of U.S. sanctions programs, see the relevant section of the Treasury Department website (www.treas.gov/offices/enforcement/ofac/programs/index.shtml).
15. 27 USC 287c.
16. See U.S. Treasury Department, "United States Code Annotated," (n.d.). Available online (www.treas.gov/offices/enforcement/ofac/legal/statutes/ieepa.pdf).
17. 50 USC 1601 et seq.
18. See President Bill Clinton, "Executive Order 12947—Prohibiting Transactions with Terrorists Who Threaten to Disrupt the Middle East Peace Process," January 23, 1995. Available online (www.presidency.ucsb.edu/ws/index.php?pid=51612).

19. See President Bill Clinton, "Executive Order 13099—Prohibiting Transactions with Terrorists Who Threaten to Disrupt the Middle East Peace Process," August 20, 1998. Available online (www.presidency.ucsb.edu/ws/index.php?pid=54808).
20. The SDGT list blocks "all property and interests in property of designated individuals or entities that are in the United States or that come within the United States, or that come within the possession or control of U.S. persons." See President George W. Bush, "Executive Order 13224—Blocking Property and Prohibiting Transactions with Persons Who Commit, Threaten to Commit, or Support Terrorism," September 23, 2001. Available online (www.presidency.ucsb.edu/ws/index.php?pid=61505).
21. See U.S. Treasury Department, "What You Need to Know about U.S. Sanctions," (n.d.). Available online (www.treasury.gov/offices/enforcement/ofac/programs/terror/terror.pdf).
22. See U.S. State Department, "Foreign Terrorist Organizations," (n.d.). Available online (www.state.gov/s/ct/rls/other/des/123085.htm).
23. See Lawyers' Committee for Civil Rights of the San Francisco Bay Area, "Government Releases Complaints from Consumers Wrongly Linked to Terrorism and Drug Trafficking on Credit Reports," March 18, 2008. Available online (www.lccr.com/3-18-08%20Press%20Release%20OFAC.pdf).
24. See 9/11 Public Discourse Project, "Final Report on 9/11 Commission Recommendations," December 5, 2005. Available online (www.9-11pdp.org/press/2005-12-05_summary.pdf).
25. John Cassara, "Is the U.S. Treasury Department Cooking the Books?," *Complinet*, September 15, 2008. Available online (http://johncassara.com/articles/Article1.pdf).
26. See FATF, *Third Mutual Evaluation Report on Anti–Money Laundering and Combating the Financing of Terrorism: United States of America* (Paris: FATF, June 23, 2006), p. 58. Available online (www.fatf-gafi.org/dataoecd/44/9/37101772.pdf).
27. See "Questions for the Record—Questions from Max Baucus, Chairman; Questions for Stuart Levey," hearing before the Senate Finance Committee, April 1, 2008. Available online (http://homeland.cq.com/hs/flatfiles/temporaryItems/20090113levey.pdf).
28. Cassara, "Is the U.S. Treasury Department Cooking the Books?"
29. Hector Tobar and Carlos Martinez, "Mexico Meth Raid Yields $205 Million in U.S. Cash," *Los Angeles Times*, March 17, 2007. Available online (www.latimes.com/la-fg-meth17mar17,0,709967.story).
30. See FATF, *Third Mutual Evaluation Report*, p. 53.
31. Ibid., p. 57.
32. Ibid.
33. Ibid., p. 53.
34. U.S. Treasury Department, Office of Foreign Assets Control, "Terrorist Assets Report 2002: Annual Report to the Congress on Assets in the United States of Terrorist Countries and International Terrorism Program Designees," (n.d.). Available online (www.treas.gov/offices/enforcement/ofac/reports/tar2002.pdf).
35. See "Uniting and Strengthening America by Providing Appropriate Tools Required to Intercept and Obstruct Terrorism (USA PATRIOT) Act of 2001," October 26, 2001. Available online (http://frwebgate.access.gpo.gov/cgi-bin/getdoc.cgi?dbname=107_cong_public_laws&docid=f:publ056.107).
36. 31 USC 5318A (b)(1)–(5). Once a designation of this sort has been issued, U.S. financial institutions and government agencies are to take one of five "special measures." Intended to provide the government with a wide range of options to counter money laundering and terrorism financing, these measures can be imposed "individually, jointly, in any combination, and in any sequence." They include "(1) Recordkeeping and reporting of financial transactions; (2) Collection of information relating to beneficial ownership; (3) Collection of information relating to certain payable-through accounts; (4) Collection of information relating to certain correspondent accounts; and (5) Prohibition or conditions on the opening or maintaining of correspondent or payable-through accounts." In general, financial institutions have strongly opposed measures 1 through 4 because of the associated costs. Instead, they have preferred that the government take measure 5, which in essence prohibits a financial institution from establishing, maintaining, administering or managing any correspondent account on behalf of any designated entity. For a complete discussion of

the range of possible countermeasures, see the notice at 68 FR 18917 (April 17, 2003), which proposed the imposition of special measures against Nauru. See also Sen. Patrick Leahy, "The United and Strengthening America By Providing Appropriate Tools Required to Intercept and Obstruct Terrorism (USA PATRIOT) Act of 2001, H.R. 3162 Section-by-Section Analysis," (n.d.). Available online (http://leahy.senate.gov/press/200110/102401a.html).

37. See FinCEN, "311 Special Measures," (n.d.). Available online (www.fincen.gov/reg_section311.html).
38. See U.S. Treasury Department, "Designation of Nauru and Ukraine as Primary Money Laundering Concerns," press release, December 20, 2002. Available online (www.ustreas.gov/press/releases/reports/designation.pdf).
39. See U.S. Treasury Department, "Treasury Department Designates Burma and Two Burmese Banks to Be of 'Primary Money Laundering Concern' and Announces Proposed Countermeasures under Section 311 of the USA PATRIOT Act," press release, November 19, 2003. Available online (www.treas.gov/press/releases/reports/js1014attachment.pdf).
40. The bank conducted numerous transactions that were indicative of money laundering and terrorism financing, including for bin Laden. It also held accounts that contained proceeds from the illicit sale of Iraqi oil. See U.S. Treasury Department, "Treasury Designates Commercial Bank of Syria as Financial Institution of Primary Money Laundering Concern," press release, May 11, 2004. Available online (www.treasury.gov/press/releases/js1538.htm).
41. Infobank was accused of laundering money from "schemes to circumvent the UN Oil-for-Food program." This money was eventually used to purchase weapons or finance military training. The First Merchant Bank of the "Turkish Republic of Northern Cyprus" (TRNC), also privately owned, served as a conduit for laundering criminal proceeds and had links to organized crime. See U.S. Treasury Department, "Treasury Employs USA PATRIOT Act Authorities to Designate Two Foreign Banks as 'Primary Money Laundering Concerns,'" press release, August 24, 2004. Available online (www.ustreas.gov/press/releases/js1874.htm).
42. Multibanka was used by Russian and other shell companies to facilitate fraud and financial crime by allowing criminals to disguise illegal proceeds in countries known for lax enforcement of AML laws. VEF Bank lacked adequate controls and procedures to detect and combat money laundering and had dealings with foreign shell companies. See Daniel Glaser (deputy assistant secretary, Office of Terrorist Financing and Financial Crime, U.S. Treasury Department), testimony before the Senate Committee on Banking, Housing, and Urban Affairs," September 12, 2006. Available online (www.treas.gov/press/releases/hp93.htm).
43. David Lawder, "Macau Bank Struggles to Shake Off North Korea Links," Reuters, December 21, 2006. Available online (www.reuters.com/article/newsOne/idUSSP15073620061221).
44. See "Who must comply with OFAC regulations?" in the "Frequently Asked Questions" section of the OFAC website (www.treas.gov/offices/enforcement/ofac/faq/answer.shtml#10).
45. See FATF, *Third Mutual Evaluation Report,* p. 53.
46. Such guidance is included in the Federal Financial Institutions Examination Council (FFIEC) *Bank Secrecy Act Anti–Money Laundering Examination Manual* (available on FinCEN's website at www.ffiec.gov/bsa_aml_infobase/pages_manual/OLM_002.htm).
47. Title 31 of the U.S. Code of Federal Regulations, chapter 5, sections 594.201 (note 3) and 501.807 (31 CFR §§ 594.201 and 501.807).
48. See U.S. Treasury Department, "Office of Foreign Assets Control: Mission," (n.d.). Available online (www.treas.gov/offices/enforcement/ofac).
49. Letter from Virginia Canter (Associate Director of Resource Management, OFAC) to Thomas Burke (Davis Wright Tremaine LLP), "RE: Lawyers' Committee for Civil Rights of San Francisco Bay Area v. United States Department of the Treasury, No. C 07-2590 (PJH)," March 18, 2008. Available online (www.lccr.com/3%2018%2008%20Treasury%20Dept%20Cover%20Letter.pdf).
50. Brian Orsak, "Legal Challenges Loom for Targeted Sanctions in Europe," Moneylaundering.com, May 5, 2008. Available online (www.amleurope.org/materials/reference_Materials/Legal%20challenges%20loom%20for%20targeted%20sanctions%20in%20Europe.pdf).

51. See Lawyers' Committee for Civil Rights of the San Francisco Bay Area, "Government Releases Complaints."
52. See Watson Institute, "Targeted Sanctions Project."

The U.S. Financial War against the Iranian Banking Community

1. See President George W. Bush, "Executive Order 13382—Blocking Property of Weapons of Mass Destruction Proliferators and Their Supporters," June 28, 2005. Available online (www.fas.org/irp/offdocs/eo/eo-13382.htm).
2. Lionel Beehner, *U.S. Sanctions Biting Iran* (New York: Council on Foreign Relations, 2007). Available online www.cfr.org/publication/12478).
3. The ban does not apply to independent foreign subsidiaries of U.S. companies.
4. See *Iran Sanctions: Impact in Furthering U.S. Objectives Is Unclear and Should Be Reviewed* (Washington, DC: U.S. Government Accountability Office, December, 2007); available online (www.gao.gov/new.items/d0858.pdf). See also Robin Wright, "GAO Report Challenges Effect of Longtime U.S. Sanctions on Iran," *Washington Post*, January 17, 2008; available online (www.washingtonpost.com/wp-dyn/content/article/2008/01/16/AR2008011603711.html).
5. Ibid.
6. See FINCEN, "Guidance to Financial Institutions on the Continuing Money Laundering Threat Involving Illicit Iranian Activity," March 20, 2008. Available online (www.fincen.gov/statutes_regs/guidance/html/fin-2008-a002.html).
7. See U.S. Treasury Department, "Iran's Bank Sepah Designated by Treasury: Sepah Facilitating Iran's Weapons Program," January 9, 2007; available online (www.ustreas.gov/press/releases/hp219.htm). See also U.S. Treasury Department, "Prepared Remarks of Stuart Levey, Under Secretary for Terrorism and Financial Intelligence, on the Designation of Bank Sepah for Facilitating Iran's Weapons Program," press release, January 9, 2007. Available online (www.ustreas.gov/press/releases/hp220.htm).
8. See U.S. Treasury, "Iran's Bank Sepah Designated."
9. See U.S. Treasury Department, "Treasury Cuts Iran's Bank Saderat Off from U.S. Financial System," press release, September 8, 2006; available online (www.ustreas.gov/press/releases/hp87.htm). See also U.S. Treasury Department, "Fact Sheet: Designation of Iranian Entities and Individuals for Proliferation Activities and Support for Terrorism," October 25, 2007; available online (www.ustreas.gov/press/releases/hp644.htm).
10. U.S. Treasury, "Fact Sheet: Designation of Iranian Entities." See also U.S. Treasury Department, "Treasury Designates Iran-Controlled Bank for Proliferation: Future Bank Controlled by Iran's Bank Melli," press release, March 12, 2008; available online (www.ustreas.gov/press/releases/hp869.htm).
11. See U.S. Treasury, "Fact Sheet: Designation of Iranian Entities."
12. Ibid.
13. See FATF, "FATF Statement on Iran," October 11, 2007. Available online (www.fatf-gafi.org/dataoecd/1/2/39481684.pdf).
14. See FATF, "FATF Statement," February 28, 2008. Available online (www.fatf-gafi.org/dataoecd/16/26/40181037.pdf).
15. See UN, "2008 UN Security Council Resolutions," (n.d.). Available online (www.un.org/Docs/sc/unsc_resolutions08.htm).

Victor Bout: The "Merchant of Death"

1. Doug Farah and Stephan Braun, "The Merchant of Death," *Foreign Policy* (November–December 2006). Available online (www.foreignpolicy.com/story/cms.php?story_id=3600). See also their excellent book on Bout, *Merchant of Death: Money, Guns, Planes, and the Man Who Makes War Possible* (Hoboken, NJ: John Wiley, 2007).
2. Bruce Falconer, "Viktor Bout's Last Deal," *Mother Jones*, March 18, 2008. Available online (www.motherjones.com/news/feature/2008/03/viktor-bout.html).

3. Farah and Braun, "The Merchant of Death." See also Falconer, "Viktor Bout's Last Deal." See also Ian MacKinnon, "'Lord of War' Arms Trafficker Arrested," *Guardian,* March 7 2008; available online (www.guardian.co.uk/world/2008/mar/07/thailand.russia).
4. Matthew Brunwasser, "Victor Anatoliyevich Bout: The Embargo Buster, Fueling Civil Wars," PBS Frontline World, May 2002. Available online (www.pbs.org/frontlineworld/stories/sierraleone/bout.html).
5. Judy Pasternak and Stephen Braun, "Emirates Looked Other Way While Al Qaeda Funds Flowed," *Los Angeles Times,* January 20, 2002; available online (http://web.archive.org/web/20030301165639). See also Stephan Smith et al., "On the Trail of the Elusive Victor Bout," *Guardian,* April 17, 2002; available online (http://s3.amazonaws.com/911timeline/2002/guardian041702.html). See also "On the Trail of a Man Behind Taliban's Air Fleet," *Los Angeles Times,* May 19, 2002; available online (http://articles.latimes.com/2005/apr/27/nation/na-bout27).
6. Farah and Braun, "The Merchant of Death." See also Brunwasser, "Victor Anatoliyevich Bout."
7. Farah and Braun, "The Merchant of Death." See also Michael Casey, "Thais Detain Alleged 'Merchant of Death,'" Associated Press, March 6, 2008; available online (ww.boston.com/news/world/asia/articles/2008/03/06/russian_arms_dealer_arrested_in_thailand). See also Thomas Bell, "'Merchant of Death' Arrested in Thailand," *London Telegraph,* March 8, 2008; available online (www.telegraph.co.uk/news/worldnews/1581035/'Merchant-of-Death'-arrested-in-Thailand.html). See also "International Manhunt Begins for Victor Bout," CNN, February 23, 2002; available online (http://transcripts.cnn.com/TRANSCRIPTS/0202/23/smn.02.html).
8. Brunwasser, "Victor Anatoliyevich Bout."
9. See U.S. Treasury Department, "Treasury Designates Viktor Bout's International Arms Trafficking Network," press release, April 26, 2005. Available online (www.treas.gov/press/releases/js2406.htm).
10. Falconer, "Viktor Bout's Last Deal."
11. See DEA, "International Arms Dealer Arrested on Terrorism Charges in Bangkok," press release, March 6, 2008; available online (www.usdoj.gov/dea/pubs/pressrel/pr030608.html). For a detailed description of the charges against Bout, see the formal complaint filed with the U.S. Southern District of New York on February 27, 2008; available online (www.usdoj.gov/opa/pr/2008/March/bout-complaint.pdf).

Chapter 11

1. If a country is a member of multiple international organizations, it can choose to request a joint Mutual Evaluation. In 2005–2006, for example, the United States underwent a joint evaluation with FATF and the Asia/Pacific Group on Money Laundering (APG).
2. See FATF, "Mutual Evaluations Programme," (n.d.). Available online, (www.fatf-gafi.org/pages/0,2966,en_32250379_32236982_1_1_1_1_1,00.html#process).
3. The length of onsite visits can vary depending on a country's size, complexity, and so forth.
4. See FATF, "Mutual Evaluations Programme."
5. The IMF and World Bank conduct more-general assessments of the financial sector—AML/CFT is just one of the components they evaluate. For more on the 2002 decision, see IMF/World Bank, "IMF Advances Efforts to Combat Money Laundering and Terrorist Finance," August 8, 2002. Available online (www.imf.org/external/np/sec/pn/2002/pn0287.htm).
6. These standard-setters included the World Bank, IMF, Basel Committee on Banking Supervision, International Association of Securities Commissioners (IOSCO), International Association of Insurance Supervisors (IAIS), and Egmont Group. It is worth noting that the 2002 methodology consisted of 120 criteria covering each of the FATF 40 + 9 Recommendations. See IMF, "International Monetary Fund and World Bank: Twelve-Month Pilot Program of Anti–Money Laundering and Combating the Financing of Terrorism (AML/CFT) Assessments," March 16, 2004. Available online (www.internationalmonetaryfund.org/external/np/aml/eng/2004/031604.pdf).
7. In comparison, FATF and the IMF/World Bank currently conduct approximately 20 assessments per year. See IMF, "Twelve-Month Pilot Program."

8. This revised methodology contained more than 200 essential criteria, 20 subcriteria, and 35 additional criteria. See ibid.
9. It should be mentioned that FATF regularly updates the methodology.
10. See FATF, *AML/CFT Evaluations and Assessments: Handbook for Countries and Assessors* (Paris: FATF, June 2006), p. 7. Available online (www.fatf-gafi.org/dataoecd/3/26/36254892.pdf). It should be mentioned that countries must submit their laws/regulations in both their native language and either French or English.
11. Ibid.
12. Ibid.
13. A full list of "authorities and businesses" that should be included in such meetings can be found in the Assessors Handbook. See ibid., pp. 8–9.
14. In rare cases, a country may receive a rating of "Not Applicable" when all or part of a requirement does not apply due to the country's structural, legal, or institutional features (e.g., if the country lacks a particular type of financial institution). See ibid., p. 10.
15. Stanley Morris, "Mutual Evaluation, and the Inter-American Convention on Corruption: Challenge and Opportunity" (Organization of American States, Department of International Legal Affairs, Office of Legal Cooperation, n.d.). Available online (www.oas.org/juridico/english/mutual_evaluation_stanley_morris.htm).

Chapter 12

1. See U.S. Treasury Department, "Prepared Remarks of Daniel L. Glaser, Acting Assistant Secretary for Terrorist Financing and Financial Crimes, before the Annual Meetings Program of Seminars: The Importance of Expanding Targeted Financial Sanctions Programs around the Globe—Challenges and Opportunities," September 14, 2005. Available online (www.treas.gov/press/releases/js2941.htm).
2. See FATF, Recommendation 21, in "The 40 Recommendations." Available online (www.fatf-gafi.org/document/28/0,2340,en_32250379_32236930_33658140_1_1_1_1,00.html#40recs).
3. As described in chapter 3, FATF first extended the associate membership option in June 2005. FSRBs that meet the criteria for this status are permitted to participate in FATF Mutual Evaluations, among other benefits.
4. Prepared in accordance with section 489 of the Foreign Assistance Act of 1961, as amended (the "FAA," 22 USC 2291). See also the State Department's "Narcotics Control Reports" webpage (www.state.gov/p/inl/rls/nrcrpt).
5. It should be mentioned that when U.S.-designated entities fit the 1267 criteria, the United States submits them for potential listing by the 1267 Committee as well. In order to get a name added to the 1267 list, there must be complete unanimity in the committee. If consensus cannot be achieved, however, the submitting member state has the option of putting the name in a separate resolution and presenting it to the Security Council—where, as described, the requirement is only nine "yes" votes and no vetoes rather than unanimity.
6. Paul Allan Schott, *Reference Guide to Anti–Money Laundering and Combating the Financing of Terrorism* (Washington, DC: World Bank, 2006), chapter V, p. V-9. Available online (www1.worldbank.org/finance/html/amlcft/docs/Ref_Guide_EN/v2/05-Ch05_EN_v2.pdf).
7. Ibid.
8. Predicate offenses are listed in section 1956(c)(7). All of the "Racketeer Influenced and Corrupt Organization" (RICO) predicates listed in 18 USC 1961(1) are included as well.
9. See FATF, *Third Mutual Evaluation Report on Anti–Money Laundering and Combating the Financing of Terrorism: United States of America* (Paris: FATF, June 23, 2006), p. 33. Available online (www.fatf-gafi.org/dataoecd/44/9/37101772.pdf).
10. See "Combating Money Laundering and Terrorist Financing Act of 2006," (n.d.); available online (www.govtrack.us/congress/bill.xpd?bill=s109-2402).

About the Author

Avi Jorisch is founder and president of Red Cell Intelligence Group (www.redcellig.com), a consulting and training firm that specializes in national security issues relating to terrorism, illicit finance, and radical Islam. A former policy advisor in the Treasury Department's Office of Terrorism and Financial Intelligence, he currently serves as a senior fellow at the Foundation for Defense of Democracies, where he leads the Center for Combating Threat Finance, a project dedicated to assisting countries, agencies, and financial institutions in the fight against money laundering and terrorism financing. He is also an adjunct scholar with the Washington Institute for Near East Policy.

During his career at the Treasury Department, Mr. Jorisch served as head of the U.S. delegation to the Financial Action Task Force's Typologies Working Group. He also acted as a Treasury liaison to the Department of Homeland Security's Immigration and Customs Enforcement Trade Transparency Unit. In addition, he has served as an Arab media and terrorism consultant for the Department of Defense.

Prior to joining the government, he was named executive director of the Coalition Against Terrorist Media, an alliance of Muslim, Christian, Jewish, and secular organizations concerned about the role terrorist groups play in funding various media outlets. These concerns also shaped his work as a Soref fellow at The Washington Institute, where he wrote *Beacon of Hatred: Inside Hizballah's al-Manar Television* (2004). Based on extensive interviews with Hizbollah members and Arab media experts in Lebanon and elsewhere, the book included a CD-ROM containing footage from some of al-Manar's most objectionable programming. Both the book and the advocacy campaign that followed resulted in significant policy changes worldwide: al-Manar programming was removed from ten satellite providers based in Australia, Barbados, Brazil, France, China, the Netherlands, Spain, Thailand, and the United States; the station was designated as a terrorist entity by the U.S. government, outlawed by the European Union, and barred from business activities in Germany; Western corporate sponsors including Coke, Pepsi, and Proctor & Gamble ceased advertising on al-Manar programs; the station's Washington, D.C., bureau was closed down; and the al-Manar website ceased to be hosted in the United States.

Mr. Jorisch has traveled extensively in the Middle East, including Syria, Lebanon, Jordan, Israel, Gaza, the West Bank, Egypt, Qatar, Turkey, and Morocco. He has written at length about Hizbollah, al-Manar, and related terrorism issues, with articles appearing in prominent publications such as the *Los Angeles Times, Washington Times, Jerusalem Post,* and *Middle East Quarterly.* In addition, he has been interviewed by more than fifty media outlets, including CNN, ABC News, Fox News, the *New York Times,* and numerous Arabic publications. He has also briefed the U.S. military, U.S. and European government officials, members of Congress, and counterterrorism officials on a range of issues, as well as provided key evidence in a successful terrorism case against U.S.-based supporters of Hizbollah.

Mr. Jorisch holds a bachelor's degree in history from Binghamton University and a master's degree in Islamic history from the Hebrew University of Jerusalem. In 2000–2001, he studied Arabic and Islamic philosophy through the Center for Arabic Studies Abroad program at the American University in Cairo. He also earned a certificate in Arabic from al-Azhar University, the preeminent institution of Sunni Islamic learning.

About Red Cell Intelligence Group

Red Cell Intelligence Group provides consulting and training services on national security issues relating to threat finance, counterterrorism, radical Islamist movements at war with democratic societies, and national security. Our clients include governments, military personnel, intelligence and law enforcement agencies, financial institutions, industry associations, and nonprofits.

Red Cell IG brings to bear decades of private and public sector experience. Through a holistic and highly interactive instructional approach, we deepen our clients' understanding of today's most pressing national security threats. Our goal is simple: to educate clients on how our adversaries think and the ideologies that drive them.